DATE DUE

DEMCO 38-296

THE REDEMPTIVE WORK

THE REDEMPTIVE WORK

Railway and Nation in Ecuador, 1895–1930

A. Kim Clark

SR BOOKS

A Scholarly Resources Inc. Imprint
Wilmington, Delaware

© 1998 by Scholarly Resources Inc.
All rights reserved
First published 1998
Printed and bound in the United States of America

Scholarly Resources Inc.
104 Greenhill Avenue
Wilmington, DE 19805-1897

Library of Congress Cataloging-in-Publication Data

Clark, A. Kim, 1964–
  The redemptive work : railway and nation in Ecuador, 1895–
1930 / A. Kim Clark
      p.   cm. — (Latin American silhouettes)
  Includes bibliographical references (p.   ) and index.
  ISBN 0-8420-2674-6 (cloth : alk. paper)
    1. Compañía del Ferrocarril de Guayaquil a Quito—
History. 2. Railroads—Social aspects—Ecuador.
3. Nationalism—Ecuador. 4. Liberalism—Ecuador.
5. Ecuador—Economic conditions. 6. Ecuador—Social
conditions. I. Title. II. Series.
HE2960.C65C54   1997
385'.09866—dc21   97-14679
                                                        CIP

⊗The paper used in this publication meets the minimum requirements of the American National Standard for permanence of
paper for printed library materials, Z39.48, 1984.

Acknowledgments

L ike most authors, I have accumulated many different kinds of debts in the process of researching and writing this book. Some are difficult to specify, given the many conversations I have had, over time, with friends and colleagues in Ecuador and elsewhere about Ecuadorian history and society and about social analysis in general. A list of everyone who has influenced my thinking on these issues would be too long to publish, but I do thank them all. My debts to others are more specific to this book, and I would like to thank those individuals by name. First, I am grateful to the people who facilitated my access to archives in Ecuador. At the Biblioteca Aurelio Espinosa Pólit in Cotocollao, I thank Father Julián Bravo, S.J. (director of the BAEP), the staff of the archive, and especially Wilson Vega Vega. I thank the curator of the Archivo Histórico del Banco Central (Quito), Ramiro Avila, and the curator of the photography archive at the Banco Central, Cosme Vásquez. I am also grateful to the Facultad Latinoamericana de Ciencias Sociales, which provided me with institutional affiliation during my research, and to the former director of the Quito campus, Amparo Menéndez-Carrión.

In Alausí, my debts are more extensive. In the Jefatura Política, I thank the former Jefe Político, Manuel Orellana, and, for their assistance and companionship, Giomar Ribadeneira and Marlene Cabezas. In the Concejo Municipal, I thank the former Municipal President, Milton López, the Vice President, Jesus Camañero, and the Municipal Secretary, Galo Quisataxi, and I extend special thanks to the Municipal Librarian, Olga Mejía. I would also like to thank Patricia de Robalino, who allowed me access to her notarial archives. Other people in Alausí facilitated my work in less direct ways. I am especially grateful to my landlords, Luis Barragán and Aida Cuesta, and to my neighbors Margarita Ribadeneira, Kepler Cuesta, and their children, Carlos, Francisco, and, especially, Mercedes, who gave up part of her summer vacation to help me transcribe documents.

I could not have undertaken the research for or writing of this book without doctoral funding provided by the Social Sciences and Humanities Research Council of Canada (June 1990 to May 1993) and the New School for Social Research (September 1991 to May 1992), for which I am grateful. In addition, subsequent postdoctoral grants from the Social Sciences and Humanities Research Council of Canada and the Wenner-Gren Foundation for Anthropological Research allowed me to extend my research on Ecuador in both chronological and thematic terms. Although my postdoctoral research is seldom reflected directly in this manuscript, the deeper understanding it fostered does emerge. Also, for permission to republish passages in Chapters 5 and 6 that had previously appeared in an article in the Ecuadorian journal *Procesos*, I thank the journal's editor, Guillermo Bustos Lozano.

I wrote this volume in three stages, and at each point along the way different people provided me with suggestions and criticism. Its first stage was a Ph.D. thesis, and I would like to thank the members of my dissertation committee: William Roseberry, Deborah Poole, Rayna Rapp, and Diane Davis. The influences of Bill and Debbie in particular permeate this work in ways that are difficult to define. My thanks also go to Chandana Mathur for her comments on several chapters and to Lindsay DuBois, who read and commented on the entire dissertation as well as encouraged me generally. I am grateful to Carlos de la Torre Espinosa, who offered crucial feedback and intellectual challenges at many points in the research and writing; my dissertation would have turned out differently without our many conversations about it. At its second stage, when I began to rethink this project as a book, Patricia de la Torre Arauz, Andrés Guerrero, and Hernán Ibarra provided encouragement and gave me suggestions for revisions. And at a third stage, William Beezley and Judith Ewell provided the ideal combination of enthusiasm and sternness to push me to rethink the book in its entirety, with results that I would not have expected. The result is a far cry from the manuscript I first sent, and I credit them with catalyzing its transformation. I also would like to thank Richard Hopper and Michelle Slavin of Scholarly Resources for their encouragement and friendly assistance in making this a better book. Responsibility for the final version nonetheless rests with me.

In addition to those whom I have already named, I am grateful to several people who gave me more general encouragement and support during the research, writing, and rewriting of this book: Marilyn Clark, Phil Clark, the late Carlos de la Torre Reyes, Noemí Espinosa, the late Eduardo Larrea Stacey, María Clemencia Martínez, and Ricardo Muratorio. And I thank Blanca Muratorio, who introduced me to the study of Ecuador as well as to the country itself; over the years, she has been for me a model for engaged research and analysis. Finally, I count myself lucky to have so many good friends among my colleagues at the University of Western Ontario, who offer daily doses of good-humored support. I dedicate this book to the two people who, in very different ways, have provided continual and unconditional support for my work: Irene Ardley and Fernando Larrea.

Contents

1

Introduction

The Political Economy and Culture of the Ecuadorian Nation and the Guayaquil-Quito Railway

This study of the political economy and culture of the Ecuadorian nation during the liberal period from 1895 to 1925 and in its immediate aftermath focuses on a particular issue— the construction and operation of the Guayaquil-Quito Railway —as a vehicle for analyzing the contradictions in the processes of national incorporation in Ecuador. For Ecuadorian liberals, and for a wide range of other groups, a railway between the port of Guayaquil and the capital city of Quito would be Ecuador's *obra redentora*, or redemptive work, the cornerstone of a broad program of economic, political, social, and even moral reform. The Ecuadorian railway was more important for national incorporation than were many other Latin American railways, which more often were built to move export products from their zones of origin directly to a port rather than to integrate national territory. At the turn of the century, Ecuador's five largest cities were located in a small triangle (the corners being Quito, Guayaquil, and Cuenca) of barely more than 300 kilometers' distance. By 1908 four of these cities were linked by rail. Jean-Paul Deler has argued that although Peru and Colombia had many more kilometers of railways than Ecuador, their systems did not provide nearly the same degree of national integration.[1]

Three principal aspects of the formation of the nation in Ecuador are analyzed in relation to the railway. First, the construction of the railway was associated with important political-economic transformations in Ecuador, as it stimulated the increased movement of people and goods around the national territory. Railway construction thus was instrumental in both the formation of a labor market and of an internal market for agricultural products, which in turn was linked to the expansion and modernization of highland agriculture. Second, the railway, and the broader discourse of movement and connection that surrounded it, allowed for consensus about the nature of national development. Consensus was possible because the two principal dominant groups in Ecuador—the landowning elite of the highlands and the agro-export elite of the coast—could identify certain of their own interests in the railway, although their underlying goals were not always compatible. Third, the processes of national economic, political, and social integration through the railway had contradictory and uneven effects on different social groups and regions. These issues are further explored by an examination of the various experiences of and perspectives on these processes in a specific region, the canton of Alausí, in the central-highlands province of Chimborazo.

When liberal politicians spoke of creating a steel embrace, in the form of a railway, between the regions of Ecuador, they had in mind primarily a connection between Quito and Guayaquil, a connection that was completed in 1908.[2] Work on a railway to link the southern and northern highlands with the Quito-Guayaquil axis was a distinctly second step in integrating the national territory, and rapid and efficient communications with other regions (including other parts of the coast beyond the Guayas River basin) had to wait much longer. Work on the line north of Quito was completed as far as Ibarra by 1929. It did not reach the northern coast of Esmeraldas province until 1957. While work on the line to the southern highlands as far as Cuenca was begun in 1915 and had reached El Tambo by 1930, the railroad was not inaugurated in Cuenca until 1964. The many other lines that were projected but never built included one to run east from Ambato into the Amazon region.

From an anthropological perspective, one reason that the Guayaquil-Quito Railway was chosen to be the focus of this study was that, by its very nature, a railway continually draws attention to relations between different spaces. Anthropologists have found it difficult to move beyond the assumptions of community studies, especially the idea that a community can be studied as a bounded unit. Anthropology's move toward regional studies, for instance, often simply expanded the area considered, without questioning the assumption that the spatial unit of analysis had to be clearly delimited at some level. The work of Eric Wolf and Sidney Mintz, in contrast, fundamentally challenged the tenets of community and area studies.[3] Wolf and Mintz proposed new ways of thinking about the spatial dimensions of anthropological projects. Rather than limit their analysis to specific communities, they undertook pioneering research that examined the processes that link different spaces and communities, with an emphasis on commodity flows over space and through time. Their work has challenged anthropologists to take the connectedness of their anthropological subjects with wider processes—indeed, their formation within such processes—as a central concern. Similarly, this book uses the railway as a means to study a region as it was transformed through its connections to other spaces and to wider processes, and in relation to broader, and sometimes competing, definitions of community.

Such rethinking of spatial connections also has implications for how one understands history and power. If a community is not seen as bounded and isolated, then one must ask about the nature of its connections, over time, with other spaces and about the conflicts that may underlie those links. As Philip Corrigan and Derek Sayer point out in their magisterial study of British state formation as cultural revolution, "Sociologists have, in general, treated 'integration' far too neutrally, ignoring its differential aspects: who is seeking to integrate whom, to what ends, by what means, and in what forms; and who suffers, which ends are denied, which means declared illegitimate, which forms suppressed, whose histories rewritten, thereby?"[4] These are precisely some of the questions explored here.

What does it mean to call this book an anthropological political economy, a study of political economy and culture? This study examines political economy through those processes of national incorporation that are simultaneously economic and political. The approach proposed here emphasizes uneven development, as the various regions of Ecuador were incorporated into the world economy in different ways and at different tempos. In addition, analysis of the differential effects of broad political-economic processes on various social groups is a central concern. Thus, in the chapters that follow, the aspects of political economy that are most evident are the formation of a labor market, the formation of an internal market, and the transformation of the state. Present throughout is a sensitivity to issues of class, as we see different groups struggling to impose their own goals on others under changing conditions dictated in part by broader economic processes. Economic issues are thus inseparable from conflict and struggle; it is essential to emphasize the *political* dimensions of political economy. The economic "structure" is not separate from the human actions that produce it—structure and agency are not autonomous dimensions of social reality. As Corrigan and Sayer state, "We cannot, even methodologically, sever social forms and 'structures' from the class (and other) struggles through which they are brought into being *and sustained*, without doing great violence to our understanding. Social forms *are* class struggles."[5]

To see economic structures as the result of political conflict also leads to issues of culture, because struggle is always rooted in culturally constructed perceptions of our own interests. The concern here is to explore how people understand their worlds—how they construct meaning, how they act on those meanings, and, in doing so, how they change those worlds. In this sense, culture is seen as constrained, because people's social locations are themselves structured. People differentially participate in, and are affected by, the processes of national economic, political, and social incorporation because of their differing social locations. As a result, in some cases, precisely those processes that "liberate" certain people simultaneously limit the possibilities available to others. In addition, people's interpretations of those processes are also constrained by social location and by their past experiences, which in turn had been constructed out of prior human actions, including their own. To say that different meanings derive from different social locations is not to say that they are mechanistically determined, but rather that they are produced in interactions characterized by domination. Thus, this book aims to examine the practices of differently situated actors within contradictory social relations.

In this conception, culture is not to be studied apart from political economy; the two dimensions must be studied in conjunction. Culture is seen as material and not merely symbolic, dissolving the distinction between material base and ideal superstructure. "Culture is at once socially constituted (it is a product of present and past activity) and socially constitutive (it is part of the meaningful context in which activity takes place)."[6] To the extent that there is a kind of determinism here, it is a historical determinism, "the determination of action and the consequences of action by the conditions in which that action takes place, conditions that are themselves the consequences of prior activity and thought."[7]

It is important to make clear the way in which determination is understood in this book, because it would be easy to take the Ecuadorian liberal perspective from the end of the nineteenth century at face value and see the railway itself as the cause of historical change in Ecuador. Technology alone is not the motor of history, however; social and political struggles are. Sayer has argued that the conceptualization of forces of production as "things" rather than as social relations is a misreading of Marx's historical materialism. For Sayer, the base/superstructure metaphor in Marx's work was applied not to a model of different societal levels, but rather to the relation between social being and social consciousness.[8] Thus, Marx's analysis focused not on technological changes, but on the activities and struggles of definite people in definite relations, producing their subsistence in definite ways.

The notion of culture used in this book does not assume that everyone shares equally in producing the culture of a given society: while all people have an equal capacity for culture, the cultural conceptions common to a particular society will be determined more by some social groups than by others. The concept of dominant culture,[9] or cultural hegemony, proposes that the social groups who dominate a given society will attempt to impose their own ideas as general ones, although that does not mean that this project is easily accomplished. Moreover, because the dominant culture is consistent with the experiences of dominant groups, the experiences of subordinate groups can only be partially represented in the dominant culture.

While dominant social groups attempt to transform their own ideology into a hegemonic process, this process can never be complete, for two reasons. First, a dominant culture is not all encompassing because people continually experience the world in ways that can contradict it. Some parts of dominant culture seem to connect with people's lives, while other aspects of it will be contradicted by their lived experiences. Under certain conditions, this may be the basis for new forms of discourse and alternative meanings, only some of which the dominant culture will be capable of absorbing. Altogether, it is necessary to look both for common, shared meanings and for those understandings that result from differential experience, which are continually produced in class-based social formations because of the very contradictions such formations entail. In addition, in some cases people may selectively use ideologies produced by or seemingly "proper to" other social groups, transforming these

ideological and discursive resources as they apply them to their
own projects and, in the process, stretching the limits of dominant ideologies. In resisting and accommodating themselves to
changing circumstances, subordinate groups may, for instance,
engage to their own ends legal resources that may have been
created for quite different reasons (see Chapter 6). Thus, the
boundaries between dominant and subordinate cultures are not
fixed walls, but rather "permeable membranes."[10]

Second, there are lines of cleavage and conflict among elite
sectors, leading to elements of tension and contradiction within
dominant cultures.[11] Elite projects are subject to contention
among and even within dominant groups, and it is important to
examine what is at stake in some of these debates and conflicts.
Surely, in the majority of cases, it is not easy for elite groups to
impose their own interests and visions of society on others, due
to opposition from both other elites and from subordinate
groups. Recognizing the importance of conflict in these processes, William Roseberry has proposed that rather than equate
hegemony with ideological consensus, we should use the concept of hegemonic process:

> *not* to understand consent but to understand struggle, the ways
> in which the words, images, symbols, forms, organizations,
> institutions, and movements used by subordinate populations
> to talk about, understand, confront, accommodate themselves
> to, or resist their domination are shaped by the process of domi-
> nation itself. What hegemony constructs, then, is not a shared
> ideology but a common material and meaningful framework
> for living through, talking about, and acting upon social or-
> ders characterized by domination. That common material and
> meaningful framework is, in part, discursive, a common lan-
> guage or way of talking about social relationships that sets
> out the central terms around which and in terms of which con-
> testation and struggle can occur.[12]

Roseberry refers to hegemonic process, then, as involving the
emergence of an accepted language of contention. His view is
also compatible with a reworking of hegemony by John and Jean
Comaroff, who argue that while ideologies make up the *content*
of debate and struggle, hegemony lends it its *form*.[13]

The Guayaquil-Quito Railway had a central role in the formation of a language of contention in liberal Ecuador. Chapter 3 examines the characteristics of a discourse regarding the
need to transform the nation through movement and connec-

tion (and especially a railway), which, at the turn of the century, allowed a consensus to emerge about national renewal among elites from the coast and the highlands and among liberals and conservatives. In the railway project and the broader discourse associated with it, elites from both of these regions could identify some —although not all—of their own interests. However, underlying this shared language were different projects of movement and connection: coastal elites were more interested in the kind of movement embodied in the formation of a labor market, whereas highland elites were concerned with the movement of goods around the national territory, especially with the marketing of highland agricultural products on the coast.

Although the railway would promote both processes, at times they contradicted each other. The potential conflicts underlying the general discourse of national reform outlined in Chapter 3 becomes clear in Chapters 4 and 5 through an analysis of the differing regional elite projects and interests subsumed within this general project. Chapter 6 then examines the contradictions of national incorporation through movement, connection, and the railway at the local level, in Alausí—contradictions experienced, at different moments and in different ways, by both subordinate and elite groups. The aim of this analysis is to recuperate the particular and differential experiences of social groups, experiences that the unifying view of national incorporation from the center tends to erase. Chapter 6 also explores how this unifying view was understood from "below": local social groups attempted to stretch the boundaries of liberal discourse, with varying degrees of success, precisely in order to combat some of the effects of the liberal project at the local level. Clearly, conflict was not eliminated, but the very fact that liberal discourse, law, and national ideology were adopted by local groups in their struggles indicates the broad success of processes of incorporation. Chapter 7, in contrast, briefly explores evidence that some groups remained beyond the reach of liberal discourse and, in particular, felt little attachment to the railway as a "redemptive work." Altogether, this book explores a hegemonic project that was only ever partially successful, given the modifications and challenges posed by both elite and subordinate groups. While we can analytically separate a discussion of culture and political economy, then, an anthropological political economy must examine both simultaneously.

Studies that take an anthropological approach to political economy have often examined the formation of communities.

Such studies date back at least to the 1950s work of Eric Wolf on the intersections of global processes and local histories that led to the formation of closed and open peasant communities.[14] The concept of community lends itself well to an analysis encompassing both culture and political economy, because "community" condenses two meanings: (1) a group of people living and producing together; and (2) a sense of belonging, of common identity. The national community is also a likely subject for an anthropological political economy, for the formation of a nation involves both political-economic changes, such as the circulation of products and labor around the national territory, and debates about who belongs to that national community.

The conceptualization of nations as imagined political communities was set forth in 1983 by Benedict Anderson, who argued that communities are necessarily imagined ones when all of their members do not personally know each other.[15] Communities are distinguished, however, by the style in which they are imagined. For Anderson, the nation is distinctively conceived as an inherently limited and sovereign community. It is thus imagined as a deep, horizontal one whose members share a national territory, beyond the boundaries of which exist other parallel, but distinct, nations.[16] Some of the historical changes that allowed this style of imagining political community to emerge involved the decline of dynastic realms and religious communities, the development of print capitalism (the mass production of books and newspapers) and the spread of vernacular administrative languages, and the movement of native colonial administrators within a delimited territorial sphere.

A central assumption of Anderson's work is that the national community is defined inclusively; usually, exclusions are reflected in silences rather than made explicit. The use of an idiom of inclusiveness for the national community bears closer analysis. In the case studied here, it is the inclusiveness, the very universalizing tendencies of the idiom through which the national community is imagined, that allows various social groups to see different populations and regions as either central or not to the national community. Importantly, not only are there different shadings or emphases in elite imaginings of the national community, but also even those individuals who are only partially or marginally perceived as members of that community can use its inclusive language to make claims for equal treatment.

Pushing Anderson's analysis further, Richard Fox has suggested that if we are to think about nations as imagined communities, we surely must also ask who does that imagining.[17] This question directs us away from a conception of imagined national communities as arenas of shared identity and interests, and toward an analysis of the conflicts among different interests, and struggles to impose projects that are involved in the formation of national communities. Gavin Smith has argued (following Sabean) that belonging to a community can perhaps best be defined not in terms of sharing interests and identity, but rather as being engaged in the same argument.[18] We can extend this concept beyond the more clearly defined community of Huasicancha, Peru, to which Smith refers, to think about how it could apply to the kind of "arguments" and conflicts that occur in national communities. This is quite consistent with the concept of a language of contention.

National ideologies and projects are fraught with tensions, and these should be seen in light of the contradictions of liberalism. To clarify what is meant by liberalism, and in what sense it is studied in this book, two distinctions should be made. First, economic liberalism and political liberalism should be distinguished from each other. The former involves laissez-faire economic policies, both beyond and within national territories.[19] The latter includes such ideals as the equality of citizens before the state, the dissolution of corporate groups, the separation of the state and civil society, and the establishment of law rather than privilege as the fundamental principle governing people's interactions (all ideals which are closely related). Together, economic liberalism and political liberalism set out the bare bones of a national project. Minimally, this involves both the economic integration of a national territory to ensure the free movement of goods, labor, and capital and the dual individualization and universalization of people as citizens rather than as members of inherently unequal and separate corporate groups (a powerful change presupposed in the emergence of that deep, horizontal community that Anderson depicts).

While economic liberalism and political liberalism can be distinguished analytically, they tend to be associated in complex ways historically. This association leads to one of the founding contradictions of liberalism. Political liberalism argues that individuals are equal (before the state); economic liberalism, however, implies the continual production of inequality, associated as it is with the emergence of societies divided into classes. Although this is fundamentally contradictory,[20] political liberalism should not be seen as simply masking the inequalities promoted by economic liberalism. Indeed, classically, rather than representing some conspiracy to fool subalterns about the class nature of the bourgeois project, the equality of individuals as assured by law has been essential to creating conditions of equal economic competition, given the peculiar character of the bourgeoisie as a class whose members are in constant competition with one another.[21] In the particular arrangement of forces characteristic of early twentieth-century Ecuador, the liberal national project implied economic changes that entailed class conflict but at the same time provided precisely some of the political and discursive resources to deal with those conflicts.

Second, Ecuadorian liberalism is analyzed here not as a series of government fiscal or trade policies, but as a discursive formation (involving practices as well as words). This does not mean that the economic implications of liberalism are not examined: in fact, the railway points us directly to a series of important economic changes. However, a set of ideas about the proper relations between the state and citizens and what constitutes modernity and progress also informed policy making. In particular, this study examines liberal discourse, a language shared by elites beyond the halls of government and, at times, also appropriated by subordinate groups in Ecuador.

Liberal discourse in Ecuador was part of a political-economic "field of force," to use E. P. Thompson's phrase—that is, a field in which social groups were mutually constrained over time by the actions and projects of others, as informed by their perceptions of what social relations should be.[22] In his studies of moral economy, paternalism, and law, Thompson provides eloquent examples of how actions are informed by past experiences and how shared yet contested understandings become the locus of social struggle.[23] In conceptualizing a mutually conditioned and historically constituted field of force that is produced by, but also exerts pressures and limits on, social actors, it becomes difficult to separate structure and agency, or the discursive and the political-economic fields. Two examples from this book will suffice for the moment. First, for highland landowners to push through legislation in the 1910s designed to facilitate the expansion and modernization of agricultural production, it was also necessary for the highlands to be perceived as a source of national wealth and well-being rather than as a drag on national progress and development (see Chapter 5). In the second example, attempts at the local level to modernize and expand production were constrained by a field of force of particular social relations. Thus, modernization attempts were constrained both by historically constituted conceptions of proper agrarian relations (constructed over time in part through the engagement of broader ideological resources and definitions) and by new discursive resources that allowed social groups to selectively employ aspects of law and national ideology to promote their own interests (Chapter 6).

The railway and more generally the Ecuadorian liberal project clearly "meant" different things to different people. These distinct experiences and the perceptions that accompanied them were not randomly distributed, of course: their multiplicity reflects the differentiation of society. That differentiation is also revealed in the fact that it is easier today to reconstruct certain experiences of liberalism rather than others, revealing the capacity of some social groups to express their points of view and impose their interests more forcefully, while the actions and perspectives of other groups can only occasionally be glimpsed in the historical record. As a result, it is easier to reconstruct the projects of the liberal state, or coastal or highland elites (Chapters 3, 4, and 5), than to interpret why indigenous day laborers in Alausí resisted sanitation measures during a bubonic plague epidemic or what was at issue for peasants in agrarian conflicts in Alausí during the 1920s (Chapter 6).

The relation between center and locality also requires rethinking in this context. For instance, the discrepancies between the liberal ideology as expressed by the president or a cabinet minister and the way in which local authorities carried out the project surely cannot be attributed merely to the dilution and distortion of liberalism as it trickled down to the local level—not least because it trickled down to subordinate groups quite well, as shown by their petitions and complaints to supralocal authorities. Instead, such discrepancies reflect a more fundamental problem for the state. Central to the liberal project was the effort to impose homogeneity on local, historically constituted diversity. Rather than homogenize identities, this project involved efforts to create homogeneous administrative processes and to make state action felt evenly across the national territory. Space and spatial connections represented a fundamental problem in this regard, because difficulties in transport, travel, and communications (see Chapter 2) directly affected the possibility of creating this kind of homogeneity. One way in which homogeneity in this restricted sense was achieved was when subordinate groups having problems with local landowners or political authorities solicited fair and equal treatment from the central state. From the local perspective, the contradictions of economic liberalism and political liberalism provided part of the tension through which the national project was established, called on, articulated, and utilized. By doing research, then, at several locations, the local case functioned not as a microcosm of society or even as a representative example, but rather as a demonstration of some of the very problems (economic, political, and discursive) that were most centrally at issue during Ecuador's liberal period. The reorganization of Ecuadorian space from 1895 to 1930 is returned to in Chapter 8.

Notes

1. Jean-Paul Deler, *Ecuador: Del espacio al estado nacional* (Quito: Banco Central, 1987), 199.

2. The U.S. company that built the railway was called the Guayaquil and Quito Railway. When construction began in the 1870s, the railway was known as the Ferrocarril del Sur (Southern Railway) because it was designed as a short line linking a highland wagon road with the Guayas River basin (see Chapter 2). Later, under Eloy Alfaro, it was occasionally referred to as the Ferrocarril Trasandino, emphasizing the fact that it was designed to scale the Andes and to run along the inter-Andean corridor. Most often during the liberal period, however, it was simply called the Ferrocarril de Guayaquil a Quito (Railway from Guayaquil to Quito).

3. See especially Eric R. Wolf, *Europe and the People without History* (Berkeley: University of California Press, 1982); Sidney W. Mintz, *Sweetness and Power: The Place of Sugar in Modern History* (New York: Penguin Books, 1985).

4. Philip Corrigan and Derek Sayer, *The Great Arch: English State Formation as Cultural Revolution* (New York: Basil Blackwell, 1985), 195.

5. Ibid., 42 (emphasis in original).

6. William Roseberry, *Anthropologies and Histories: Essays in Culture, History, and Political Economy* (New Brunswick, NJ: Rutgers University Press, 1989), 42.

7. Ibid., 54. See also the useful discussion of structure and agency in the preface and introduction to Philip Abrams, *Historical Sociology* (Ithaca: Cornell University Press, 1982), xi–17.

8. Derek Sayer, *The Violence of Abstraction* (Oxford: Basil Blackwell, 1987), 92.

9. See Raymond Williams, *Marxism and Literature* (New York: Oxford University Press, 1977).

10. T. J. Jackson Lears, "The Concept of Cultural Hegemony: Problems and Possibilities," *American Historical Review* 90 (1985): 574.

11. A classic exploration of these issues is found in Antonio Gramsci's "Notes on Italian History," in his *Selections from the Prison Notebooks*, edited and translated by Quintin Hoare and Geoffrey Nowell Smith (New York: International, 1971), 44–120.

12. William Roseberry, "Hegemony and the Language of Contention," in *Everyday Forms of State Formation: Revolution and the Negotiation of Rule in Modern Mexico*, edited by Gilbert M. Joseph and Daniel Nugent (Durham, NC: Duke University Press, 1994), 360–61 (emphasis in original).

13. John Comaroff and Jean Comaroff, *Ethnography and the Historical Imagination* (Boulder, CO: Westview Press, 1992), 28–29.

14. Eric R. Wolf, "Closed Corporate Peasant Communities in Mesoamerica and Central Java," *Southwestern Journal of Anthropology* 13 (1957): 1–18; idem, "Types of Latin American Peasantries," *American Anthropologist* 57 (1955): 452–71; idem, "The Vicissitudes of the Closed Corporate Peasant Community," *American Ethnologist* 13 (1986): 325–29.

15. Benedict Anderson, *Imagined Communities: Reflections on the Origin and Spread of Nationalism* (London: Verso, 1983).

16. See also Daniel A. Segal, "Nationalism, Comparatively Speaking," *Journal of Historical Sociology* 1, no. 3 (1988): 301–21.

17. Richard G. Fox, Introduction, to *Nationalist Ideologies and the Production of National Cultures*, edited by Richard G. Fox (Washington, DC: American Ethnological Society, 1990), 7.

18. Gavin Smith, "The Production of Culture in Local Rebellion," in *Golden Ages, Dark Ages: Imagining the Past in Anthropology and History*, edited by Jay O'Brien and William Roseberry (Berkeley: University of California Press, 1991), 195.

19. Nonetheless, we now know that state intervention was crucial to the creation and maintenance of the conditions under which the market could operate "freely," both in the classic European case and in other contexts. See Christopher Hill, *Reformation to Industrial Revolution* (New York: Pantheon, 1968); Joseph L. Love and Nils Jacobsen, eds., *Guiding the Invisible Hand: Economic Liberalism and the State in Latin America* (New York: Praeger, 1988); Karl Polanyi, *The Great Transformation: The Political and Economic Origins of Our Time* (Boston: Beacon, 1944); Steven Topik, "State Interventionism in a Liberal Regime: Brazil, 1889–1930," *Hispanic American Historical Review* 60 (1980): 593–616.

20. On the inherently contradictory nature of liberalism see H. J. Laski, *El liberalismo europeo* (Mexico: Fondo de Cultura Económica, 1992); Uday S. Mehta, "Liberal Strategies of Exclusion," *Politics and Society* 18 (1990): 427–54.

21. Philip Corrigan and Derek Sayer, "How the Law Rules: Variations on Some Themes in Karl Marx," in *Law, State, and Society*, edited by Bob Fryer et al. (London: Croom Helm, 1981), 29; Derek Sayer, "The Critique of Politics and Political Economy: Capitalism, Communism, and the State in Marx's Writings of the mid-1840s," *Sociological Review* 33, no. 2 (1985): 240–45.

22. E. P. Thompson, "Eighteenth-century English Society: Class Struggle without Class?" *Social History* 3, no. 2 (1978): 133–65.

23. Ibid.; E. P. Thompson, "The Moral Economy of the English Crowd in the Eighteenth Century," in *Customs in Common: Studies in Traditional Popular Culture* (New York: New Press, 1991), 185–258; idem, "The Moral Economy Reviewed," in *Customs in Common*, 259–351; idem, *Whigs and Hunters: The Origin of the Black Act* (New York: Pantheon Books, 1975).

2

Historical Overview of the Ecuadorian Economy and Geography

Ecuador is located on the Pacific coast of South America. It is crossed by both the intangible line of the equator and the all-too-solid lines of the Andes, as Ecuadorian elites perceived these mountains at the turn of the century. As a result, Ecuador has a remarkable diversity of climatic zones, varying by altitude, within short distances of one another. Its three continental regions are the tropical coast (*costa*), the temperate highlands (*sierra*), and the eastern Amazonian lowlands (*oriente*); the fourth region is the Galápagos Islands. The western coastal area of plains and low hills has a humid tropical climate (contrasting with the dry climate of the Peruvian coast), with somewhat drier areas in the central coastal zone of Manabí. The highlands are characterized by two parallel chains of the Andes that define a high-altitude plateau (see Map 1). In the southern highlands, the two mountain ranges lose their clear definition. In the north-central highlands, several high, snow-covered peaks rise above the two general ranges, forming an "avenue of volcanoes" (some rising more than 6,000 meters above sea level). Altogether, the long inter-Andean corridor undulates in a sequence of thirteen valleys and river basins, ringed and divided by high-altitude grasslands (*páramos*) and transverse mountain ridges. The Ecuadorian highlands thus have the form of a ladder, with the ridges forming the rungs and the cordilleras, the sides. Each valley contains a provincial city surrounded by rural areas. The inter-Andean valleys, at altitudes of 2,200 to 2,800 meters, tend to have stable, pleasant climates that have been characterized as "perpetual springtime," given their greater temperature changes from day to night than from season to season.

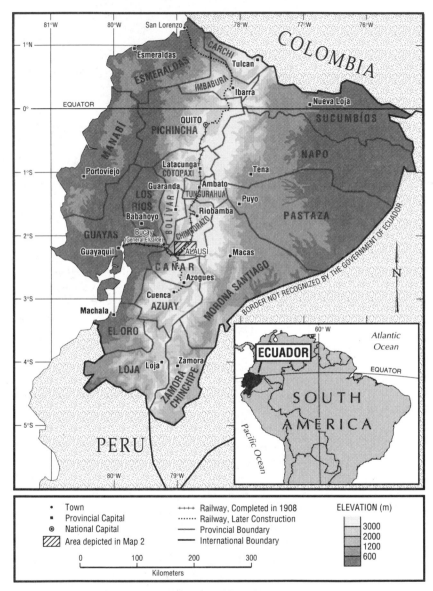

Map 1. Political Divisions and Topography of Ecuador

Travel in Nineteenth-Century Ecuador

The difficulties of travel during the nineteenth century could be summed up by the fact that Ecuadorian paths were known as *caminos para pájaros*, or roads for birds.[1] In 1892 the German geographer, Teodoro Wolf, who lived in Ecuador for more than twenty years, published a book on its geography in which he included a description of travel routes. As Wolf explained, "In Ecuador, trails are so minimally artificial that we could almost consider them to be a natural phenomenon, intimately bound to the topography."[2]

During the nineteenth century the coastal region had few roads or trails, as transit was easiest by river. In the most populated areas there were some trails that could be used in the dry season, but in most of the zone there were no paths of any kind; and, when a path was opened, it would quickly disappear under the growth of tropical vegetation. In the highlands, toward the end of the century, there was only one good road, which connected Quito and Sibambe. The principal road that linked the entire highland region from Carchi to Loja could be considered reasonably good only where it crossed the provinces of Pichincha, Tungurahua, León (later Cotopaxi), and Chimborazo. In other areas, the road was adequate in the dry season but almost impassable in the rainy season. Meanwhile, the trails from the highlands toward the Amazon could be traveled only on foot; wealthy travelers were carried on the backs of Indians. None of the trails initiated between the northern highlands and the coast (that is, between Pichincha and Imbabura, and Manabí and Esmeraldas) was completed, which was understandable given the lack of population on the northern coast that would allow for a profitable interregional trade. In contrast, the more densely populated areas of the coast (principally the Guayas River basin) had a more active trade with the central highlands and, therefore, had a number of mule trails, which linked them to the Andean region.

Thus, during the latter nineteenth century, there were several routes from the southern coast to the central highlands, although the most common route was from Guayaquil to Babahoyo (also called Bodegas de Babahoyo because government warehouses were located there), to Guaranda, through Ambato, and on to Quito. The first leg of the journey, from Guayaquil to Babahoyo, involved an 80-kilometer trip by water, followed by a 340-kilometer trek by horse or mule to Quito.

Prior to the 1860s, travelers had to wait for the tide to carry them upriver by bamboo or balsa raft since in the extensive and flat coastal basin, the Guayas River ebbed and flowed with the marine tides, reversing its course every twelve hours, with the current reaching speeds of five miles per hour.[3] It took two days to reach Babahoyo from Guayaquil. Between 1860 and 1890, however, steamboats were introduced into the Guayas River system, increasing the speed and comfort of this segment of the trip, which now took only six to eight hours. The arrival of the steam age in the Guayas basin reduced transportation time by a factor of five. In addition, the smallest steamboat could carry at least twice as much cargo as could the largest raft. Around 1880, river navigation ensured daily service between Guayaquil and Daule and Guayaquil and Babahoyo, as well as between Guayaquil and Yaguachi, where the short railway toward the highlands began. The steam era would come later to the highlands proper, with the improvement and completion of the railway, which would prove to be much more costly and difficult than the development of transport routes on the coast.[4]

Depending upon the season, the weather, and the changing condition of trails, the time it took to travel from Guayaquil to Quito varied, but for most of the nineteenth century the trip took from ten to fourteen days. The discomfort of travel was augmented by there being few inns along the route, and these rarely offered more amenities than basic shelter. For six months of the year, during the rainy season, the trip was almost impossible. If cargo arrived in Guayaquil destined for Quito during the rainy season, the owner often had to wait six or eight months for it, until the trails became passable. Most people avoided traveling during the rainy season if they could, with the exception of the letter carriers.[5] The route from Babahoyo to the foothills of the Andes crossed tropical swamps, but the most difficult part of the trip began after the ascent to Guaranda, situated at 2,668 meters above sea level, which could be undertaken only by foot or on mule. The trail rose to 3,660 meters above sea level to scale the western range of the Andes, causing altitude sickness among travelers.

The various routes between the coast and highlands all followed the same general pattern.[6] Along the coastal plain, the muleteers often had to use machetes to open a path through the dense tropical forest. From this plain, the trail penetrated the highlands via one of the river valleys that extended from the western slopes of the Andes. At first the valley was wide, the river slow running, and the ascent gradual. Steadily the valleys narrowed and the rivers quickened, and the traveler began a sharper climb, entering the humid climate of the tropical forest along the western slopes. The humidity of the Ecuadorian coast contrasts with the dryness of the coastal desert of neighboring Peru. The cold Humbolt current, which runs along the Peruvian coast, causes rain to fall out at sea, whereas the warmer El Niño current runs along the Ecuadorian coast so that the rain falls when clouds encounter the western slopes of the Andes. On these slopes, the nineteenth-century traveler climbed along muddy cliffs overlooking the river valley, in constant danger of sliding and falling into the swift-running stream. At times it was necessary for the traveler to cross the same river several times. The tropical forest complicated his journey through the narrowing valleys, as tree roots tripped the animals and fallen trunks blocked the trail. Indeed, "the nearer one approaches the base of the ridge of the Andes the larger and taller the trees become, until, in the gorges of the western spurs, one finds the hothouses of nature, which, steaming under a tropical sun, force into existence a rank and prodigal vegetation, where each plant and tree has to wage desperate war for existence, and where, when some monarch of the forest lifts his crest above his fellows, tons of lianas, mosses, and parasites tug at trunk and branch until the exhausted giant is borne to earth."[7]

The zone's humidity soaked travelers and their mules in sweat. At around 600 to 800 meters above sea level, usually in a place where several valleys and rivers met, the trail abandoned the valley to rise in a zigzag up to a mountain ridge, the division between two valleys. Here the real ascent began, as the climb became increasingly steep, with few ledges to allow a rest. In addition, in these zones the soil was soft, and with the almost continual fall of rain, the trail turned into muddy ruts. Here, too, the traveler encountered the worst of the *camellones*, deep furrows—often two- or three-feet deep and full of mud and water—worn into the soil by the passage of mule trains. Despite the discomfort caused by the floundering of horses and mules through such ruts, "these camellones are of great benefit to the traveler on the steep acclivities and descents of the mountain roads, where they prevent the horse from sliding and falling, and hurling its rider into one of the precipices below."[8] One traveler in the 1870s was rebuked in Quito for complaining about the ruts in the road; and, "upon asking my monitor what he considered a bad road, he said, 'A road is bad when the beasts

tumble into mud holes and vanish right out of sight.' "⁹ When
animals became stuck in these ruts, the cargo had to be removed
so that the animals could be pulled out and then reloaded. From
these zones, pack animals, passengers, and cargo emerged covered with mud.

These travel conditions continued to an altitude of some
2,000 meters, where the ground became more solid and dry and
the temperature more pleasant, with a cool breeze. The tropical
forest gave way to temperate zone vegetation in the ascent from
2,000 to 3,000 meters above sea level. Above 3,000 meters, the
páramo grasslands began, with numerous rises and falls of the
trail. The ground again became as slippery as soap with the
slightest rainfall, causing the animals to slide and fall. When
this occurred during an ascent, the pack and mount animals
would fall backward, which was particularly dangerous; on a
descent, they could at least see where they were going as they
slid forward. Animals that were experienced on these trails knew
how to slide under control:

> coming to the top of an eminence, they stop, and having placed
> their forelegs in a slanting position, they put their hind legs
> together, drawing them a little forward, as if going to lie down.
> In this attitude, having, as it were, taken a survey of the road,
> they slide down with startling velocity. Their dexterity in fol-
> lowing the various windings of the road is really astonishing,
> for by a gentle inclination of the body they turn first to one
> side and then to another, keeping the most perfect equilibrium,
> which is the only means of saving themselves and their riders
> from being hurled headlong forward, or being dashed to pieces
> by a fall. All the rider has to do is to keep himself fast in the
> saddle without checking his beast. Any unguarded motion on
> his part, by disordering the equilibrium of the mule, might
> lead to fatal consequences.¹⁰

Although these moments on the trail were hair-raising, in
sóme ways the worst was still to come. In the final ascent over
the western cordillera, travelers suffered from cold, wind, fatigue, and, often, altitude sickness. This was particularly true
on the ascent around Chimborazo mountain:

> The trail at many points is scarcely wide enough for a horse to
> pass, and there we scramble over craggy rocks, overlooking
> an abyss, while the wind blows with an irresistible impetus.
> The horse frequently stops suddenly and clings to the ground
> in order not to be swept off his feet by the wind that passes

whistling through the grasses in a terrifying manner; and then the passenger, who at any moment expects to be flung from his saddle, sighs with relief when he only loses his hat and a few pieces of luggage; but it often happens that all his efforts are futile and he and his horse topple over the precipice. . . . Twice I have crossed Chimborazo in the windy season and on both occasions I feared at every instant that I would be dashed on the rocks. . . . More than once I have seen small donkeys carrying voluminous but light cargos such as hats, fall to the abyss of a ravine, carried away by the irresistible force of the winds.[11]

These conditions continued until the traveler reached one of the principal Andean trails leading over mountain ridges and through inter-Andean valleys, to arrive, exhausted, in Quito, many days after having embarked.

The overall project of Ecuadorian governments after the 1895 Liberal Revolution was expressed in terms of both movement and connection. The coastal region was seen as already characterized by these attributes. The extensive area of the Guayas River basin was connected through a network of navigable rivers. As already mentioned, not only was the Guayas River navigable, but it also reversed its flow every twelve hours, which facilitated travel by raft powered by human muscle. Thus, this core coastal area was far more integrated internally than were the highlands. This region was also the dynamic center of trade with the international market, through the export of the overwhelmingly important product of cocoa as well as other top export products. For instance, in 1900, Ecuador's four most important exports (by percentage of total value exported) were cocoa (70.7 percent), *tagua*, or vegetable ivory (10.4 percent), rubber (7.0 percent), and coffee (5.4 percent).[12] The coast was also the center of the import trade. The fabulous profits of tropical export agriculture allowed for luxury consumption in the coastal region, which imported most of the basic food products consumed there.

If the highlands were seen in a very different light, as disconnected and less dynamic, this too had some basis in reality. They had been the center of the area's economy during much of the colonial period, but in the decades following independence (1830–1870), the highlands underwent processes of dearticulation, deurbanization, and depopulation. From its more integrated economy earlier in the colonial period, the region saw a return to production for local markets in each of the highlands' thirteen intermont basins, along with a general dearticulation of transportation routes and regional economies. Deurbanization was also caused by a series of catastrophes that occurred in the late eighteenth and nineteenth centuries, which added to the overall experience of this time as one in which the country was decomposing and in decline. Serious epidemics afflicted the highland towns, including measles in 1785–86 and smallpox in 1816. But the nineteenth century was also an era of great earthquakes and volcanic eruptions (of Cotopaxi and Tungurahua), where again towns had the highest mortality rates, often due to the collapse of stone buildings. Eruptions also had long-term effects on highland agriculture, as crops were damaged by ash. In 1797 an earthquake destroyed Riobamba, killing twelve thousand people, including over 60 percent of the urban population. Earthquakes also occurred in Cayambe in 1859, Imbabura in 1868 (causing more than ten thousand deaths), and Latacunga in 1876.[13] Similarly, troop demands for food, fodder, and livestock during the independence battles also led to deurbanization, as people attempted to escape these exactions. Military conscription for the independence wars took its demographic toll as well. Thus, in 1825 the sex ratio (number of men per 100 women) was 67.3 in Latacunga and 61.8 in Riobamba, while these figures had been, respectively, 87.4 and 70.5 in 1780.[14] Nonetheless, the image of the highlands as stagnant and disconnected throughout the nineteenth century and the claim that the liberals would be the first to connect the region internally and with the coast were not entirely accurate, as an overview of Ecuadorian economic history makes clear.

Overview of Ecuadorian Regional Economic History

The territory that is now Ecuador was in the process of being incorporated into the Inca state at the time of the Spanish conquest. In some ways, the colonial period saw a continuation of its peripheral status. Rather than being the site of important mineral wealth that could enrich the royal coffers in Spain, the Audiencia de Quito (now Ecuador) principally produced textiles and agricultural crops for other regions of the empire. Thus, Ecuador produced for the internal colonial market rather than for Europe, sending its textiles to the silver-mining center of Potosí and selling basic foodstuffs within the protected area of Spanish colonialism. Associated with textiles, sheep raising and, to a lesser extent, cotton cultivation were also important. Indians were recruited through rotating labor drafts (*mita*) for work in textile sweatshops (*obrajes*). The goods made in Ecuadorian *obrajes* included "coarse brown sackcloth, wadding, white or black woolen cloth, blankets, cordova hats, straw hats, fiber sandals, and ship riggings of high, medium, and ordinary quality."[15]

The market for the output of the *obrajes* began to contract in the eighteenth century. Potosí, the principal market for Ecuadorian products and, in general, the central axis around which Andean space was articulated during the colonial period, suffered a strong decline in silver production in the first half of the eighteenth century, in turn undermining textile manufactures. In addition, with the opening of the Cape Horn route in the 1740s and an increase in French contraband, Ecuadorian textiles began to lose their share of the reduced Peruvian market. The Bourbon reforms of the 1770s, which to some extent opened up Latin American markets to competition from European goods, further intensified the crisis.

Another element of these reforms—the opening of the port of Guayaquil, which had previously served only intracolonial trade—created the conditions for the expansion of cocoa production on the coast. As the highland manufacturing economy declined, a new dynamism emerged in the sparsely populated coastal region, based on the first cocoa boom, which lasted from 1780 to 1820.[16] Cocoa production had begun to expand on the coast prior to the Bourbon reforms, although the reforms greatly stimulated this growth. Carlos Contreras has argued that coastal elites began to explore export possibilities based on coastal products with the decline in highland manufacturing output at midcentury. Unlike the colonial areas that produced metals (especially Bolivia and Mexico), colonial Ecuador could gain access to specie only through its exports to other Latin American or to Spanish markets. Thus, the crisis of the late colonial period in Ecuador implied a decline in the role that textiles had played in organizing both urban and rural space. This decline led to a long economic downturn involving both the ruralization and the demonetarization of the highlands, while the relative importance of the coast increased.

In 1830, Ecuador became fully independent with the breakup of Gran Colombia. Much of the fighting for Peru and Bolivia's independence was launched from the southern highlands of Ecuador and drew on Ecuadorian resources. When Gran Colombia disintegrated, Ecuador was assigned a disproportionate share of the British independence debt (contracted primarily for the purchase of armaments). The English were interested in increasing their share of the Latin American market for their exports, and, because of the foreign debt, Britain was given preferential access to this market. The entry of British textiles, especially of cotton goods, into Ecuador further undermined the local textile economy in the nineteenth century. Whereas poor transportation and communications between regions had provided natural protection for locally produced goods early in the century, this protection began to decrease as communications were improved after the 1860s. The result would be a crisis in artisan-peasant production in the north-central highlands.

After independence, Ecuador's political boundaries were set by granting equal representation to three "divisions" centering on the cities of Guayaquil on the coast, Quito in the north-central highlands, and Cuenca in the southern highlands. In some ways, Ecuador in the early nineteenth century was made up of regions that were oriented away from rather than toward each other. The coast produced cocoa for the world market. The southern highlands' economy was directed toward Peru. The north-central highlands, characterized by large haciendas, were oriented toward Colombia. The circulation of Peruvian currency in the southern highlands and of Colombian currency in the northern region reflects this outward orientation. To a large extent, these three regions operated according to separate economic rhythms for much of the nineteenth century. It was rare to encounter elites who had economic interests in more than one of these regions before 1870,[17] when the landowning elite of the northern highlands began to consolidate its power within the Andean zone.[18] The lack of integration of Ecuador's principal regions was to become particularly manifest in 1859 when four governments, based in Quito, Guayaquil, Cuenca, and Loja, claimed to rule the national territory.

In the context of the near dissolution of the country in 1859, Gabriel García Moreno came to power with a strong centralizing vision. Paradoxically, the conservative and Catholic García Moreno had an essentially liberal project: to modernize the state, to forge an internal market by connecting the various regions of the country through an ambitious road and railway construction program, to develop a technical elite (he established the Escuela Politécnica Nacional in Quito), and to reform policing and prison policies (he built the Panopticon in Quito). García Moreno has been characterized as a caudillo who used the church instead of the military to further his goals.[19] Thus, he pursued his national project by bringing church and state closer together rather than by separating them, as had happened in several other Latin American countries where the foundations of a secular state had been laid during the nineteenth century.[20] García Moreno perceived that in a country as Catholic as Ecuador, the church could be employed to dominate opposition to his broad campaign to modernize the state and form an internal market. It has been persuasively argued that García Moreno used the church as his tool and that he strengthened it for his own political purposes.[21] His association with the Catholic Church has led scholars at times to see him as establishing a "theocracy" in Ecuador. It should be noted, however, that his policies brought him into conflict with local clergy, which he resolved by promoting the immigration of foreign orders. García Moreno also experienced conflict with highland landowners when their control over local indigenous laborers was undermined by the labor demands of his extensive road construction programs.[22]

The first work on a railway in Ecuador was undertaken under García Moreno. His goal was to connect Guayaquil with Quito, cities which at the time were linked only by a mule trail. He began by improving the old colonial route along the inter-Andean corridor, developing it as a wagon road between Quito and Riobamba. In his overall infrastructure project, branch roads were designed to unite the highland provinces to the main road, thereby improving communications with the northern province of Imbabura and the southern provinces of Azuay and Loja, as well as between the capital and port. By 1872 a mule trail had reached Sibambe in the canton of Alausí, and García Moreno conceived of the plan to unite Sibambe and Yaguachi by rail. From Yaguachi, steamboats would carry goods and travelers down the Yaguachi River (which was dredged for the purpose), to the Babahoyo and then Guayas rivers, and on to Guayaquil. In October 1873 the first two locomotives arrived in Ecuador; in May 1874 railway traffic was officially inaugurated on the short extension between Yaguachi and Milagro. By 1875, when García Moreno was assassinated, the rail line was 45 kilometers long.

Partly in the context of the stimuli to production and transport under García Moreno, the north-central highlands began to recover in the 1860s (the southern highlands were less affected by these processes). One sign of the recuperation of the highland economy was the establishment of additional periodic markets in highland towns between 1860 and 1870, demonstrating the new vitality of regional trade.[23] While the earlier part of the century saw the coexistence of large properties with numerous small ones in the north-central highlands, after 1870 the consolidation of the large haciendas began. This occurred in part in response to the incentive offered by the new possibilities of the internal market, which were associated with improved transportation and the gradual recovery of urbanization. In the north-central highlands, there began to be an emphasis on livestock raising, requiring large tracts of land, thus stimulating the land market. The consolidation of the large livestock properties coincided with the crisis in artisanal production, generating labor migrations toward the coastal region where cocoa production was entering a second phase of expansion.

Meanwhile, on the coast, cocoa entered a second boom period after 1870. At the beginning of the 1830s there had been approximately five million cocoa plants in Ecuador; between 1890 and 1910 the number of plants increased from thirty-three million to eighty million.[24] Cocoa was cultivated on plantations on the southern coast, primarily in the Guayas River basin, where land was plentiful but labor was scarce. The second cocoa boom depended largely on the growth in Europe of new groups of urban consumers with their rising standard of living and taste for exotic goods. Coastal cocoa production generated labor migration from the highlands, given the relatively high wages offered (80 centavos per day in coastal export agriculture, in contrast to 20 centavos per day in highland agriculture, by 1906). In the early twentieth century, the construction of the Guayaquil-Quito Railway would facilitate the formation of a labor market, not only because workers followed the rail line to the coast but also because work building the railway offered higher wages than did highland agriculture (see Chapter 4).

The financing of cocoa production remained in the hands of Ecuadorians rather than foreign investors. Because cocoa production involved minimal backward and forward linkages, it did not encourage the overall development of Ecuadorian manufacturing capacity through the establishment of facilities such as processing plants.[25] Indeed, it did not even promote the construction of roads; steamboats were used for transportation within the Guayas River basin. There was also very little reinvestment of earnings in the plantations, whose growth relied on expanding cultivation into new lands rather than on improving efficiency. Rather than being reinvested in agro-export or in other productive activities, earnings from cocoa left the country through capital flight and were spent on luxurious living in Guayaquil as well as on foreign debt payments.

In the early period of cocoa production at the end of the colonial era, food production within the coastal region had provisioned the local markets. With the expansion of cocoa, as both subsistence lands and labor were drawn into the export economy, and as the city of Guayaquil grew rapidly, it became necessary to obtain food staples from elsewhere. Given the high costs of transport from the highlands at the end of the century, it was cheaper for Ecuadorians living on the coast to import basic goods such as wheat and barley from Chile or even California than to bring them in from the highlands. Thus, as cocoa production expanded on the coast, it did not mean that highland food production was developed through a transfer of earnings from the export sector to the nonexport economy. Rather, as the coastal market grew, so did imports, until the disruption of trade during the First World War.

Guayaquil experienced growth that paralleled the expansion in cocoa output. After doubling its population between 1780 and 1820, the city's growth slowed between 1830 and 1870 due to repeated epidemics of yellow fever and a decline (in relative terms) in cocoa production. However, in the half century from 1870 to 1920, Guayaquil's population grew from twelve thousand inhabitants to ninety thousand. Ecuador's third largest city at the beginning of the nineteenth century passed Cuenca in the 1830s and Quito in the 1880s.[26] Still, while Cuenca's population doubled between 1840 and 1920, the population of Quito, Riobamba, and Ambato—the beneficiaries of increased trade associated with road and railway construction—quadrupled in this period.[27]

As already described, internal travel and transport were arduous throughout the nineteenth century, with travel between Quito and Guayaquil often taking two weeks or more and almost impossible during six months of the year. This also implies an increasing divergence of life-styles between the elites of Quito and Guayaquil, who were not closely linked through intermarriage or business relations. Quito was a very Catholic city, with little conspicuous consumption, not only because of the difficulties of moving imported goods inland but also because highland earnings from producing for the regional economy were limited compared to coastal earnings from agroexports. Guayaquil, in contrast, was becoming a bustling city whose elites had significant disposable incomes and access to imported goods of all kinds. Also, Guayaquil was the center of banking and finance as well as of the import-export economy. Thus, the history of Ecuador in the nineteenth century can be seen as a tale of two cities (unlike the history of many other Latin American countries at the turn of the century, which could be seen as tales of one city).

In addition to the north-central highlands, centered around Quito, and the coastal region, around Guayaquil, the other distinct regions in nineteenth-century Ecuador were the southern highlands, around Cuenca, and the Amazon. At the end of the colonial period, the southern highlands produced cascarilla bark for the world market, cotton textiles for the internal colonial market (Lima and northern Peru, Chile, Panama), and agricultural foodstuffs for Ecuador's coastal region. From 1825 to 1850 the southern highlands became more isolated, focusing on agricultural and livestock production for local markets. From 1850 to 1885 the region increased its output of cascarilla (used for quinine) and, to a lesser extent, "Panama" hats for the world market. These years also saw the remonetarization of the region, allowing for investment in new economic activities such as the production of quinine and textiles, some mining, and an upsurge in road construction. Following a decline in cascarilla exports from 1885 to 1900, the search for economic alternatives led to a further expansion in Panama hat making. In addition, the continued improvement of the routes to the coast from the southern highlands resulted in some agricultural production for that market as well as the increased movement of workers to that zone.[28]

There were important differences among highland regions in the resources available for agricultural and livestock production.[29] The northern highlands (Carchi, Imbabura, Pichincha, and Cotopaxi) had the most fertile lands, with valleys, a broad sub-Andean belt, and vast extensions of *páramo* grasslands. The central highland provinces (Tungurahua, Chimborazo, and Bolívar) had similar characteristics, but with relatively smaller agricultural and livestock zones compared to those in the north. Finally, the southern provinces (Cañar, Azuay, and Loja) had less fertile, more volcanic soil, with fewer possibilities for agricultural development. Wherever agriculture was undertaken in the south, an intense process of soil erosion occurred. The result was an early disintegration of the hacienda in the southern provinces and the emergence of a smallholding peasantry. In part, these peasants were able to purchase land because of their access to money through artisanal production of Panama hats and, later, through migrations to the coast.

Unlike the highlands and the coast, where economic processes were increasingly coordinated in the nineteenth century, the Ecuadorian Amazon was significantly less articulated. Early in the colonial period, during its gold boom from 1540 to 1580, this region had been more closely tied to the highland core area. By the end of the sixteenth century, however, the combination of indigenous attacks on Spanish settlements and a colonial policy that defined the Audiencia de Quito as a textile and agricultural producer led to the abandonment of efforts to colonize the zone. For most of the colonial period the Ecuadorian Amazon was left to the care of religious communities such as the Franciscans and the Jesuits. The expulsion of the Jesuits in 1767 led to a further decline in the Spanish presence in the region.

By the nineteenth century, the southern Amazon in particular saw more influence from Peru than from the Ecuadorian core. This early nineteenth-century "marginality" from the perspective of the world economy or national integration was nonetheless experienced by the region's indigenous peoples as an era of demographic recovery and recuperation of territory. Around 1850 the economy was rearticulated with broader economic processes through the search for rubber, with the first areas affected being those closest to Peru. Rubber exploitation took off after 1875, reached its peak between 1890 and 1900, and was practically exhausted by 1914. Unlike what occurred in the Colombian Putumayo region, where rubber was extracted by large companies who used a labor system resembling slavery, in the Ecuadorian Amazon smaller producers were involved, and they negotiated with indigenous groups for labor, establishing the basis for subsequent patron-client relations. Throughout the nineteenth and twentieth centuries, there has been great variation in the ways and extent to which the indigenous societies and areas of the Ecuadorian Amazon have been affected by missionaries, hacendados, and colonists.[30]

In the 1860s limited networks of exchange connected the highland provinces to each other, with the coast, and with the southern and northern borders.[31] Imbabura province sold textiles and salt to southern Colombia, and textiles, sugar, cotton, and lard to Pichincha, León (later Cotopaxi), Tungurahua, and Los Ríos. León in turn had commercial relations with Pichincha and Los Ríos, selling them agricultural products, livestock, and textiles. Tungurahua sold agricultural products, lard, bread, shoe leather, shoes, and articles made from agave fiber (*cabuya*) to the coastal provinces. Chimborazo sold salt and textiles to Pichincha, Imbabura, and Colombia. Azuay had privileged relations with Guayaquil, for it was possible to travel to the coast by the Naranjal trail all year round, whereas the road through Babahoyo was impassable between May and December. Loja's principal economic ties were with Peru, to which the province sold agricultural, livestock, and artisanal products. Despite the establishment of these networks of production and circulation, however, most nineteenth-century commerce between the highlands and the coast was still limited to the transport of luxury articles for highland landowners and the movement of a few articles (such as sheep hides and shoe leather) destined for Guayaquil and external markets. Because it was still too expensive to move large quantities of low-value goods between regions, highland agricultural production continued to be primarily for local urban consumption.[32]

As has been made clear, Ecuador was a heavily agricultural country, and the limited industry that developed in the late nineteenth century was very much tied to agriculture. In the last three decades of the century, larger producers, taking advantage of the new opportunities in regional markets that came with improved transportation, undertook some manufacturing. The forms of "industry" that they established in the late nineteenth and early twentieth centuries in the north-central highlands included flour mills and leather working. At the turn of the century, with railway construction, there was also an important expansion in dairy products. After World War I, there was renewed expansion of textile manufacturing. Similarly, on the coast, sugar production and processing, which began near the end of the century, were stimulated by the First World War. Thus, in Ecuador, industrialization, such as it was, was not separate from agriculture but was based directly upon it.

The Liberal Period and the Railway

Throughout most of the nineteenth century political power in Ecuador was concentrated in the highlands, in the hands of large landowners closely linked to the Catholic Church. Thus, the nineteenth century has been considered the era of the "large landowners' state," the *estado terrateniente*.[33] In 1895 coastal liberals, whose economic power had been growing for some time, finally seized political power. In a sense, different political ideologies were "naturally" rooted in the distinct economic and social terrain of the coast and the highlands. The coast, with its import-export trade and production for the world market, was principally liberal. Thus, coastal elites sought fewer barriers to trade. In addition, the coast was much less influenced by the conservative ideology of the Catholic Church: the church owned few rural properties on the coast (reducing its economic and political power in the region) and had relatively few churches and even fewer convents or monasteries there as well. In contrast, given that their textile industry had been undermined by British imports, highland elites tended to favor more protectionist policies. In addition, the Catholic Church was an overwhelming presence in the highlands, where it was one of the largest landowners, where the majority of its convents were located, and where members of the clergy were often elected to congress or the senate.

In the aftermath of the scandal that triggered the Liberal Revolution in 1895, President Luis Cordero was compelled to resign.[14] His resignation was forced by a conservative uprising, but, once they had initiated it, the conservatives could not maintain control over the process. The country disintegrated into factions, and coastal elites called on General Eloy Alfaro to return from exile and assume command. Alfaro led the liberals to power and became the great leader of the Liberal Revolution. Born in Manabí in 1842, Eloy Alfaro had begun his career as a revolutionary in 1864 when he participated in an uprising against García Moreno. With the failure of that movement, he was forced to flee to Panama, where he became a successful businessman. He went on to use his wealth to finance liberal insurrections against conservative governments in Ecuador. In 1883–84 he led Manabí and Esmeraldas provinces in a guerrilla war against the governments of Ignacio Veintimilla and José María Plácido Caamaño. By 1895, Alfaro had achieved international renown as a soldier, having fought in civil wars not only in Ecuador but also in Central America and in the Cuban independence movement. Liberal civilians invited the "Viejo Luchador" (old warrior) to lead the liberal forces in 1895. He was joined by other civilian and military liberals, including General Leonidas Plaza Gutiérrez, who had fought with him in 1884. Plaza had also been born in Manabí and had similarly lived in exile, fighting in civil wars in Costa Rica and El Salvador. In August 1895 the liberal army won decisively against government forces, and Alfaro took command of the government in September, when he arrived in Quito for the first time in his life. His rule was legitimized by a constituent assembly that took place in Guayaquil in late 1896. While peasants of the coast and highlands fought in the Liberal Revolution, the history of subaltern projects in this war has yet to be written.[35]

The first administration of Alfaro was plagued by repeated insurrections by conservatives funded by the Catholic Church. In 1901, Alfaro was succeeded as president by Leonidas Plaza, who had been elected despite Alfaro's misgivings. Although Alfaro agreed that a military president was needed given the threat of civil war, he doubted Plaza's authenticity as a liberal because of the latter's accommodating attitude toward conservatives. Indeed, Plaza went on to include conservatives in his government. Nonetheless, or perhaps precisely because he was able to construct a broader elite consensus, Plaza succeeded in enacting and institutionalizing a number of the most important reforms associated with the liberal project, particularly the measures leading to the separation of church and state. Plaza, who was from a coastal commercial family, had married into the important highland landowning family of the Lassos. Following his marriage, he had experimented with the modernization of dairy production on the Lasso properties in Cotopaxi province. Thus, Plaza embodied a pact between highland and coastal elites in his person; similarly, Plaza's government represented the merging of interests of these two dominant groups, to a much greater extent than had occurred under Alfaro.

In many ways, Alfaro may have been the leader whom the liberals needed in 1895, but Plaza was the leader who was capable of consolidating the revolution as an elite project. Alfaro had international renown as a liberal revolutionary, contacts throughout the coast, long military experience, and an ability to mobilize the popular bases of liberalism. In addition, because he had spent most of three decades in exile, he had not collaborated with previous governments, which gave him an unsullied image. For these reasons he was able to seize power in 1895. However, Ayala has argued that Alfaro quickly generated resistance to his government among elites because they feared that he would mobilize subordinate groups for more radical reforms.[36] In addition, there were incidents of violence and of repression of the press during his first government. Under Plaza, in contrast, there was freedom of the press and an opening to many elite sectors who participated directly in his government.

In 1905, Plaza promoted the election of a civilian, Lizardo García, as his successor. Plaza himself left for Washington as ambassador to the United States. Soon thereafter, García was overthrown by Alfaro, in part on the pretext that García was not committed to completing the railway. In 1906, Alfaro called another constituent assembly, which wrote a new constitution and again elected him president. Alfaro's second term (1907–1911) was fraught with tension, not least because he provided additional government funds to the railway company to ensure the success of that project. The railway was inaugurated in Quito a year late, on June 25, 1908 (Alfaro's birthday). In 1911 he supported the election to the presidency of Emilio Estrada, a successful Guayaquil businessman and banker, although he had misgivings after the elections were held. Fearing that he would not allow the transfer of power at the end of August 1911, military leaders forced Alfaro to resign three weeks before the end of his term. He made a public vow not to intervene in future politics and left for Panama.

The unexpected death of Estrada in December 1911 provoked a civil war. Again the insurgents called Alfaro back from Panama, this time to moderate in the conflict. This war, which was not entirely settled until 1916, led to more casualties than Ecuador had ever seen: in January 1912 alone, three thousand soldiers died. Public indignation against Alfaro and the insurgents was ignited. The rebel leaders, including Eloy Alfaro and his nephew, Flavio Alfaro, were arrested at the end of January 1912 and sent from Guayaquil to Quito by train, to be held in the García Moreno Penitentiary. There, they were attacked and killed by a mob and their bodies were then dragged through the streets and burned in the famous *arrastre*, or dragging, of the Alfaros.

In the subsequent power vacuum, Leonidas Plaza was again elected president. Civil war continued during his second term (1912–1916), although fighting was mostly limited to the province of Esmeraldas. This period saw the establishment of an implicit agreement between coastal and highland elites, known as the oligarchic pact. During the First World War, the cocoa export economy began to suffer from changing international market conditions, undermining the power of the coastal agro-export elite. In contrast, the changing market conditions increased the power of the coastal banking and emerging agro-industrial elite, which was based in part on sugar planting and processing. Three civilian presidents, all associated with this rising elite, followed Plaza: in 1916, Alfredo Baquerizo Moreno came to power, then José Luis Tamayo in 1920, and Gonzalo Córdova in 1924. From 1895 to 1925 all of Ecuador's presidents had been from the coast. This changed, however, in 1925, when Córdova was overthrown in the July Revolution (Revolución Juliana) by junior military reformers and the middle classes. After a brief period during which a military junta governed Ecuador, Quito physician Isidro Ayora became president. He remained in office until 1931. In the late 1920s the political spectrum in Ecuador became more complex with the creation, in 1926, of the Socialist Party.[37] In the 1930s, in the context of an extended political and economic crisis, Ecuadorian politics was further transformed by the eruption of populist politics and the direct involvement of the urban lower classes in the political arena.

One of the principal achievements of Ecuador's liberal period was the construction of the Guayaquil-Quito Railway, which was promoted tirelessly by General Alfaro. For a quarter century prior to the Liberal Revolution, Ecuadorians had been trying to build a railway. After García Moreno's death in 1875, few important advances were made on railway construction until 1885, when the government of José María Plácido Caamaño contracted with English engineer Marcus Kelly to administer and extend the Yaguachi line. At that time, "we could say that of everything that had been done to date, there only existed a few thousand rails covered with jungle foliage and incapable of supporting the passage of a train. The bridges had been destroyed, some for strategic reasons and others by the rigors of the climate. The materials in the most part had been stolen or destroyed, and almost all of the wooden ties were useless."[38] In 1886, Kelly raised over the Río Chimbo a large iron bridge built by the Paris firm of Eiffel (just prior to the raising of the tower that would make them famous). He also surveyed routes to extend the rail line and began construction toward the Andes. Because the transport of construction materials from Guayaquil to Yaguachi by river was expensive and slow, Kelly proposed that a rail line be built on the coastal plain from Yaguachi to Durán, across the Guayas River from Guayaquil.[39] By 1887 the line connected Durán with Chimbo, in the foothills of the Andes in Bolívar province. However, the train carried few passengers and even less cargo because Chimbo was not on the preferred route to Quito and because it was difficult to acquire horses and pack animals in Chimbo to continue the journey to the highlands. In 1888, Kelly began to experience financial and labor difficulties, worsened considerably by the destruction of a large part of his work during the rainy season.

Kelly was on the verge of bankruptcy by 1890 when French count Thadée d'Oksza appeared on the scene to propose that his European syndicate take over Kelly's obligations. In 1891, however, the recently signed contract with d'Oksza was canceled because the count had not deposited the required 2 million francs in a Paris bank to guarantee his solvency. The cancellation decision was bolstered by the argument that the contract had been abusively expensive in the first place. In any case, President Antonio Flores (1888–1892) had expressed grave doubts about Ecuador's ability to construct a railway; his administration laid much greater emphasis on improving the old mule trail from Babahoyo to Guaranda. Inaugurated in 1891, the Vía Flores reconfirmed the Babahoyo-Guaranda route's importance as the principal artery of national traffic. This new trail, and the improvement of the García Moreno wagon road, reduced the duration and discomfort of the trip from Guayaquil to Quito. Nonetheless, travel between the highlands and the coast was almost as difficult at the end of the century as it had been at independence.

If Eloy Alfaro succeeded in building a railway where others had failed, it was no doubt due to a combination of rising customs revenues from cocoa exports (used to guarantee the payment of railway bonds) and his unshakable political will. In 1895, while the final battles of the Liberal Revolution were still being fought, Alfaro sent an Ecuadorian engineer to initiate railway exploration in the Alausí area. In 1896, even before receiving approval from the constituent assembly scheduled for October, Alfaro began to solicit railway contractors. On March 13, 1897, railway entrepreneur Archer Harman and his secretary, Eduardo Morley, arrived in Quito from the United States to negotiate. On June 14, 1897, the first contract with Harman was signed.

It is not clear how Harman came to be interested in building the railway in Ecuador. One story states that Alfaro had asked Ecuadorian diplomats in North America and Europe to solicit interest among entrepreneurs abroad. Luis Carbo, an Ecuadorian diplomat in New York, was in a café one day discussing his country's railway project when one of his companions called out to a friend playing billiards across the room, "Hey, Harman, do you want to build a railway?"[40] The following, at least, is known.[41] Archer Harman was born in Virginia, the son of a colonel in the Confederate Army. His family had been financially ruined by the Civil War, and he had to support himself from an early age. He began to work for railway contractors, and at age thirty he obtained the contract for building the Colorado Midland Railroad. After becoming interested in the Ecuadorian railway project, he spent most of his time from 1897 to 1911 in Ecuador, New York, and London attending to the business of the Guayaquil and Quito Railway Company, of which he was president at the time of his death in October 1911.

When the 1897 contract was signed, the railway's estimated cost of $17,523,000 was six or seven times the annual customs revenues of Ecuador, or five times the total annual government revenues at the time. The cost of the rolling stock, estimated at 600,000 sucres (only 3.5 percent of the total cost), was equal to all of the capital invested in the fifteen steamboats that plied the waters of the Guayas basin at the beginning of the 1890s.[42] Given that it was not clear that the railway would be profitable and that Ecuador had a poor international credit reputation due to repeated suspensions of payment on the independence debt to Great Britain, Ecuador could not hope to obtain international financing on its own. The government was compelled to seek foreign investors for the line. Thus, Harman spent several months in London in 1897–98 renegotiating Ecuador's foreign debt to ensure financing. In these dealings, Harman's Guayaquil and Quito Railway Company (incorporated in Trenton, New Jersey) became the principal debtor to the foreign bondholders, and the Ecuadorian government in turn became the guarantor of the debt. In 1925, well before its concession had ended, the company sold majority control of the railway to the government after landslides during the rainy season destroyed the track between Bucay and Tixán and it decided it was not worthwhile to repair the line.

The Ecuadorian railway was expensive and very difficult to build. As Teodoro Wolf pointed out in 1892, the real problem lay in the ascent up the western slopes of the Andes, given the humidity and the shifting nature of the soil.[43] The major difficulty was not due to the superficial topography, but rather to the climatic conditions and the nature of the rocks. Wolf argued that the enormous project of the Oroya railway in Peru was relatively easy in comparison because it was constructed on solid ground. If Ecuador's vegetation and humidity could have been eliminated, and the western slopes given the arid climate of Peru, the same kind of solid ground would have resulted and the decomposition of the underlying rock would cease. No route from

Guayaquil to Quito could avoid this problem. In 1900 the work done to date by Harman was indeed destroyed by landslides in the rainy season (as had occurred in 1888 and would again in 1925). As a result, the original route to ascend to the highlands through the Chimbo Valley was modified in favor of construction in the valley of the Chanchán River. The Chanchán was crossed twenty-six times by the rail line, which ascends 3,050 meters in 80 kilometers, around the double switchback built on the mountain face known as the Nariz del Diablo, the Devil's Nose. The Guayaquil-Quito Railway turned out to be one of the most expensive railways in the world. In fact, it only operated at a profit for a few years in the 1920s and again in the 1940s. Nonetheless, this railway was to become the principal artery of national integration in Ecuador. Not only did it allow the economic integration of the national territory, but it also provided a political and discursive field within which Ecuadorian elites could build consensus about their national project.

Notes

1. Dawn Wiles, "Land Transportation within Ecuador, 1822–1954" (Ph.D. diss., Louisiana State University and Agricultural and Mechanical College, 1971), 1.

2. Teodoro Wolf, *Geografía y geología del Ecuador* (1892; reprint ed., Quito: Editorial Casa de la Cultura Ecuatoriana, 1975), 247.

3. Bureau of the American Republics, *Ecuador* (Washington, DC: Government Printing Office, 1892), 82.

4. Deler, *Ecuador*, 192–93.

5. Friedrich Hassaurek, *Four Years among the Ecuadorians* (1867; reprint ed., Carbondale: Southern Illinois University Press, 1967), 13.

6. This description is based on a number of nineteenth-century sources, principally: Julio Castro, "Páginas de una cartera de viaje: Un viaje con García Moreno en 1861," *Boletín de la Academia Nacional de Historia* 82 (1953): 174–219; Hassaurek, *Four Years*; Edward Whymper, *Travels amongst the Great Andes of the Equator* (1892; reprint ed., Salt Lake City, UT: Peregrine Smith Books, 1987); T. Wolf, *Geografía y geología*.

7. Bureau of the American Republics, *Ecuador*, 9.

8. Hassaurek, *Four Years*, 22.

9. Whymper, *Travels amongst the Great Andes*, 187.

10. Hassaurek, *Four Years*, 25.

11. Castro, "Páginas de una cartera de viaje," 201.

12. Linda Alexander Rodríguez, *The Search for Public Policy: Regional Politics and Government Finances in Ecuador, 1830–1940* (Berkeley: University of California Press, 1985), 178–79.

13. Rosemary D. F. Bromley, "Urban-Rural Demographic Contrasts in Highland Ecuador: Town Recession in a Period of Catastrophe, 1778–1841," *Journal of Historical Geography* 5, no. 3 (1979): 281–95; Yves Saint-Geours,

"Economía y sociedad: La sierra centro-norte, 1830–1875," in *Nueva historia del Ecuador*, vol. 7, *Epoca republicana I*, edited by Enrique Ayala Mora (Quito: Corporación Editora Nacional and Grijalbo, 1990), 47–48.

14. Yves Saint-Geours, "La sierra centro y norte (1830–1925)," in *Historia y región en el Ecuador: 1830–1930*, edited by Juan Maiguashca (Quito: CERLAC, FLACSO, and IFEA, 1994), 150.

15. John Leddy Phelan, *The Kingdom of Quito in the Seventeenth Century: Bureaucratic Politics in the Spanish Empire* (Madison: University of Wisconsin Press, 1967), 67. See also Robson Brines Tyrer, *Historia demográfica y económica de la audiencia de Quito* (Quito: Banco Central, 1988).

16. Carlos Contreras, *El sector exportador de una economía colonial: La costa del Ecuador (1760–1830)* (Quito: Abya Yala and FLACSO, 1990). Regarding the cocoa economy in general see Manuel Chiriboga Vega, *Jornaleros y gran propietarios en 135 años de exportación cacaotera (1790–1925)* (Quito: Concejo Provincial de Pichincha, 1980); Lois Crawford de Roberts, *El Ecuador en la época cacaotera: Respuestas locales al auge y colapso en el ciclo monoexportador*, translated by Rafael Quintero and Erika Silva (Quito: Editorial Universitaria, 1980).

17. Saint-Geours, "Economia y sociedad," 45.

18. Jorge Trujillo, *La hacienda serrana, 1900–1930* (Quito: Abya Yala and Instituto de Estudios Ecuatorianos, 1986), 123–42.

19. George Blanksten, *Ecuador: Constitutions and Caudillos* (Berkeley: University of California Press, 1951), 13.

20. Examples include Mexico's midcentury Reforma and later reforms in Chile, Argentina, and Brazil. See John Lynch, "The Catholic Church," in *Latin America: Economy and Society, 1870–1930*, edited by Leslie Bethell (New York: Cambridge University Press, 1989), 301–69.

21. Enrique Ayala Mora, *Lucha política y origen de los partidos en el Ecuador* (Quito: Corporación Editora Nacional and Taller de Estudios Históricos, 1978); Marie-Danielle Demélas and Yves Saint-Geours, *Jerusalén y Babilonia: Religión y política en el Ecuador, 1780–1880* (Quito: Corporación Editora Nacional and Instituto Francés de Estudios Andinos, 1988); Saint-Geours, "Economía y sociedad."

22. Saint-Geours, "Economía y sociedad," 59.

23. Rosemary D. F. Bromley and Robert J. Bromley, "The Debate on Sunday Markets in Nineteenth-Century Ecuador," *Journal of Latin American Studies* 7, no. 1 (1975): 85–108.

24. Jean-Paul Deler, "Transformaciones regionales y organización del espacio nacional ecuatoriano entre 1830 y 1930," in *Historia y región en el Ecuador: 1830–1930*, edited by Juan Maiguashca (Quito: CERLAC, FLACSO, and IFEA, 1994), 298.

25. This is a characteristic of what Bulmer-Thomas calls the commodity lottery. Latin American countries had suitable climates for different kinds of agro-export production, while the commodity lottery also favored certain countries with important mineral deposits. Thus, some commodities that fueled the export-led model of development in the nineteenth century allowed for or required early industrialization, while others did not. For instance, meat production in Argentina fostered the establishment of processing plants where beef was cured to enable its transport. Beef production in the Argentinian pampas also required the construction of railways. Neither cocoa nor, later, banana production in Ecuador

had significant backward or forward linkages. See Victor Bulmer-Thomas, *The Economic History of Latin America since Independence* (Cambridge: Cambridge University Press, 1994), 15.

26. Deler, *Ecuador*, 180.

27. Ibid., 184.

28. Silvia Palomeque, *Cuenca en el siglo XIX: La articulación de una región* (Quito: FLACSO, 1990).

29. Trujillo, *La hacienda serrana*, 124.

30. Regarding regional differentiation within the Ecuadorian Amazon see Blanca Muratorio, *The Life and Times of Grandfather Alonso: Culture and History in the Upper Amazon* (New Brunswick, NJ: Rutgers University Press, 1991); Anne-Christine Taylor, "El Oriente ecuatoriano en el siglo XIX: 'El otro litoral,' " in *Historia y región en el Ecuador: 1830–1930*, edited by Juan Maiguashca (Quito: CERLAC, FLACSO, and IFEA, 1994), 17–68.

31. Hernán Ibarra, "Ambato: Las ciudades y pueblos en la sierra central ecuatoriana (1800–1930)," in *Ciudades de los Andes: Visión histórica y contemporánea*, edited by Eduardo Kingman Garcés (Quito: CIUDAD, 1992), 226–27.

32. Trujillo, *La hacienda serrana*, 46.

33. Rafael Quintero, "El estado terrateniente del Ecuador (1809–1895)," in *Estados y naciones en los Andes*, vol. 2, edited by Jean-Paul Deler and Yves Saint-Geours (Lima: Instituto de Estudios Peruanos and Instituto Francés de Estudios Andinos, 1986), 397–418.

34. This scandal was precipitated by the so-called sale of the flag, when Ecuador lent its flag for the illegal sale of a Chilean warship to Japan during the Sino-Japanese War. Chile had declared itself neutral in that conflict.

35. Enrique Ayala Mora, *Historia de la revolución liberal ecuatoriana* (Quito: Corporación Editora Nacional, 1994), states that there was important subaltern participation in the Liberal Revolution but provides little information about the nature of the subalterns' project, if indeed they had an autonomous one. Ecuadorian historiography has concentrated much more on elite projects and on the political history of this era; there is nothing resembling the accounts of subaltern projects in Peruvian and Mexican civil wars in the nineteenth century. See Florencia E. Mallon, *The Defense of Community in Peru's Central Highlands* (Princeton: Princeton University Press, 1983); idem, *Peasant and Nation* (Berkeley: University of California Press, 1994); Nelson Manrique, *Yawar mayu: Sociedades terratenientes serranas, 1879–1910* (Lima: IFEA and DESCO, 1988); and for the early twentieth century, a vast literature on the Mexican Revolution.

36. Ayala Mora, *Historia de la revolución*, 149.

37. Leonardo J. Muñoz, *Testimonio de lucha: Memorias sobre la historia del socialismo en el Ecuador* (Quito: Corporación Editora Nacional, 1988).

38. A. L. Yerovi, "Refutación de un informe," in *Ferrocarril del sur: Juicios imparciales* (Guayaquil: Imprenta de "El Tiempo," 1892), 10.

39. The establishment of the coastal rail terminal in Durán rather than across the river in Guayaquil was, therefore, not a carefully deliberated decision on the part of the Ecuadorian government but the result of a proposal made for convenience by Kelly. During the liberal period, the Guayaquil and Quito Railway Company would offer transport by steamboat from the rail terminal to Guayaquil proper. Today, one of the difficulties with

rehabilitating and modernizing the railway is precisely the fact that it cannot be easily or economically connected with the port of Guayaquil, thus reducing its use for the transport of heavy imported goods such as machinery.

40. Alfredo Maldonado Obregón, *Memorias del ferrocarril del sur y los hombres que lo realizaron, 1866–1958* (Quito: Talleres Gráficos de la Empresa de Ferrocarriles del Estado, 1977), 54.

41. This information is drawn from Harman's obituary, *New York Times*, October 10, 1911.

42. Deler, *Ecuador*, 200.

43. T. Wolf, *Geografía y geología*, 256–57.

3

The Railway, the Reform of the Nation, and the Discourse of Liberalism

Without a railway between the coast and the interior of our country, nothing, nothing are the toils, the struggles, and the sacrifices of true republicans since the birth of our nation. Without a railway, sovereign and unceasing motor of positive progress, how paltry and irremediable are the fortunes of our inter-Andean sections! Without a railway, so much individual strength, thirsty for productive occupation and finding it nowhere, is wasted; so many lives end in misery, for lack of work. Naturally the result could be none other, both in economic and political terms, than this chaos throughout our being since the dawn of our existence. Without a railway, without facility for life, without average well-being for ninety percent of our brothers, how can we speak of true liberty . . . and true dignity, without which the genuine Republic cannot cease to be a mere myth?

Liberal evolution, in Ecuador, must be essentially social, and without a railway, without that arena open to all aptitudes, to all intelligences, to all activities, by way of the broad, non-communal development of agriculture, industry, and commerce, we cannot even conceive of the moral, intellectual, and physical transformations that the law of progress requires for the triumph of the radiant life of true democracy. Without a railway, then, I have always thought that any revolution is ephemeral, inefficient and laughable any endeavor for progress, and thus, my dream, my delirium, my only program is concentrated in this single word: RAILWAY!

—President Eloy Alfaro[1]

The railway was a great symbol of modernity throughout Latin America. In many cases, railways served to integrate export regions with the world market,[2] which it was thought would guarantee prosperity in the late nineteenth-century model of export-led development.[3] Argentina, Brazil, Chile, and Mexico constructed railways that were instrumental in developing their resources for export. In contrast, in the late nineteenth century, Peru built "railways to nowhere," as Paul Gootenberg has characterized them, regional lines between the highlands and the coast.[4] In principle, Peru's regional railways were considered a way to transfer resources generated by the guano boom into more permanent development of the interior and not into the extraction of new export products.

The Ecuadorian railway provides a contrast to what occurred in other Latin American countries. As in Peru, the Guayaquil-Quito Railway was not constructed to transport export products. Likewise, it was considered a way to transfer resources generated by the coastal agro-export economy to the highlands. In Ecuador the railway ran from the principal port to somewhere important, the national capital, and it linked the most densely populated portions of the national territory. The connection of Ecuador's two largest cities, and with several important highland provincial capitals as well, was thus a significant nation-building exercise.[5]

The Guayaquil-Quito Railway, however, was not only a national project in the sense that it connected an important portion of the national territory and stimulated the movement of labor and goods around that territory. It also provided a discursive field within which different social groups could come to an uneasy consensus about the nature of national development and modernization. In a sense, the railway became the discursive as well as the physical and economic link that would incorporate different spaces and populations. The discourse of movement, connection, work, and energy as developed around the railway was ambiguous enough to appeal to a variety of audiences: different social groups could see in this discourse something of interest to them. "Movement" and "connection," in particular, were keywords for the liberal discourse in the sense that Raymond Williams uses "keywords,"[6] pointing us toward conflicts over meaning that are obscured through the use of a common term. The meanings of keywords are not set but are articulated and transformed through struggles over specific political-economic and cultural projects. Thus, keywords give the appearance of consensus, although they may well evoke different things for different people.

The Reform of the Nation
through Movement and Connection

The construction of a railway from Guayaquil to Quito was promoted as the key to a whole series of economic, political, and
social transformations, the cornerstone of a broad project of
national renewal. As it was characterized during the inauguration ceremony in Quito in 1908, the railway was "the project
that synthesizes an entire program of social reforms."[7] Similarly,
there were frequent references to the "moral and material importance" of railway construction. The railway was perhaps most
often referred to as a "redemptive work" for Ecuador; as such,
it was "the great enterprise of our desires and sacrifices."[8] The
nature of the redemption was specified on the front page of the
Quito daily, *El Comercio*, on June 25, 1908, the date of the railway's
inauguration in the capital:

> In a broad sense the railway has been called . . . a redemptive
> work, because it will stimulate our activity, encourage our
> timid initiatives, broaden the field of our resources and rela-
> tionships. . . . Commerce, agriculture, industry of every kind,
> the sciences, the arts, all the useful manifestations of human
> activity, everything that tends to facilitate the struggle for life
> and to affirm the sentiments of nationality in a people like ours,
> that is still anarchic and divided: here is the vast field in which
> one must admire the incalculable benefits of this redemption.
> . . . The project of the inter-Andean railway thus represents,
> for Ecuador, her moral resurrection and emancipation as a
> people.[9]

The liberal period saw the promotion of an important project
of modernization, broadly conceived. Liberals themselves con-
trasted the liberal period and the long period that they associated with conservatism prior to the 1895 revolution (although it
was in fact much more varied) as being characterized by, respectively, "the light of progress" and "obscurantism." These
traits were also expressed in evolutionary terms, so that Conservatives were called the "historic party," while the liberals were
seen as having placed the country on the threshold of something entirely new. With the construction of the railway in particular, "the nation will be reborn, rising like the phoenix from
its own ashes."[10] Ecuadorians were urged to "bid farewell to the
past, in order to greet the future."[11] Indeed, "Ecuador belongs

to yesterday, to a yesterday so immediate to today, that in the clepsydra of time they become confused." With the coming of liberalism and the railway, however, "the beautiful Ecuadorian territory will be the land of the future."[12] In this conception, the past was associated with stagnation, inertia, routine (*rutina*), and backwardness, where regions were disconnected and closed in on themselves. In contrast, the future would be characterized by movement, connection, growth, and expansion. Given that "movement" and "connection" were keywords for the liberal project, it is understandable that the cornerstone of that program should be the construction of a railway.

Discussions about the railway continually referred to the need to "awaken" the dormant nation to productivity and progress by connecting regions and stimulating movement and energy. "Where communication is assured by easy and expeditious routes, where movement does not find itself hindered by insuperable obstacles, neither the work of industry nor commerce would be detained by difficulties of expansion. There we would be able to say that progress is not a vain word."[13] Capital too would become more mobile, "stimulated by the railway, [so that] great enterprises, that today slumber in stasis due to the lack of capital, will provide every kind of benefit to the country."[14] But the economic project encompassed by the railway had much broader implications. The railway represented "the most secure well-being of the nation, her prosperity and wealth, the peace of citizens, the aspiration of the towns, the delirium, in sum, of society, are all embodied in the railway, as the sole raft that can rescue us from the shipwreck in which Ecuador finds herself."[15] As Ecuador's minister of the interior observed in his 1904 special report on the railway, "I judge that tied to the termination of this project are all of the social reforms of the country, even the most advanced ones of which we dream . . . since the onward march of the locomotive, bringing with it the immigration of men, commerce which is wealth, and movement which is life, brings also the exchange of ideas, challenges previously unknown in public life, the discovery of unexplored industries, and, as a result, the inevitable and peaceful imposition of new systems."[16]

As an inhabitant of Riobamba explained in 1905, in arguing that it was essential to have the main line pass through his city, the railway would have far-reaching effects on Ecuadorian society:

> I have a sublime impression of the railway. It seems to me that its laborious advance is because it comes loaded with a whole world of ideas, of reforms and of life, to dispense them wherever it arrives. I believe that it is precisely for this reason, to ensure that they do not lose their share during this distribution, that people crowd around it anxiously when its march is suspended. I believe that the steam of the locomotive recomposes minds, and has something magnetic about it that facilitates their perfect functioning. I believe that with its resonant and intense whistle that echoes in the mountains and ravines, cities awaken from the lethargy in which they reposed, and rise to their feet to accompany it on the path to civilization and progress. I believe that even the strip of land along which the railway passes becomes fertile. And I imagine, in sum, that even corpses could be resuscitated by the heat expended by that blessed monster (*monstruo bendito*).[17]

In liberal discourse, movement, which could not be generated without links between regions, was closely associated with connection—and connection would allow modernity to penetrate Ecuador. The railway represented "the desire to see free and prosperous the Ecuadorian nation that only yesterday was isolated from the pulse of modern life. . . . The railway, the stupendous wonder, the divine monster, has knocked at our door and announced itself the secure and perpetual messenger of our future and our national prosperity."[18] Connection would also be important in consolidating national harmony. Long-time liberal legislator Abelardo Moncayo described the railway during the 1908 inauguration ceremonies as "the indissoluble link, the steel embrace between all of the zones of Ecuador," that would eliminate "degrading regionalisms."[19] Connection would allow people to become closer culturally as well as physically. Indeed, it was argued that after George Stephenson's invention of the steam locomotive, England had seen "the diminishing of hatreds, the triumph of mutual affection, the dazzling propagation of love in all human hearts." Without doubt, "universal brotherhood is one of the first consequences" of Stephenson's invention.[20] Similarly, Flavio Alfaro, a liberal military leader and Eloy Alfaro's nephew, suggested at the inauguration that "what we behold today seems like a dream! Yesterday an immense and rugged distance divorced our Andes from the shores of the ocean and now we see ourselves brought closer, united, we old and fond brothers."[21] If the railway was to destroy regionalisms and end fratricidal conflicts, it would be because people would learn more about each other and even become more alike through the new chances offered by the railway to move around the national territory.

By connecting regions, the railway would promote the movement of people, products, and ideas. Because of the importance of the circulation of ideas, educational reforms were central to the liberal project. And the railway, by its very presence, was seen as spreading new ideas: in broad terms it was considered to be a means of communication. For instance, the expansion of the press would be encouraged by the railway. Soon after the railway was inaugurated, congress decreed (on November 7, 1909) that blank newsprint could be transported by train at the lowest cargo rate, that newspaper vendors would travel for free, and that each daily newspaper was entitled to free use of the telegraph lines built alongside the tracks, for up to 200 words daily.[22] Indeed, during the liberal period, given that it was relatively inexpensive to start a newspaper, a sphere of "public opinion" began to emerge, as issues of national importance began to be debated in the press and not only in congress and gentlemen's clubs.[23] As Benedict Anderson points out, the emergence of a community of readers is central to the imagining of national communities.[24]

President Alfaro hoped that with the railway "all the towns of the republic, united by an iron clasp, will consolidate national unity, causing the disappearance of provincialism and elevating the country from its economic prostration, opening up to individual effort new and beautiful horizons."[25] His reference to individual effort was clearly part of the liberal project to establish a society based on effort and work rather than on privilege. This was an argument against corporate groups, and it would be engaged to undermine the privileges of the Catholic Church. The overall discourse of movement and connection in the liberal project, as applied to the nation, was also developed in the individual in such fields as prison reform and education, where the invigorating, hygienic influences of work and movement were proposed. Thus, the liberal discourse about the moralizing influence of work went well beyond the railway, as liberals were also in the process of broadly constructing their own identity. In some ways, what the railway was to do for the nation was mirrored by what new policies in policing and education were to do for individuals, awakening them from inertia through moral reform by work.

In regard to policing and prisons, liberal discussions emphasized the importance of work both for providing the security that would make labor worthwhile (by protecting its result, property) and in positing the value of the work itself as a moralizing force, that is, the police were to protect those who did work, and they were to rehabilitate criminals through teaching them the value of work. For the Guayaquil police chief,

> Society does not prosper except when life and property rest peacefully in the shadow of a good system of government, when a man knows that if he commits a crime he will immediately be apprehended and punished. Then work increases and with this, the wealth of the masses, because the virtuous dedicate themselves quietly to their business; and those of wicked instincts, seeing how difficult it is to gain from bad speculations, seek the means to honestly earn their sustenance. Evil does not progress when the Police is there, ready to strangle it in its cradle. . . . In [the Police] rests not only the security of citizens and their goods, but also the progressive march of industry and commerce, since it cannot be doubted that when there is not sufficient security, the spirit to enter into great undertakings diminishes.[26]

But the police were not simply supposed to punish crime; they aimed to eliminate it altogether by attacking vices at their origin. To ensure the "advance of our civilization, we must seek the cause of social vices and cut them out at the roots, with no vacillation whatsoever," declared Quito's police chief.[27]

The attractiveness of idleness, in particular, was perceived as underlying a great deal of crime. Certainly gambling was a problem, in part because it represented "the voluptuousness of profit without work . . . one of the causes that most lowers the moral and educative level of a people."[28] One of the most pervasive causes of crime was vagrancy, and so it was criminalized. Trade schools for idle boys were established with funds collected by imposing fines on gambling houses. The liberal state also turned its attention to beggars in its campaign against vagrancy. After all, "often begging is a disguise that masks laziness, malice, robbery, espionage, vengeance, and so many other ruinous passions of the perverse."[29] However, the state was concerned with distinguishing carefully between those who begged because they could not work and those who begged because they did not want to work: "The first is a misfortune, the second is a vice. Adopting special repressive laws against vagrancy, more than half of the petty daily infractions in the population would be eliminated. In this respect, the labor of beggars in workshops overseen directly by the Police and under its jurisdiction, would be the best corrective that, redeeming children and adults, would also benefit future generations."[30]

Those individuals whose vices were not reformed at the roots would be corrected once they were imprisoned. That the inmates in jails and prisons passed their days in "consummate idleness" was thus of particular concern. Work undertaken in prisons was seen not as a form of punishment, but as a moralizing influence. Indeed, "the first step toward moral improvement is to acquire the habit of work. Its effect is prodigious even over the spirit of the most indolent and wicked who have never felt their brows moistened with the sweat of honest labor. Thus, the reign of poverty and vice is extirpated, and old and inveterate thieves become honorable and hard-working citizens. A reformative system should be based on continuous, active, diligent, and honorable labor."[31]

The value of work and movement for individuals was also a theme in education. Liberals proposed that the educational system be reformed to provide more adequately for the nation's needs in two ways: by dedicating government resources principally to primary and practical education, and by making manual work and physical exercise essential components of primary education. As with the police, who were expected to extend their gaze evenly over the national territory, everywhere encouraging virtue while discouraging vice, in education too the emphasis was to be placed on that element that extended most widely, primary education. Officials and politicians consistently argued for committing funds to the promotion of primary education rather than for more advanced facilities. Primary education affected all Ecuadorians, while advanced education benefited only a small elite.[32] Hence, "the unmistakable necessity of attending preferentially to primary education, the source from which will resplendently emerge, modest lawyers and doctors, trustworthy artisans, honorable laborers, and citizens, in sum, useful to their country."[33] One must "carry Instruction to the lowest strata of society, as a means to moralize the crowds and an impulse to intelligent labor."[34] There were specific measures taken to achieve this goal, such as night schools for adult workers.

In addition to preparing citizens for useful work, primary education policies also promoted manual labor and physical exercise at the earliest ages: "Manual labor in primary schools

. . . purifies customs, strengthens virtue and is the best defense of innocence. Labor is the basis of social morality and of the betterment of peoples. . . . It is in primary school where the first steps of future workers must be taken, who will later dedicate themselves to commerce and agriculture, to the manufacturing industries and even professional careers. Manual labor must necessarily be united with the other elements of education, if we want to secure the foundations of greatness and prosperity for the Republic."[35]

Schools not only should cultivate children's intelligence but also should perfect the "living machinery" of the human body through physical education for children. The underlying philosophy was summed up in the Latin maxim "Mens sana in corpore sano," also popular among police and prison wardens. Thus, it was only so that education would become "a true means of social transformation," the "most efficient means to regenerate a people."[36] In 1905 the secretary of education claimed that military drills and gymnastics, "the bases of energy and valor," were being taught in the majority of primary schools in the country. "The authorities must be vigilant to ensure that the child is not simply educated in the sciences, but also to make of him a strong, healthy element, capable of fighting and triumphing in the battles of war and in the fertile tasks of labor," he cautioned.[37]

The liberal project to redeem individuals from inertia and stagnation was also evident in discussions of the problem of *rutina* in education. In this context, *rutina* was seen as the dissemination of an outdated worldview as well as, more narrowly, the instructional emphasis on rote learning rather than on stimulating intelligence and interest. This discourse regarding the disciplinary benefits of work, movement, and manual labor was assimilated into an argument against church control over education. Leonidas Plaza made explicit the connections between educational reform, the moralizing influence of work, and the separation of church and state:

> the overly elevated mind will never allow the hands to touch the earth: the sweat of labor is a curse for the church, not a blessing. Here again we discover that the exercise of a right appears in the guise of a penalty. He who imposes it does not himself suffer it: the church does not labor, it prays. Let us redeem man from this punishment. Let us teach him that to work is legitimate! The need to reform Public Education is urgent. . . . Subjects of study that have no application in practical life should be eliminated. Philosophy for our youth is

merely phantasmagoria; in place of these life-denying gymnastics of the mind, let us implement gymnastics of the
muscles.[38]

Altogether, for the liberal state, the discourse about movement,
work, and energy was incorporated into a wide variety of fields
of social, economic, and political reform.

Toward a Consensus on Regional and National Reform

While it appears that the railway was to reform the nation, on
closer examination it is clear that the implicit object of reform
was not the entire nation but rather a particular region. President Eloy Alfaro was explicit in the speech that opens this chapter: it was the Andean region that required transformation. An
editorial in *El Imparcial* in 1908 celebrating the inauguration of
the railway in Quito decried that "the isolation of the Andean
peoples, in the era of steam and electricity, was a blasphemy
against civilization; even more, an infamy."[39] The coastal region
was not the primary object of the liberal project of movement
and connection because it was seen as naturally characterized
by these processes. As already mentioned, the extensive area of
the Guayas River basin was connected through a network of
navigable rivers. The coast was also closely integrated into the
international market through both the export and import trades.
The particular region that required movement and connection,
both internally and with the coast, was the highlands.
     In the late nineteenth century the coast had seen very vis-
ible forms of modernization, especially in Guayaquil, with its
gas lighting, streetcars, and bustling commercial activity. As discussed in Chapter 2, the highlands were not stagnant and un-
changing in the nineteenth century; nonetheless, the changes that
occurred there were not highly visible. More pervasive in the
highlands was the sensation of chaos caused by the deurbanization, economic depression, and natural disasters that had
occurred. Only after the construction of the railway would
"progress" in the highlands become more clearly apparent. The
railway would allow the modernization of cities by, for instance,
transporting machinery needed for the installation of electricity and moving large amounts of construction materials.[40] In
another example, before the building of the railway, there had
not been any automobiles in Quito. Following 1908, the city rap-

idly modernized. This particular kind of movement would directly benefit the coastal import-export elite, because machinery of various kinds was usually ordered through their trading companies.

Given the lack of visible modernization in the highlands, there was at the turn of the century a widespread image of highland backwardness and stagnation. During the d'Oksza controversy in the early 1890s, an Ecuadorian who promoted railway construction with national capital compared the two regions. The coast was "laborious, advanced, prosperous, full of life, in possession of almost all of the century's advances; on its own apt for carrying out any enterprise, it appears full of confidence and faith in its destiny," whereas the highlands were "unproductive, submerged in misery, full of natural elements but impotent to exploit them, lacking credit in the exterior; a dead center, in sum, where work finds no stimulus and existence itself resembles lethargy."[41] After considering and rejecting several explanations for this situation, he concluded that it was due to the highlands' lack of transportation routes, and especially a railway.

The analyses of the many scholars and politicians who attempted to understand the differences between the dynamic coast and the seemingly inert highlands were often surprisingly similar, despite areas of disagreement. One of the most original discussions of the problems posed by the highlands was the analysis by Quito intellectual Belisario Quevedo, a liberal (but an anti-Alfarista) who is regarded as one of the precursors of socialism in Ecuador.[42] Quevedo attempted to understand the influence of climate on progress, although Ecuador seemed to contradict the European theory of climatic determinism. That theory argued that harsher climates molded hardier peoples: for instance, in their struggle to subsist in a difficult climate, European peoples had had to work hard to survive. As a result, they grew strong and developed habits of hard work and inventiveness that led them to high levels of social development and economic productivity. In contrast to the energetic Europeans, tropical peoples were seen as passive, living in lush environments that provided them with all that they needed without any effort on their part.[43]

In Ecuador, Quevedo wrestled with the dilemma that elsewhere the greatest civilizations, the most advanced economies, and the highest levels of progress had been attained by peoples living in temperate zones. How, then, could one explain that in

Ecuador it was in the temperate climate of the highlands that progress had been stalled,

> while under the ardent climate of the coast there is more ac-
> tivity, liberty, energy, frankness, self-confidence, perseverance,
> and other virtues that scholars deny entirely to tropical cli-
> mates. . . . The contradiction is manifest. Under an enervating
> climate, in the midst of prodigious nature, identified by schol-
> ars as the field of inertia and misery, we see a portion of Ecua-
> dorians, overflowing with vitality, confront vigorously and
> resolve triumphantly the problems of existence, while another
> portion of Ecuadorians does not rise to the same level before
> the challenges of life, living as they do under a temperate cli-
> mate, proclaimed by science as the theater proper to the most
> splendid development of the vigorous and active characteris-
> tics of the human species. One same race shows effects pre-
> cisely opposite to those that all climatic indicators would lead
> one to expect.[44]

Quevedo, caught between accepted theory and the Ecuadorian reality, concluded that the backwardness and listlessness of the highlands must be caused by the fact that the highland climate, which combined high altitude with proximity to the equator, "has the grave inconvenience of being monotonous, unvarying, perpetual springtime." It was not simply a temperate climate that led to national greatness elsewhere; rather, it was the varia- tions in the temperature and the "ever changing struggle of seasons" that stimulated productive energies. "Our eternal springtime maintains us in a paradise of idleness. In a climate that is always even, at no moment are we pressed into activity and work, so efforts become dispersed, they trickle away, they disappear, and tasks that can be done at any hour either are never done or are done little by little and poorly. Eternal springtime is the most efficient discipline to arrive at inactivity and enerva- tion." The solution was to open up the highlands to outside in- fluences, products, ideas, and people, particularly through the construction of routes of transport and communication.

Despite numerous differences in their perspectives, Guaya- quil physician and social reformer Alfredo Espinosa Tamayo also believed that the disparities between the coast and highlands were attributable to the presence or lack of movement and con- nection. According to Espinosa Tamayo, "The coast, more in con- tact with the outside world, is much more cosmopolitan and less attached to traditional customs than the highlands, where the difficulties of communications and the scarcity and poor quality of roads hinder and paralyze energies. There one lives a static life, in opposition to the more active and agitated existence of the coastal towns."[45] The effects were especially clear in highland agriculture, in which outdated methods of cultivation did not yield sufficient harvests to allow for the profitable movement of products to other regions and abroad. "The lack of roads and the difficulty and high cost of constructing them, which often is not compensated by the limited produce available to transport," compounded the problem, which "has impeded the development of industry, rendering difficult if not impossible the transport of raw materials and machinery across the crags and ravines of the high cordillera of the Andes, and has used up the energies of many generations."[46] For both Quevedo and Espinosa Tamayo, the stagnation and inertia of the highlands were seen as caused by the region's natural attributes such as climate and landscape. Nonetheless, these problems were not seen as insurmountable. Appropriate state action could wrest the highlands from this submission to nature. In particular, the construction of transportation routes would be a central element in the transformation of the highlands by enabling human beings to master nature and turn it to their use.

General aspects of the basic liberal discourse of movement and connection were widely held in both the coast and the highlands. In addition, they were common to both liberals and conservatives. The participation of conservatives in this shared discourse is clear in a 1909 debate between Alejandro Andrade Coello,[47] a member of the new liberal intelligentsia associated with the normal school (Colegio Mejía) established in Quito by the liberals,[48] and Cuencano poet and essayist Remigio Crespo Toral, the most renowned conservative intellectual of his generation. Politically, the two scholars were directly opposed.

They also arrived at very different conclusions about the results of the Liberal Revolution. Andrade Coello wrote *La Ley del Progreso* in response to an article by Crespo Toral evaluating one hundred years of independence (dating from the first independence movement in 1809). In this book Andrade Coello set out to demonstrate that there had been far more progress in Ecuador in the fifteen years since the Liberal Revolution than there had been in the eighty-five years prior to that. Crespo Toral argued that very little had been achieved in the entire one hundred years since independence, but he consoled himself with the thought that, after all, what was a mere century in the life of a society? Their evaluations of the railway also diverged. Andrade Coello declared that the railway alone could be considered the work of a century, given its transformative effects: "Its whistle gladdens hearts, and its plume of smoke disinfects us of prejudices and chases away bats from our forgotten hamlets. At its passing, there are radiant awakenings and new life. . . . We were submerged in barbarousness and at the point of being eaten by worms: with only the railway we could call ourselves civilized and rest on our laurels."[49] Crespo Toral, in contrast, argued that in view of the forty years it had taken to build the railway, "its progress has been slower than a camel in the desert."[50]

Despite the different projects and positions of Andrade Coello and Crespo Toral, the parallels between their perspectives are often striking. For instance, Crespo Toral accepted all of the liberal tenets for a national project but insisted that the Ecuadorian president who had done the most to carry through that project was not the liberal Eloy Alfaro but the conservative Gabriel García Moreno. Both scholars also argued for the importance of the increased movement of people and of regional connection and for the need to stimulate energies and work in order to destroy inertia and transform society. Thus, Crespo Toral argued:

> A poor territory, with habits of work among its inhabitants, can reach a high prosperity. Everyone must be persuaded that it is necessary to work without rest, in order to be prosperous as individuals and as a nation. One works for today, one works for tomorrow, one works for the remote posterity: hence the solidarity of work in all eras, in order to form history and create greatness. . . . Work, work, prayer of work, religion of work! and we will be a people, and we will be brothers, we will have formed a nation, we will have triumphed. . . . Movement is life, inertia is putrefaction and death; work is movement, heat, and light; it is the dynamic and singular formula for progress. . . . There is no agent who cannot move, no being foreign to activity. The spirit of work generates heroism; and if we had been workers, like the Spanish of the sixteenth and seventeenth centuries, the mountain would now be a succession of towns and cities, and our people would be wealthy and happy. We fear movement, and nature with her majesty dominates us: we are still slaves. The jungle is virgin, virgin the mine, virgin

the free force of water: we are stragglers, miserable in the midst
of abundance, condemned to the ranks of the inferior. . . . Let
us construct the house, sanitize the town, provide it with electricity and water, design an infinite network of roads, multi-
ply colonizations; let us plant, let us save our strength for
science, let us invent and make ours, very much ours, the soil,
the subsoil, the spring, the electrical current; and let us force
heaven to make us happy.[51]

The image here, presented by the foremost conservative intellectual of this period, is one of nature that must be dominated
by machines. The "virginity" of the mine and of the waterfall is
an image not of purity, but of passivity, infertility, and wasted
resources. Crespo Toral expressed the widespread belief that Ecuador was sleeping a dream of misery on a mountain of riches,
from which the country was unable to benefit.

It is striking that in Ecuador there does not appear to have
been a romantic critique of the railway as a destructive machine.
If the railway was not seen as a harbinger of industrial ills, this
was because the effects of industrialization had been so limited
in Ecuador. There were none of the polluted cities, blackened
smokestacks, or misery of the industrial working classes that
provoked both conservative and radical critiques of industry in
Great Britain. While Ecuadorians made frequent reference to the
locomotive as a "monster," it was not a monster that threatened
the peace of a pastoral garden, because rural areas were not perceived in pastoral terms.[52] The Ecuadorian countryside was not
a romanticized landscape that offered alternative, spiritual, or
authentic values to a weary, conflict-ridden industrial society,
but rather an area widely seen as characterized by colonial and
feudal relations of stagnation and inertia. The railway would
liberate people and regions from this fate, through the transformative effects of the "monster of progress," "the divine monster," "the blessed monster" of the locomotive.

The language of movement and connection that developed
around the railway during the liberal period meant different
things to different people, appealing to both coastal and highland elites. This overall discourse was perfectly appropriate for
a nation whose economic prosperity was linked to the movement of a primary product out to the world market. Nonetheless, this product—cocoa—was not moved by the railway. But
the agro-export elite of the coast was closely integrated with

import interests, and the construction of a railway between the port and the capital did suggest the possibility of selling imported products to the highlands. Perhaps most important, however, from the perspective of coastal elites, was the hope that the railway would break down the insularity of the highlands and thus stimulate the creation of a labor market. The movement of people, in the form of highland workers, was very much in the interest of coastal plantation owners (see Chapter 4). In general, the construction of the railway was part of the broader project of coastal elites to transform the highlands to both undermine church power and free indigenous labor and thus to attain modernity and progress.

The movement of indigenous workers toward the coast was not in the interests of the highland landowning elite, but another kind of movement was. Highland elites were particularly concerned with the possibility of forging an internal market, that is, with moving highland agricultural and livestock products to the coast by train. Ultimately, they also hoped to export some of these products. While the image of the highlands developed in liberal discourse was unflattering, at least some highland elites agreed with the need to transform their region. Ideally, the elite of the northern highlands sought an independent route to the northern coast, with a port they could control (Esmeraldas) rather than having to rely on Guayaquil. Unsuccessful efforts to achieve this were undertaken throughout the nineteenth and twentieth centuries.[53] Nevertheless, the route between Quito and Guayaquil would provide them with new opportunities and, in fact, was much more important for provisioning the internal market than any other route to the coast would have been.

The railway also represented a transfer of resources from the coast to the highlands, given that its construction was guaranteed by customs receipts. Not only did the vast majority of imported goods enter the country through Guayaquil, but also the majority of export products were produced on the coast. If this was a form of transferring or redistributing resources, it was a redistribution between regionally based elites, not one between the wealthy and the poor. The latter redistribution would have to wait for incipient social policy in the late 1920s and 1930s, after subordinate groups took a more central role in national politics and when attention began to be paid to the need to create more consumers for national industry. While liberals did not generally pass laws favoring highland elites and, in fact, aimed to undermine these elites' power over labor, the construction of the railway nonetheless did favor highland landowners in other ways. And despite the fact that the railway was the definitive liberal project in Ecuador, and that liberalism was an elite project based in the coastal region, coastal elites themselves had reservations about the railway. They resented the fact that resources that they believed to be the result of their own effort and ingenuity were being used to guarantee the railway bonds for a project that did not directly benefit them. Indeed, the acquisition of rolling stock as provided for in the original railway contract was equivalent in expense to the entire capital investment in the fifteen river boats that served the Guayas basin at the beginning of the 1890s, which was only a minimal part of the total cost of the railway construction project.[54] Clearly, the railway represented a range of possible advantages and disadvantages for both the coastal agro-export elite and the landowning elite of the highlands. Neither group could impose a project entirely in its own interest, but each could hope to gain something from the railway. The railway, and the broader language of movement, connection, and progress articulated around it, can be seen then as a field within which an uneasy agreement could be reached between Ecuador's two dominant classes.

While the railway and the associated language of movement and connection allowed the constitution of a tenuous consensus between liberals and conservatives, and coastal and highland elites, a critical area of contention continued to exist: the relations between church and state. For the liberals, an important characteristic of the language of movement was that it could also be used to push through the establishment of the secular state, which was essential to their economic and political power as well as to their vision of a modern society. Indeed, the two significant achievements of the liberal governments during the fifteen years following the Liberal Revolution were the construction of a railway and the separation of church and state. These projects were linked through the language of movement and connection as well as through the use of religious imagery in describing the railway as a "redemptive work" and the locomotive as a "divine monster." Although the railway was Alfaro's principal project, several of the most important steps in the establishment of a lay state were undertaken by Leonidas Plaza, whose ability to forge an alliance between highland and coastal elites (rousing Alfaro's suspicions about his credentials as a liberal) was undoubtedly part of the reason that he was able to institutionalize these reforms.

The Church as an Agent of Inertia and Tradition

At the end of the nineteenth century, coastal liberals were
blaming the stagnation, inertia, and disconnectedness of the
highlands in part on the Catholic Church. The church was overwhelmingly centered in the highlands, where the majority of
the country's population had lived since precolonial times. The
relative presence of the church in the highlands versus the coast
is revealed in such issues as the number of convents in each zone.
Already by the early seventeenth century so many convents
had been founded in Quito that ecclesiastical authorities petitioned the Royal Council of the Indies to prohibit the establishment of any more. In contrast, no convent was built in Guayaquil
until 1858.[55] By the end of the nineteenth century, only 53 of the
458 churches in Ecuador were located on the coast and only 6 of
Ecuador's 47 convents and monasteries.[56] One result was that
the clergy were primarily recruited from the highlands, where
they often had kinship connections with elite families.

The various orders of the Catholic Church together made it
the largest landowner in the highlands during the nineteenth
century. At the end of the century the landed properties of religious communities numbered eighty-six in eight highland provinces, with a total value of more than ten million sucres.[57] This
was not simply a colonial remnant: the church had actually *increased* its presence in highland agriculture after the 1864 concordat between the Vatican and the Ecuadorian government
signed under García Moreno. This agreement allowed the church
not only to acquire properties but also to preserve and expand
them under the protection of the state. Thus, protests against
rutina in highland agriculture were often directed, either implic-
itly or explicitly, at the church.

The church was seen as opposed to innovations that would
lead to increases in agricultural production or reinvestment of
profits to improve productive systems. Liberals condemned the
inactive nature of church wealth. The nationalization of the properties of religious orders in 1908 was commonly referred to as
the *ley de manos muertas*, where the state seized estates from the
"dead hands" of the Catholic Church.[58] The church was relatively less influential on the coast because it did not own rural
properties there: its real estate holdings were limited to urban
buildings in coastal towns and cities. Anticlericalism on the coast
during the nineteenth century was also due to the increasing
proportion of coastal contributions to church revenues through

the payment of tithes that amounted to 10 percent of gross production. Although tithes were made voluntary in 1889, they were replaced by another tax on rural properties to support the church.

Relations between church and state in Ecuador during the nineteenth century were such that the state promoted Catholicism to the exclusion of all other religions. This relationship reached its zenith when President García Moreno made Catholicism a condition for citizenship (in the constitution that became known among liberals as the Black Charter). In addition, according to the 1882 concordat between the government and the Vatican, education, from primary school to university level, had to be in accordance with Catholic doctrine. The church also had rights of censure; through pastoral letters and decrees it could prohibit either the publication or the importation of books that offended Catholic doctrine and morals. The government, in turn, was required to adopt the appropriate means to ensure that such publications did not circulate in the republic. This requirement was clearly contrary to liberal ideals of freedom of expression, and liberals suffered politically from these measures. For instance, Felicísimo López, a liberal from the coast, was excommunicated for referring to Catholicism, in a published article, as a sect (suggesting that it was one among many religions). Although he was elected senator for Esmeraldas province in 1894, congress was required by the concordat to disqualify him because he had been excommunicated. In contrast, in 1896, after the Liberal Revolution, he again was elected to congress, and this time he was permitted to take his seat. In 1901, López was named minister of development.[59]

During the fifteen years after 1895, the liberal state secularized education, declared freedom of religion, passed civil marriage and divorce laws, established the civil registry of births, marriages, and deaths, secularized cemeteries, nationalized the properties of religious orders, and expelled foreign members of religious orders.[60] In the constitution of 1897 the state guaranteed the freedom of education, making primary education obligatory and free of charge. While parents could still choose to send their children to religious schools, for the first time the state insisted on licensing teachers before they could legally teach in any school, whether state, municipal, private, or religious. Under the 1899 Ley de Patronato, Catholicism continued to be the official religion of Ecuador, with the important limitation that its practices could not oppose state institutions. Congress was given the right to appoint many church officials, and they in turn were required to present themselves before congress or the council of state to take a constitutional oath before assuming office. In addition, the state would determine the appropriate resources for the support of the clergy, who could no longer independently impose any tax or contribution for the support of the church. The passage of comprehensive laws at the national level, under central state control—with an argument about unifying legislation so that all citizens would be treated equally, and be equally protected from abuses—was in part how the struggle against the church was played out. This process occurred not only in education but also in the laws of civil marriage (1902) and divorce (1902 and 1910), the civil registry of births and deaths (1900), and the secularization of cemeteries (1902). With the passage of these laws, the state also wrested from the church at least some control over life-cycle rituals.

In discussing the separation of church and state, liberals repeatedly referred to the need to circulate new ideas as well as people. The church was perceived as inhibiting both of these processes. Regarding the former, the church was seen as holding a monopoly over thinking, one that allowed no questioning or creativity. The church had the right to censure the press and prevent the entrance into the republic of any printed matter with which it disagreed. Thus, with the growth of a press free of censure during the liberal period, it was claimed that finally "it is widely believed that everyone has the right to think, and it is now incomprehensible that thinking should be the privilege of a particular class, much less a monopolized industry."[61] The church also dominated education. Attacks on traditionalism, *rutina*, and intolerance in church-dominated education characterized it as "that chain which binds us to the Middle Ages. How can we expect the triumph of Democracy and Liberty, if we entrust the education of our youth, that is, the formation of our future citizens, to those who have combatted and still combat without cease liberal principles? How can we expect the enlightenment of the people, if we confide the diffusion of light to those who have fought without rest to maintain the empire of shadows?"[62] President Leonidas Plaza insisted that, "as far as I am concerned, . . . the state of backwardness and contemptible passivity in which the Republic has vegetated for so many long years, is the fault and absolute responsibility of the perverse education we have received."[63]

In regard to the circulation of people, the church was without doubt highly resistant to the immigration of non-Catholics.

Until passage of the civil marriage law in 1902 there was no institution by which non-Catholics could marry in Ecuador, nor could non-Catholics be buried prior to the secularization of cemeteries. As a landowner, the church was also seen as rigidly controlling labor in the highlands, workers whom liberals believed would be better employed on the coast. But more generally there was a perception that the church aimed to keep people "in their place," both by promoting a hierarchical society and by discouraging any physical movement of the faithful that might expose them to new ideas.

It is important to understand the role of anticlericalism in Ecuador because this has been seen as the principal characteristic of Ecuadorian liberalism. A thorough discussion of the complex church-state relations during the liberal period is beyond the scope of this book. Nonetheless, it is necessary to at least briefly explore how some of the conflicts between the Catholic Church and the liberal state were expressed since these indicate very different conceptualizations of society, the state, and the citizen or individual. Three examples of such conflicts follow.

First, an important part of the liberal project was the establishment of a society governed by contractual relations among individuals (this ideal was also central to the formation of a labor market). This model became subject to much conflict during the establishment of civil marriage. In its protests over civil marriage, the church insisted that the contractual aspect of marriage was inseparable from the sacramental. This position was clearly contrary to the emergence of a society made up of individuals who could freely enter into contracts with each other, which also implied that they could later withdraw through mutual agreement, that is, through divorce.[64] Marriage was a key institution for the creation of such a society. Not only did marriage govern reproduction, but it also provided one of the most important bases for the transfer of property. (The parallel creation of the civil registry, or the centralization of records about births, marriages, and deaths, was similarly essential for the determination of property rights.) Moreover, the idea that human will (*voluntad humana*) alone could be the source of these individual rights was anathema to those who conceived of society as governed by divine law. The conflict over who was endowed with the capacity to make laws—man or God—was foreshadowed when the constitution of 1896–97 did not invoke the name of God, "the Supreme Legislator," as in previous constitutions;

rather, the document was written in the name and by the authority of the Ecuadorian people.

Second, the liberal state attempted to remove the church's influence from political matters and relegate it to civil society. Liberals argued:

> The religious element, according to ideas that predominate today, should be located, within the State, in the same role as art, science, industry, commerce, etc., insomuch as the state is required to guarantee and even favor the development of all the manifestations of human activity to their grand intellectual, moral, and social ends, without any other restriction than that which prevents such development from overstepping its bounds and invading the sphere of the State's attributions. And in accordance with these ideas, neither religion, nor art, nor science deserves special privileges from the Public Powers, nor do they constitute organisms that, in the face of the State, can dispute, using force, these rights.[65]

For the church, the state effort to place limitations on its sphere of activity implied a fracturing of the integrated Catholic individual: "We Ecuadorians neither have nor could we ever have one moral code as private individuals, another moral code as parents, and a third moral code as citizens: as private individuals, as parents, and as citizens our rule of conduct is a single one, that is, Catholic morality, and we are equally Catholics in the home as in civil life. . . . We are Catholics in the temple and in the public plaza."[66]

Third, there were important issues of national sovereignty at stake in these conflicts. The fact that the church and state held profoundly different ideas about the degree of authority that governments could hold over and within their territories was also reflected in discussions over civil marriage. The church urged Catholics to follow the pope's instruction not to accept a civil marriage ceremony prior to the religious one.[67] The state countered that Ecuadorian citizens were subject first to Ecuadorian law and that the edicts of a foreign power such as the pope could not overrule national laws. The church proceeded to argue that the pope could never be foreign to Ecuadorian Catholics:

> The Pope, so they say, is a foreigner, and does wrong to interfere in Ecuadorian politics. The Pope, is he a foreigner? How could it be that the Pope is a foreigner? Who is the Pope? The

> Pope is the representative of Jesus Christ; to say, then, that the Pope is a foreigner for Ecuadorians, would be the equivalent of asserting that Jesus Christ is a foreigner for Ecuadorians. The true God, could he be a foreigner for anyone? . . . To sustain that the Pope is a foreign ruler, for a Catholic nation, would be the same as to deny the unity of the Church, the unity that is one of the essential characteristics of the one true Church, of the Church founded by Jesus Christ. The Church, is it one? Then, the Pope is not a foreign ruler in Ecuador.[68]

On the other hand, the church also argued that although the pope was not a foreigner, neither was he subject to Ecuadorian courts. The church thus rejected the logic of the modern state's having sovereignty over its citizens within its own territory. The church urged Catholics to defy Ecuadorian law in the name of an identification that operated on a different level of abstraction but that also came into direct conflict with the state.

That the Catholic Church financed civil wars over these issues demonstrates that these were not simply philosophical differences. During Eloy Alfaro's first term as Ecuador's president (1896–1901), clergy and conservatives regrouped in southern Colombia to launch counterrevolutionary attacks against the Ecuadorian government. Pedro Schumacher, the conservative bishop of Portoviejo, was particularly active in these movements. During this era, conservatives argued that to fight on one side or the other "was not to ask where was Ecuador and where was Colombia, but rather where was Christ and where were his adversaries, where was the truth and where was the error."[69] In this conflictive atmosphere, Federico González Suárez, bishop of Ibarra, publicly stated in 1900 that to cooperate with the invaders from Colombia was a form of treason and that clergy should not sacrifice their nation to save their religion. This foreshadowed a period of accommodation to the secular state that would later be consolidated during González Suárez's tenure as archbishop of Quito, despite the ongoing debate about the form that church-state should take.[70]

It is evident that there were serious underlying issues of national sovereignty, jurisdiction, and very different ideas of the rights and duties of the state and its citizens involved in the conflicts between church and state.[71] The separation of state and civil society assumed that the equality of citizens before the state ensured the freedom to be different within civil society: to associate with others in various ways, to believe what one wished, to enter into contracts, and so on. But in principle this separation also assumed that what happened within civil society could not affect the duties of the state and citizens toward one another. If the church represented the past, tradition, and backwardness for liberals, this was because from pulpit and classroom it promoted a conception of society thoroughly incompatible with the society that the liberals were trying to establish. The church and state demonstrated two distinct styles of imagining community, involving different, and irreconcilable, definitions of the community to which one owed one's primary loyalty.

Liberals suggested that movement and connection did not occur prior to the Liberal Revolution, during the period dominated by highland elites, conservatives, and the church. But what the liberal state sought to establish was a particular form of connection, unlike that which the church had promoted. This kind of connection was one between free and equal individuals. Therefore, in this context, the railway was consistent with a much broader project to promote immigration, educational reform, new agricultural policies in the highlands, and liberty of thought and expression—all projects that the church opposed with varying degrees of vigor. Andrade Coello, expressing the liberal perspective, commented on the affinity among some of these projects:

> To extend our arms to fraternally receive individuals of all of the communions of the human family, that is to progress. Let us welcome the integrity embodied in Protestants, Catholics, Jews, Moslems, and Buddhists! With this embrace, immigration, science, industry, commerce, good manners, and the exchange of ideas will flourish. It would be ridiculous to cast out from the social bosom a useful man because he had been excommunicated, or to allow oneself to die of hunger rather than buy food in the store of the Brahmin. It is a symptom of madness, a mortal sin against the hygiene of the body and soul, to prevent air and light from penetrating the gloomy and fetid grotto. . . . With such absurd measures, can we even conceive of clarity, health, moral and physical development?[72]

Why should the state worry about what religion its citizens practice? "Let each believe what he wants; let him pray, work, produce, and prosper!"[73] Thus, the overall social and economic project of liberalism—to promote movement and connection—was also compatible with anticlericalism and the separation of church and state.

Toward Redemption

Around the railway a discourse was constituted about the moral reform of the Ecuadorian nation through work, generative activity, movement, and connection. If the previous conservative period had been characterized by disconnection and locality, then the liberal period was to be about connection. To the extent that liberalism, progress, technology, and the railway were destructive, they were destroyers of smallness, isolation, backwardness, routine, and stagnation. The community that was to be forged by the railway was by its very nature a connected one— a national community.

The railway was part of an uneasy truce between Ecuadorian elites, a truce needed because of the highland elites' ongoing economic and political strength, broadly defined. Sometimes this group's power was made clear in quite specific ways. Liberals closely controlled the elections of the executive. "We will not lose by ballots what we have won with bayonets" ("no perderemos con papeletas lo que ganamos con bayonetas"), Alfaro is rumored to have said. Ample evidence exists of electoral fraud during presidential elections. Thus, the liberal army became the "great elector," particularly in the early period of liberalism, through its control of polling stations and electoral lists.[74] While liberals controlled presidential elections from 1895 to 1925, it was more difficult for them to control the elections for congress. Although the senate was composed of equal numbers of representatives per province, congress was based on proportional representation by population. The more conservative highlands had a larger population than the coast, and its resulting congressional strength meant that at times the executive and congress were at odds. In 1898 the conservative-dominated congress prohibited the executive from carrying out the first railway contract with Archer Harman. Only through intense lobbying was Alfaro able to push through the contract, albeit with some revisions (the original contract had contained many loopholes that benefited the company at the nation's cost, and some of these were removed).[75] The need to compromise to achieve liberal projects was evident here.

While there were ongoing objections to the Guayaquil and Quito Railway Company, and to specific provisions in the various contracts signed by the government and the company,[76] opposition to the overall project to construct a railway—to the idea of movement and connection—was less common. The central issue was, instead, how to achieve this project at the lowest cost to Ecuador. As *El Comercio* pointed out in 1908, "The railway has cost us, and will continue costing us, enormous sacrifices and immense privations, money, tears, and blood."[77] But even this cost would be worthwhile if the railway laid the basis for Ecuador's future prosperity and harmony, if it indeed were a redemptive work. There was general consensus that it would be. This consensus was so broad that Archbishop González Suárez ordered that the city's church bells be rung on June 25, 1908, at the moment the railway arrived in Quito (marked too by the firing of cannon) and at every hour on the hour until ten o'clock that night. He explained, "As no one could remain indifferent before an event of such transcendental consequences for the progress and advance of our Nation, we will ring the bells of the cathedral and all of the convents and chapels of Quito to contribute to the just rejoicing of the capital, which could do no less than greet with exultation the locomo-tive's ascent to the lofty summit of the Ecuadorian Andes."[78]

Although the railway was seen as having profoundly magical effects, this book argues that it was not through magic that Ecuador became economically, politically, and socially transformed during the liberal period. These processes were driven not by technology, but rather by political struggle among elites and between elites and subordinate groups. The railway changed the terrain on which these battles were fought, and it also changed the limits of the possible for various groups. It was the catalyst for the formation of a tenuous consensus among elites that would allow the liberal project to be carried out. The language of movement and connection so central to the liberal project provided a discursive field in which both highland and coastal elites could identify their own interests, even though in some cases their underlying projects would be in conflict. The extent to which the elites could achieve their projects depended on their capacity to mobilize politically, and their successes were only ever partial. Thus, even when elites have a relatively coherent hegemonic project at the level of ideas, one must always ask how compatible it is at the level of practice and underlying projects.[79]

Notes

1. Eloy Alfaro, address to congress, September 27, 1898, in *Ferrocarril (documentos oficiales)* (Quito: Imprenta Nacional, 1898).

2. William Glade, "Economy, 1870–1914," in *Latin America: Economy and Society, 1870–1930,* edited by Leslie Bethell (New York: Cambridge University Press, 1989), 42.

3. Bulmer-Thomas, *Economic History,* chap. 3.

4. Paul Gootenberg, *Imagining Development: Economic Ideas in Peru's 'Fictitious Prosperity' of Guano, 1840–1880* (Berkeley: University of California Press, 1993), 89–111.

5. Steven Topik suggests that even coffee railways in Brazil promoted some degree of integration of the national territory, but clearly this was not their primary aim. See Steven Topik, *The Political Economy of the Brazilian State* (Austin: University of Texas Press, 1987), chap. 4.

6. Raymond Williams, *Keywords* (New York: Oxford University Press, 1976).

7. Víctor Manuel Arregui, "Discurso," in *El ferrocarril del sur, 1908–1933: Breve relación de los principales festejos que se realizaron en Quito, el 24, 25 y 26 de junio de 1908, con motivo de la inauguración del tren en esta ciudad* (Quito: Imprenta "Industria," 1933), 52.

8. Ministro de lo Interior y Policía, Obras Públicas, etc., *Informe del ministro de lo interior y policía, obras públicas, etc. al congreso ordinario de 1902* (Quito: Imprenta Nacional, 1902), 18.

9. *El Comercio,* June 25, 1908.

10. Eloy Alfaro, *Mensaje especial sobre la obra del ferrocarril del sur dirigido a la convención nacional por el presidente interino de la república General Don Eloy Alfaro* (Quito: Imprenta Nacional, 1896), 4.

11. Leonidas Plaza, address to congress, August 10, 1902, in Alejandro Noboa, *Recopilación de mensajes dirigidos por los presidentes y vicepresidentes de la república, jefes supremos y gobiernos provisorios a las convenciones y congresos nacionales desde el año de 1819 hasta nuestros días,* vol. 5 (Guayaquil: Imprenta "El Tiempo," 1908), 132.

12. Alejandro Andrade Coello, *La ley del progreso* (Quito: Casa Editorial de J. I. Galvez, 1909), 22, 35.

13. Ministro de lo Interior y Policía, Obras Públicas, etc., *Informe del ministro de lo interior y policía, obras públicas, etc. al congreso ordinario de 1903* (Quito: Imprenta Nacional, 1903), 28.

14. Eloy Alfaro, cited in Roberto Crespo Ordóñez, *Historia del ferrocarril del sur* (Quito: Imprenta Nacional, 1933), 63.

15. Ministro de Gobierno, *Informe concerniente a las secciones de instrucción pública, justicia y beneficencia que presenta el ministro de gobierno a la convención nacional de 1896–1897* (Quito: Imprenta Nacional, 1897), 18.

16. Ministerio de Obras Públicas, *Informe especial del ministerio de obras públicas sobre el ferrocaril trasandino al congreso de 1904* (Quito: Imprenta Nacional, 1904), i.

17. Un Riobambeño, *Riobamba y el ferrocarril* (Quito: Tipografía de la Escuela de Artes y Oficios, 1905), 22.

18. *El Comercio,* June 25, 1908.

19. Abelardo Moncayo Andrade, "Discurso," in *El ferrocarril del sur, 1908–1933: Breve relación de los principales festejos que se realizaron en Quito, el 24, 25 y 26 de junio de 1908, con motivo de la inauguración del tren en esta ciudad* (Quito: Imprenta "Industria," 1933), 8.

20. Roberto Andrade, "Discurso," in *El ferrocarril del sur, 1908–1933: Breve relación de los principales festejos que se realizaron en Quito, el 24, 25 y*

26 de junio de 1908, con motivo de la inauguración del tren en esta ciudad (Quito: Imprenta "Industria," 1933), 59–60.

21. Flavio Alfaro, "Discurso," in *El ferrocarril del sur, 1908–1933: Breve relación de los principales festejos que se realizaron en Quito, el 24, 25 y 26 de junio de 1908, con motivo de la inauguración del tren en esta ciudad* (Quito: Imprenta "Industria," 1933), 44.

22. *Registro Oficial*, November 11, 1909.

23. Ayala Mora, *Historia de la revolución liberal*, 225.

24. Anderson, *Imagined Communities*, chap. 2.

25. E. Alfaro, *Mensaje especial*, 2.

26. Annual report of the Guayaquil police chief, reproduced in Ministro de lo Interior y Policía, Beneficencia, etc., *Informe del ministro de lo interior y policía, beneficencia, etc. al congreso ordinario de 1900* (Quito: Imprenta Nacional, 1900), n.p.

27. Annual report of the Quito police chief, in Ministro de lo Interior, Policía, Beneficencia, Obras Públicas, etc., *Informe del ministerio de lo interior, policía, beneficencia, obras públicas, etc. a la nación en 1908* (Quito: Imprenta Nacional, 1908), n.p.

28. Ministro de lo Interior y Policía, Obras Públicas, etc., *Informe del ministro de lo interior, policía, obras públicas, etc. a la asamblea nacional de 1906* (Quito: Imprenta Nacional, 1906), x.

29. Annual report of the Quito police chief, in Ministro de lo Interior y Policía, Beneficencia, etc., *Informe . . . 1900*, n.p.

30. Annual report of the Quito police chief, in Ministro de lo Interior y Policía, Obras Públicas, etc., *Informe . . . 1903*, n.p.

31. Annual report of the general director of prisons, in Ministro de Justicia y Cultos, *Informe del ministro de justicia y cultos al congreso ordinario de 1900* (Quito: Imprenta Nacional, 1900), n.p.

32. Throughout the liberal period the project of educating citizen-workers rather than elite scholars progressively came together. In 1897, Eloy Alfaro removed Latin instruction from the basic school curriculum in favor of "more useful" languages such as English and French. By 1908 his minister of education argued that many students did not even have a solid understanding of the national language and that this should be attended to prior to foreign language training. He therefore proposed that foreign languages be taught only in normal schools.

33. Ministro de Gobierno, *Informe . . . 1896–1897*, 7.

34. Ministro de Instrucción Pública, *Informe del ministro de instrucción pública al congreso ordinario de 1900* (Quito: Imprenta de la Universidad Central, 1900), viii.

35. Ibid., x–xi.

36. Ibid., 8, 14.

37. Secretario de Instrucción Pública, Correos y Telégrafos, *Memoria del secretario de instrucción pública, correos y telégrafos, etc. al congreso ordinario de 1905* (Quito: Tipografía de la Escuela de Artes y Oficios, 1905), vii.

38. Leonidas Plaza, address to congress, August 10, 1903, in Noboa, *Recopilación de mensajes*, 193–94.

39. *El Imparcial*, "Editorial de 'El Imparcial,' 24 de junio de 1908," in *El ferrocarril del sur, 1908–1933: Breve relación de los principales festejos que se realizaron en Quito, el 24, 25 y 26 de junio de 1908, con motivo de la inauguración del tren en esta ciudad* (Quito: Imprenta "Industria," 1933), 14.

40. J. Gonzalo Orellana, *Guía comercial geográfica* (Guayaquil: Imprenta de la Escuela de Artes y Oficios de la Sociedad Filantrópica del Guayas, 1922), 215.

41. Yerovi, "Refutación de un informe," 8.

42. Ayala Mora, *Historia de la revolucíon liberal*, 164.

43. Michael Adas, *Machines as the Measure of Men: Science, Technology, and Ideologies of Western Dominance* (Ithaca, NY: Cornell University Press, 1989), 255–56.

44. Belisario Quevedo, "La sierra y la costa," 1916, reprinted in *Ensayos sociológicos, políticos y morales* (Quito: Banco Central and Corporación Editora Nacional, 1981), 187–94. This and the following quotes are from pp. 191–93.

45. Alfredo Espinosa Tamayo, *Psicología y sociología del pueblo ecuatoriano* (1918; reprint ed., Quito: Banco Central and Corporación Editora Nacional, 1979), 266.

46. Ibid., 257.

47. Andrade Coello, *La ley del progreso*.

48. Remigio Crespo Toral, "Cien años de emancipación (1809–1909)," *La Unión Literaria* (Cuenca) 4th series, no. 2 (1909): 59–78.

49. Andrade Coello, *La ley del progreso*, 51.

50. Crespo Toral, "Cien años de emancipación," 66.

51. Ibid., 76–77.

52. For Europe and North America compare Adas, *Machines as the Measure of Men*, chap. 3; T. J. Jackson Lears, *No Place of Grace: Antimodernism and the Transformation of American Culture, 1880–1920* (New York: Pantheon, 1981); Leo Marx, *The Machine in the Garden: Technology and the Pastoral Ideal in America* (New York: Oxford University Press, 1964); Raymond Williams, *The Country and the City* (New York: Oxford University Press, 1973). For examples of antirailway sentiments in Mexico see William H. Beezley, *Judas at the Jockey Club and Other Episodes of Porfirian Mexico* (Lincoln: University of Nebraska Press, 1987), 103–4.

53. Since the colonial period, northern highland elites had sought an alternate route to the sea that would free them from reliance on Guayaquil's elite. Attempts to link Quito and Ibarra with Esmeraldas failed because the trails constructed were quickly engulfed by the tropical forest. The maintenance of such routes was expensive because they passed through zones of scarce population and little economic development. In 1940 an all-season road was built from Quito to Santo Domingo de los Colorados, but only in 1954 were gravel roads built to link Santo Domingo with Bahía de Caráquez and Esmeraldas.

54. Deler, *Ecuador*, 200.

55. Gregory J. Kasza, "Regional Conflict in Ecuador: Quito and Guayaquil," *Inter-American Economic Affairs* 35, no. 2 (1981): 19.

56. Claudio Mena Villamar, *Ecuador a comienzos de siglo* (Quito: Abya Yala and Letranueva, 1995), 26.

57. Trujillo, *La hacienda serrana*, 50.

58. Officially, this law was called the Ley de Beneficencia. Nationalized properties became *haciendas de asistencia pública* because the fees from renting them out were invested in public welfare institutions. The state did not directly administer such haciendas and use the profits for its programs, but rented them to private individuals for a set price.

59. Mena Villamar, *Ecuador*, 33.

60. That the paradoxical slogan "Dios y Libertad" (God and Liberty) closed official state communications during the liberal period can only be understood as a protest against the foreign origin of religious communities in Ecuador. "Dios y Libertad" was the rallying cry of the March 1845 revolution (the Revolución Marcista) against President Juan José Flores, the Venezuelan caudillo who dominated Ecuadorian politics from 1830 to 1845. Concerning the primarily foreign members of religious orders, the liberals particularly objected to their intervention in national politics, especially when they financed and promoted armed movements against the liberal government at the turn of the century. Thus, one justification for nationalizing the properties of religious communities was to deprive them of the wealth that financed counterrevolutionary movements. See Enrique Ayala Mora, "Estudio introductorio," in *Federico González Suárez y la polémica sobre el estado laico*, edited by Enrique Ayala Mora (Quito: Banco Central and Corporación Editora Nacional, 1980), 52.

61. Leonidas Plaza, address to congress, August 10, 1903, in Noboa, *Recopilación de mensajes*, 140–41.

62. Ministro de Instrucción Pública, *Informe . . . 1900*, iii.

63. Leonidas Plaza, address to congress, August 10, 1905, in Noboa, *Recopilación de mensajes*, 286.

64. Diana Barker has pointed out, however, that the marriage contract is only superficially like other contracts. It is the only kind in which the characteristics of the parties entering into it are so closely defined, for example, by gender, age, and civil status. Despite the possibility of divorce, a marriage contract cannot be nullified by mutual consent as easily as can other contracts. Moreover, unlike commercial contracts, "there can be no bargaining between spouses since the state decrees what marriage shall be. It is not, in fact, a contract between the spouses, but rather they agree together to accept a certain (externally defined) status." She continues, "While a commercial agreement between two parties does not, as such, confer rights or impose duties on any other person(s), the fact of being married affects the spouses' rights and duties in many ways." These specificities of the marriage contract do not change the fact that Ecuadorian liberals saw civil marriage as a model for other kinds of contracts. See Diana Leonard Barker, "The Regulation of Marriage: Repressive Benevolence," in *Power and the State*, edited by Gary Littlejohn (New York: St. Martin's Press, 1978), 254–55.

65. Leonidas Plaza, address to congress, August 10, 1904, in Noboa, *Recopilación de mensajes*, 226–27. The combination of laws that established the lay state were seen as having "returned to State control the individual, the citizen, the family, the society, the church itself." Leonidas Plaza, address to congress, August 10, 1905, in Noboa, *Recopilación de mensajes*, 297.

66. Federico González Suárez, "Manifiestos de los obispos del Ecuador sobre la ley de matrimonio civil," 1902–3, reprinted in *Federico González Suárez y la polémica sobre el estado laico*, edited by Enrique Ayala Mora (Quito: Banco Central and Corporación Editora Nacional, 1980), 286. See also González Suárez, "Primera instrucción pastoral sobre la participación del clero en política," 1907, reprinted in *Federico González Suárez y la polémica sobre el estado laico*, 320–21.

67. The law of civil marriage did not eliminate religious marriage ceremonies, but required that a civil ceremony be performed first. Participants could then choose whether they also wanted to be married by the church.

68. González Suárez, "Manifiestos . . . matrimonio civil," 273.

69. Conservative historian Wilfrido Loor, cited in Mena Villamar, *Ecuador*, 79.

70. In addition, the fact that Plaza's government in 1901–1905 did not provide support for liberals fighting against the conservative government in Colombia also helped to diminish Colombian support for counterrevolutionary forays into Ecuador. In contrast, Eloy Alfaro had been dedicated to supporting liberalism on an international scale.

71. See also Charles A. Hale, "Political and Social Ideas," in *Latin America: Economy and Society, 1870–1930*, edited by Leslie Bethell (New York: Cambridge University Press, 1989), 235–38.

72. Andrade Coello, *La ley del progreso*, 14–15.

73. Ibid., 41–42.

74. Ayala Mora, *Historia de la revolución*, 227–32.

75. For the various contracts signed between the government and the railway company see *El ferrocarril de Guayaquil a Quito: Contratos y otros documentos importantes, 1897–1911* (Quito: Talleres de "El Comercio," 1912).

76. See, for instance, Manuel J. Calle, *Una palabra sobre el contrato ferrocarrilero* (Quito: Imprenta de "El Pichincha," 1897); Ecuatorianos, *Doce millones de sucres: El ferrocarril de Guayaquil a Quito* (Quito: Imprenta "La Industria," 1932); idem, *Ferrocarril trasandino: Hablen los números* (Guayaquil: Imprenta de "El Tiempo," 1902); E. O. N., *Ferrocarril Alfaro-Harmann* (Lima: Imprenta del "Universo," 1897); *El ferrocarril del sur y los derechos del Ecuador* (Quito: Talleres de "El Comercio," 1916); Ernesto Franco, *La verdadera defensa nacional* (Quito: Imprenta Nacional, 1923); Un imparcial, *Breves observaciones que demuestran lo ruinoso que será para la nación el contrato del ferrocarril del sur* (Guayaquil: Imprenta de Gómez Hnos, 1897); Imparciales, *Cuestión candente* (Quito: Imprenta de la Escuela de Artes y Oficios, 1898); F. B. Stewart, *Manejos de Mr. Harman* (Quito: Imprenta de "La Prensa," 1910).

77. *El Comercio*, June 25, 1908.

78. Circular from the archbishop of Quito to the priests of the churches and superiors of the convents of the capital, Quito, June 20, 1908, published in *El Comercio*, June 21, 1908.

79. James C. Scott, Foreword, in *Everyday Forms of State Formation: Revolution and the Negotiation of Rule in Modern Mexico*, edited by Gilbert M. Joseph and Daniel Nugent (Durham, NC: Duke University Press, 1994), xi–xii.

4

Movement from the Perspective of the Coast

Liberalism, the Railway, and the Labor Market

Among the range of possible meanings of movement in Ecuador, the coastal agro-export elite was particularly interested in stimulating labor migrations from the highlands to the coast. From the colonial period onward, land had been a source of prestige and power in Ecuador, but land was worthless without control over a labor force that would produce wealth on it. Thus, the colonial settlement of Spaniards in Ecuador occurred massively in the highlands, where they had found a ready labor force. In contrast, any attempt to take advantage of production possibilities on the coast was based on stimulating migrations from the highlands. Even in the sixteenth century, however, the Spaniards of the highlands passed dispositions to prohibit the displacement of Indians toward the coast. These decrees were necessary because of the tremendous competition among Spaniards for Indian labor for agriculture and textile manufactures in the highlands, for mines in the southern highlands and the Amazon, and for agriculture and transport on the coast.[1]

In the territory that would become Ecuador, the coast was home to under 10 percent of the total population, from before the conquest through most of the colonial period. Only at the beginning of the nineteenth century did the coastal population surpass the 10 percent mark. Migrations from the highlands, a gradual trickle for most of the colonial period, accelerated in the last quarter of the eighteenth century. Jean-Paul Deler has identified a number of factors generating these migrations: the economic crisis of the highlands in the eighteenth century leading to the closure of textile factories; a series of natural

catastrophes, including earthquakes and repeated eruptions of
the Cotopaxi and Tungurahua volcanoes; cycles of drought and
excessive rainfall afflicting highland agriculture; civil disturbances, such as indigenous uprisings (related to the economic
crisis and its consequence, the expansion of large estates); and
finally, military disturbances during and after independence.[2]
These migrations increased in the last third of the nineteenth
century as cocoa entered another boom period. With the construction of the railway these migrations were further stimulated. At the beginning of the twentieth century the coast had
one-quarter of the national population, and by the end of the
1920s its share had passed one-third (see Table 1).

Table 1. Population Distribution of Ecuador, 1825–1926

Region	1825		1889		1926	
	Population	%	Population	%	Population	%
Coast						
Guayas	42,807	8.62	98,042	7.71	483,508	16.51
Other[a]	38,410	7.73	144,076	11.33	631,756	21.56
Subtotals	81,217	16.35	242,118	19.04	1,115,264	38.07
Highlands						
Northern[b]	124,330	25.02	308,940	24.29	544,142	18.58
Central[c]	169,790	34.17	377,833	29.71	797,568	27.23
Southern[d]	110,090	22.16	262,870	20.67	472,340	16.12
Subtotals	404,210	81.35	949,643	74.67	1,814,050	61.93
Amazon	11,419	2.30	80,000	6.29	n/a	n/a
Totals	496,846	100.00	1,271,761	100.00	2,929,314	100.00

Source: Adapted from Rodríguez, *The Search for Public Policy*, 202–5.
[a]Esmeraldas, Los Ríos, Manabí, El Oro.
[b]Carchi, Imbabura, Pichincha.
[c]Cotopaxi, Tungurahua, Chimborazo, Bolívar.
[d]Cañar, Azuay, Loja.

Labor and the Liberal Project

The social basis for the liberal project was the coastal elite who
produced cocoa for the world market at the end of the nineteenth century. These cocoa producers suffered from a chronic
shortage of labor because of the scarce population of the coastal
region. Even though the coastal population grew throughout the
nineteenth century, it was still low relative both to the highland
population and to the needs of cocoa plantations. This situation

of relative population scarcity was exacerbated by the high rates of mortality on the coast due to tropical diseases. In addition, the availability of unoccupied lands stimulated a continual flow of workers away from the plantations.[3]

For most of the nineteenth century the expansion of the agricultural frontier on the coast was undertaken through the contracting of a cocoa planter (*sembrador*) and his family to colonize a new area and plant cocoa trees (provided by the plantation owner) as well as subsistence crops for their own use (some of which also served as shade for the cocoa plants). *Sembrador* families lived off the subsistence crops for the five years required for the maturation of the cocoa plants and then turned these fields over to the plantation, at which point they received a nominal payment for each healthy cocoa plant (20 to 30 centavos).[4] The *sembrador* absorbed many of the risks for the plantation owner, which meant that the amounts invested in planting and maintenance were very low indeed. Moreover, before 1896, land for cocoa production could be obtained from the government at no cost (after that year, land could be purchased for a mere 4 sucres per hectare).[5] The maintenance of existing cocoa plantations was carried out by salaried agricultural workers and day laborers.

While the coast was relatively underpopulated, and coastal elites placed great emphasis on the scarcity of workers, it should be pointed out that this did not prevent the expansion of the agro-export economy. What it does appear to have caused, however, was an increase in the plantations' labor costs, particularly compared to similar costs in the highlands. The labor shortage implied that the wages paid to workers were much higher on the coast, from 80 centavos to 1 sucre daily, while the day wage in highland agriculture prior to 1895 was 2 to 5 centavos.[6] However, a part of these labor costs was recuperated by the plantation owners, chiefly through workers' debts to the company stores on the plantations. Although labor costs probably made up a relatively high proportion of the production costs on cocoa plantations, in some cases annual profits could reach up to 25 percent of the total initial capital invested in these enterprises.[7]

In their search for workers, coastal plantation owners looked to the highlands. Efforts to stimulate migrations were carried out by labor recruiters (*enganchadores*) who offered to advance wages and to pay for transportation to the coast. Despite the efforts of these labor recruiters, however, the mobilization of highland workers appears to have been limited at the turn of the century, especially in comparison with what was to follow.

It was only with the construction of the railway and with the passage of legislation that undermined the rigid control of highland landowners over the indigenous peasant population that migrations were intensified.

Coastal elites looked to the new liberal administration to stimulate labor migrations, in part by loosening labor ties in the highlands. Coastal planters saw highland landowners as artificially maintaining a monopoly over labor, thus sabotaging the prospects for national development through export production. From the perspective of the liberal agro-export elite of the coast, highland landowners used extraeconomic coercion to preserve control over labor. In this context, the liberal state attempted to take the moral upper hand over highland landowners by insisting on its own role as protector of Indians from the abuses of both "traditional" highland landowners and the Catholic Church (also a large landowner). The liberal goal of generating a labor market thus involved the development of a discourse stressing the liberty of contracts, and political measures to undermine highland landowners' power over labor, rather than the use of extraeconomic coercion to generate flows of forced labor or to dispossess indigenous peasants of their lands.

To identify the specificity of the Ecuadorian case, it is useful to compare Ecuador with Guatemala, another country with a large indigenous population, which was also incorporated into the world market through primary product exports in the 1870s.[8] In Guatemala, after 1871, the liberal government of Justo Rufino Barrios began to promote coffee production in areas adjacent to the western highlands where the majority of the Maya lived. The modernization drive initiated by Barrios entailed an attack on both native land and native labor. Although there are many ways to cultivate coffee,[9] in Guatemala large estates developed, given the speed with which land was acquired after 1871 and the means of acquisition through personal connections to the ruling elite. Because Guatemalan coffee was produced on large estates, and because the development of coffee plantations did not simultaneously dispossess smallholders, coffee planters required a seasonal work force that would provide labor when needed and that could be dispensed with in other periods. Coffee requires more labor in the harvesting season than it does at other times: in Guatemala, this labor was provided by migrant indigenous peasants, prodded by a series of political measures. One way for the plantation owners to obtain this labor was through outright coercion in the form of a draft known as the *mandamiento*, established in 1876. This draft was a state levy on Indian villages, according to which each community had to send a certain number of laborers each year for the coffee harvest. Another means to obtain labor was debt: in 1894 debt peonage was legalized, permitting the use of force to ensure that workers paid their debts. This peonage was often activated through the *habilitación*, or advanced pay for work, generating debt that peasants had to repay by working on coffee estates for very low remuneration.

In order to further encourage the flow of labor to plantations, a process of acquiring Indian land in the highlands began, especially after the passage in 1877 of a law that abolished all forms of communal property. Some highland Indians were completely dispossessed and became permanent workers on the lowland plantations. However, most Indians held on to some land but were required to work seasonally on plantations to buy the food that they could no longer produce in sufficient quantities for themselves. Finally, in 1934, a vagrancy law was passed requiring individuals holding less than a stipulated amount of land to work part of each year as wage laborers for others (those with fewer than 6.9 acres were required to work one hundred days, those with fewer than 2.8 acres worked one hundred fifty days). Only in the 1940s had Guatemalan Mayan peasants become so pauperized that it was no longer necessary for large landowners to use extraeconomic means of labor recruitment.

Despite the fact that, after 1870, Ecuador also initiated a monoexport boom that suffered from a chronic shortage of labor and that this boom took place in a zone neighboring the highlands with its dense indigenous population, processes similar to those described for Guatemala did not occur in Ecuador. The key to understanding these issues lies in the fact that the Ecuadorian highlands adjacent to the cocoa production zone were not merely an area of free indigenous communities but, more important, one of haciendas owned by a strong dominant class. The existence of two strong, regionally based dominant classes— one in the highlands, associated with haciendas producing for the internal market, and the other on the coast, producing for the world market on plantations[10]—was fundamentally important for the particular way in which labor relations developed in Ecuador. While in the nineteenth century political domination was in the hands of the highland elite, the liberal period represented the rise of the coastal elite. Nonetheless, this group was unable to impose a project that was exclusively in its own interests during the liberal period. Instead, an uneasy working relationship developed between the two dominant classes. If the coastal elite had been capable of quickly destroying the power of the highland elite, or if that group had not existed, coastal planters might have also found it easier to impose extraeconomic coercion to obtain cheaper labor rather than take the route that they did.

Ecuadorian liberals have been chastised by social scientists for their inability or unwillingness to destroy the power of the highland landowners, leading instead to compromises with them. This tendency is often seen as the weakness that prevented the liberals from carrying through more radical reforms, such as agrarian reform in favor of highland peasants. Given the nature of the era under consideration, and in the context of a comparative perspective on Latin America, it seems improbable that elite groups would have promoted a redistribution of land in favor of subordinate groups. It seems more likely that without a powerful highland class, coastal liberals would have engaged in extraeconomic coercion to obtain labor rather than undertake an agrarian reform program that might have rooted indigenous peasants even more strongly to the highlands. To understand the path not chosen, we must always keep in mind that Ecuadorian liberalism was an elite project.

The Ecuadorian case fits well into Antonio Gramsci's category of the passive revolution of capital, which he applied to Italian history. As Partha Chatterjee sums up, "Gramsci has talked of the 'passive revolution' as one in which the new claimants to power, lacking the social strength to launch a full-scale attack on the old dominant classes, opt for a path in which the demands of a new society are 'satisfied in small doses, legally, in a reformist manner'—in such a way that the political and economic position of the old feudal classes is not destroyed, agrarian reform is avoided, and the popular classes especially are prevented from going through the political experience of a fundamental social transformation."[11] However, the reformist, legalistic route to social change in Ecuador did provide important openings for subaltern action. As a result, Ecuadorian liberalism was a relatively positive experience for Indians, in the comparative context of Latin America.

The power of highland landowners could not be eliminated easily. The liberal conflict with that group engaged important ideological resources, as coastal elites and liberal legislators attempted to represent themselves as the promoters of modernity, progress, and freedom in contrast to both the highland elite and the Catholic Church. This campaign against highland power-holders was articulated precisely around the liberal state's role in protecting the rights and freedom of indigenous laborers. The "freeing" of indigenous peasant labor thus did not occur through a violent transformation of this sector into a proletariat or semiproletariat but rather through a series of legal regulations that gradually undermined the power of highland landowners as well as of the church. These legal measures, combined with railway construction, created conditions that permitted an expansion in the migration process that had begun to occur in previous decades.

Coastal elites saw indigenous labor as immobilized by hacendados, by church institutions, and by local authorities, the triumvirate of local powers seen as oppressing the indigenous peasants of the highlands.[12] During the latter part of the nineteenth century, indigenous highland peasants were required to provide several kinds of services that benefited the triumvirate, in addition to the agricultural work that they carried out in their own communities or on haciendas. One such service was the subsidiary labor tax, which was established in 1854 to promote road construction.[13] Those who could not pay the tax in cash were required to work it off on road construction gangs. Although this tax technically applied to all adult males, those who actually worked were overwhelmingly indigenous men, along with some poor mestizos. In 1871 there was an important indigenous uprising in Chimborazo against state exactions, including the subsidiary labor tax. The uprising, led by Fernando Daquilema, was brutally repressed by the government of García Moreno.[14] Elite conceptualizations of the appropriate punishment reveal the different regional perspectives in formation: while highland hacendados were convinced that the participants should be put to death as a lesson to others, coastal elites thought that it would be much more instructive if the defeated rebels were sent to work on coastal plantations.

The subsidiary labor tax was supplemented by García Moreno's 1861 Law of Municipal Administration, which specified that municipal public works would be built through the contribution of either money or labor by male inhabitants of the area. In 1869 the Ley de Caminos Vecinales was passed for the construction of local footpaths and mule trails. That law required all adult males in a given canton either to work two days per year on such tasks or to pay the wages of a replacement worker. Local archival research in the Alausí region demonstrates that this law was applied exclusively to indigenous men. Only with the reorganization of this system in association with passage of the Ley de Fomento Agrícola in 1918 is there local archival evidence that every male inhabitant of a particular area really was recruited for such work or required to pay for a replacement worker.

After the Liberal Revolution, a number of legal measures were taken to encourage the mobility of indigenous labor in the highlands. These laws were aimed mostly at undermining the power of large landowners in the zone. The first of these measures was the elimination, in 1895, of the subsidiary labor tax. However, the presidential decree of December 28, 1895, that in its first article abolished this tax, in its second permitted municipalities to create substitute contributions for the construction of municipal public works (plazas and public buildings, the cobbling of streets, and so on). In contrast to the tendency to establish unified legislation during the liberal period, in this case a national law was replaced by various municipal bylaws allowing for local labor recruitment, which rendered recruitment guidelines ambiguous.

During the liberal period, labor recruitment for municipal public works became the site of multiple struggles at the local level. During these conflicts, the central state positioned itself as the protector of indigenous rights, at a cost to the legitimacy of local authorities. As indigenous laborers petitioned central state authorities to protect them from the abuses of local officials, orders were passed down the administrative hierarchy to constrain the activities of these local authorities, leading to a gradual strengthening of the central state and undermining the local forms of political power.[15] These processes also undermined the power of local landowners because the construction of municipal public works had often favored this group, either through the common abuse of diverting to private enterprises peons who had been recruited for public works, or simply because the kinds of projects undertaken were defined by municipal councils, usually dominated by local landowners.

In 1899 a series of legal measures were taken "to protect the indigenous race" and to modify the institution of debt peonage. These included a provision that indigenous labor could only be obtained if Indians freely entered into contractual relations, a requirement that state officials oversee these contractual relations, and a prohibition on the heritability of debt. This last measure placed a limit on the length of debts, which previously had outlived the original debtor. In addition, a minimum daily wage of 10 centavos was set for the highlands, while previous salaries of peasant laborers in the region had fluctuated between 2 and 5 centavos.[16] These regulations were strengthened in 1906 when the new police code (the first such code at the national level) fixed a minimum salary of 20 centavos in the highlands and 80 on the coast as well as introduced the possibility of dissolving personal service contracts. This reinforced the mechanisms tending to introduce liberty of contract into the relations between highland peasants and the hacienda system.[17]

The church had also traditionally singled out Indians for specific labor services as well as other taxes. In exchange for the benefits of obligatory religious instruction, Indians were required to provide various services in churches and convents and on the lands and in the residences of clergy (under the names of *doctrina* and *pongo*). Tensions over the provision of these services became an arena in which church-state conflicts were played out at the local level during the first ten years of the liberal period, as a discourse of law versus custom was developed. The state argued that only those services required by law or specified in a previous contract could be demanded of anyone. The persistence of customary labor obligations exposed the church to allegations of abuse, and the liberal state quickly positioned itself as the defender of indigenous rights. Indians in turn could use these conflicts to more broadly resist the forced recruitment of their labor for local public works as well as by the church, given that the liberal state used a general discourse about freedom of contract to undermine church privileges at the local level.[18]

In 1898 the congress revoked a territorial tax on Indians aimed at supporting the church and declared tithes, first fruits, and similar contributions voluntary in that the state would no longer intervene to ensure their payment. These processes undermined the power of local officials who had participated in the collection of these taxes as well as eliminated one of the mechanisms by which Indians became indebted and thus tied to their localities. Once passed by the central state, these legal measures took effect principally because of the actions of subordinate groups, who had called upon the central state to limit local abuses. A similar strategy was to remind local authorities of the new legal measures, with an implicit threat to petition the central government. A revealing example of this process is provided in a note to the political lieutenant of Sibambe parish in Chimborazo from the indigenous authority (*regidor*) of Linge:

> In regard to your order that the people of my community should pay the collector of the territorial tax, under the threat that we will be arrested by the constable, I say to you: Happily, I was in Chimbo yesterday, and I met some gentlemen who were reading a large sign with embossed print, and who said to me, "Regidor, you are in luck, along with all those of your class. Here is a decree from the President of the Republic, exonerating you from the territorial tax, and warning all the authorities to treat you well." With this news, I returned home full of joy and advised the community, and together we gave thanks to God and the Señor President who have freed us from the continual thefts that we have suffered year after year, when we have been forced to pay any amount the collector specifies, even using the constable to help steal from us.
>
> I suggest you look around for this decree, no doubt you have it tucked away somewhere in your office; and if in spite of everything the constable is sent here, now we have some one to whom we can complain, and the thieves will suffer their punishment.[19]

Given the liberal emphasis on legal measures to undermine the highland elites' control over labor, it is not surprising that Indian complaints had a heavily legalistic tone during the liberal period. This "tendency to litigation so characteristic of our rural folk"[20] was to become a frustrating characteristic of indigenous Ecuadorians from the perspective of many elite groups.

The early liberal period also saw the beginnings, in 1905, of the debate over the elimination of debt peonage. However, debt peonage was not abolished at this time because of the combined resistance of highland landowners, who were interested in maintaining a sufficient labor reserve to expand their production to provision the coast, and of the coastal agro-export elite, who wanted to maintain control over laborers on their plantations through debt mechanisms (particularly debt to the company store). Debt peonage would not be eliminated until 1918, when changing international market conditions during the First World War had begun to undermine the cocoa agro-export elite. At that time, a new agro-industrial and banking elite associated with sugar production and processing was on the rise, and they needed a steady supply of temporary seasonal workers for the harvest.

The gradual conformation of a labor market during the liberal period was encouraged both by these legal measures and by railway construction. Infrastructure projects required a great deal of labor, which encouraged the mobility of workers due to the high salaries paid. Labor mobility was also promoted by the activities of *enganchadores*, who recruited national workers in the highlands by providing them with transportation, cash advances, and information about job opportunities that might not have been available locally. A closer examination of labor policies on railway construction illustrates some of the difficulties and contradictions involved in forging a labor market. This analysis is based in part on documentation drawn from local archives in the region of Alausí, which was a strategic location during railway construction in part because the worst labor problems for the railway company occurred on the ascent to the Andes in this zone. Moreover, railway exploration began there under direct government supervision prior to the existence of any contract for actual construction.

Labor on Railway Construction

All of the nineteenth-century contractors of the Ecuadorian railway line had been defeated by labor problems. Predictably, problems with labor emerged in the construction of the Guayaquil Quito Railway during the liberal period. The worst arose in the construction of what was known as the "mountain section," which meant not the highlands but rather the ascent to the highlands from Bucay to Alausí, up to and around the Nariz del Diablo, where a double switchback was built to scale the western cordillera of the Andes. Chief engineer Major John Harman, brother of Archer Harman, noted that among the most serious difficulties faced in construction was "the absolute lack of labor in the mountain sections."[21] Eventually, finding local labor "unsatisfactory,"[22] the James P. MacDonald Company of New York was compelled to import some four thousand Jamaican laborers for work on this section, along with an unspecified but much smaller number of Puerto Ricans and Barbadians.

One of the principal problems faced by the railway labor contractors, as well as by coastal plantation owners, was fear among highlanders of the disease-ridden tropical climate. Indeed, part of the reason that Marcus Kelly faced financial ruin in 1888 was that he was forced to pay laborers 1 sucre per day to attract them to the tropical construction zone. Despite the high wages, many of the workers fled from the embankment work on the western foothills of the Andes, afraid of the tropical forest with its malaria, ferocious animals, and snakes. The work that Kelly did manage to complete cost the lives of more than five hundred day laborers.[23] When railway construction recommenced under the liberals, "the question of labor on the line has caused serious difficulties and expense. . . . On account of the climate, [the natives] will not come down to work in the lower districts."[24] The evidence demonstrates that these fears were well grounded. There were problems with snake bites, which killed a number of workers, and jaguars, which attacked the mules and donkeys.[25] In addition, a high proportion of the workers did contract tropical diseases.

One unspecified disease attacked the workers in 1900. At an altitude of 200 meters above sea level an insect was encountered living in the shrubs along the rail line; its bite caused headache, high fever, and death. The company destroyed the shrubs, but before this had been completed, large numbers of workers had died and were buried in mass graves at Kilometer 106 of the rail line.[26] There was also an outbreak of smallpox among the Jamaicans and indigenous laborers.[27] In fact, in 1902, only 50 to 60 percent of the laborers in the construction camps were actually at work; the remainder were ill with various diseases.[28] The unhealthy climate led the Guayaquil and Quito Railway Company to make special provisions to protect the health of their foreign engineer corps, such as supplying mules and horses for their transport as well as "an unusual number" of servants.[29] In addition, the engineers' camp was established at a distance from the camps of the common laborers, reinforced by barbed wire. Despite these precautions, tropical diseases claimed the life of engineer Henry Davis in 1900 and of John Harman in 1907.

The worst problems of labor recruitment associated with climate were over by September 1902, when construction of the railway to Alausí had been completed. There was another, more tenacious problem, however, which clearly demonstrated some of the difficulties of forging a labor market: local peasant laborers were immersed in a different logic than that of the labor market as long as they were not "freed" from the means of production. Given the difficulties in obtaining workers due to both fear of disease and local laborers' inconsistent attitudes toward work on the line, some of the contradictions of liberalism began to emerge.

Spurred by Eloy Alfaro's determination to build a railway, exploration work on possible railway routes began well before contracts had been signed with investors and entrepreneurs to construct the line. By October 1895, Ecuadorian engineer Modesto López was already working on preliminary surveys in the Alausí area.[30] A German engineer, Sigvald Muller, was also contracted for a six-month period to study the line and had arrived in Alausí to supervise López by September 1896. This period of exploration continued until the contract was signed with the newly formed Guayaquil and Quito Railway Company, which began work in late 1898.

Labor recruitment for railway exploration from 1895 to 1897 thus was carried out under the direct control of the Ecuadorian government. Recruitment was undertaken in much the same way as for municipal works: the political administrator of the canton ordered the political lieutenants in the parishes to name day laborers with the help of indigenous authorities. These laborers were required to present themselves for work on the line, or risk being fined or jailed. By early 1897 it was becoming increasingly difficult to recruit laborers, who insisted that they could not be forced to work without a previous contract.[31] Local authorities warned their superiors that only through the use of force would they be able to send laborers to the line, but the higher authorities were convinced that the offer of good wages would be enough to attract workers. Here the distance between the liberal ideals of the central state and the thorny recruitment problems of the local officials become clear.

In 1897, for example, when López requested forty day laborers from Modesto Corral, the political administrator of Alausí, he contacted the surrounding villages for workers but to no avail because of the locals' fear of the climate on the mountain section. Corral then contacted the governor to find out what legal resources were available to him to supply laborers. The governor responded that given the elevated wages, he found it strange that people did not volunteer. Hoping for a more helpful answer, Corral telegraphed President Alfaro to inform him that the only possible way to obtain workers would be through force. Alfaro too responded that an agreement should be reached with the engineer, that once a daily wage was defined and advances were distributed among the laborers, it would be possible to proceed with "some firmness" to ensure compliance. An agreement was reached with the engineer: the wage to be paid was 1 sucre daily, and each peon would receive an advance of 4 sucres prior to beginning a fortnight's work. On this basis, Corral sent out orders to the political lieutenants requesting ten peons per fortnight from each parish to assist with the surveys of the line. The political lieutenants were warned that if they did not comply, they would be fined 10 sucres each, and the peons who were notified and did not work would be fined 4 sucres. Clearly, the use of force and the payment of wages were not incompatible: extraeconomic coercion was used in association with wage labor. While superior political authorities expressed high ideals in extolling the persuasive powers of wages alone, local authorities used force and imposed fines on those who declined to work as well as on the lower authorities directly responsible for recruiting.

Laborers were also recruited through the distribution of cash advances, which then legitimated the subsequent use of force. Why was force necessary? Day laborers were offered 1 to 1.20 sucres per day (from which food was deducted) for their work on surveys for the rail line. In comparison, laborers on local public works earned only 10 to 20 centavos. However, the seemingly rational economic calculation that would dictate that laborers would gravitate toward the higher wages could not be assumed as long as workers had not been separated from the means of production. Peasants were tied to the agricultural cycle, and no amount of money would induce them to leave their fields at peak periods. Thus, they went to work on the line at their own convenience, rather than in accordance with the needs of the railway project. In 1896, López complained that in certain months he had far more peons than he needed on the line, while in other months it was impossible to obtain any workers at all. Indeed, in 1897 the Indians of Alausí canton stated outright that they would rather pay a fine than go to work on the line and neglect the agricultural tasks that would provide them with their subsistence for the entire year.

With the arrival on the scene of the New Jersey-based Guayaquil and Quito Railway Company in late 1898, the labor system was overhauled. The company had a strict timetable within which construction had to be completed (although, in fact, few deadlines were met satisfactorily). Labor needs could no longer be satisfied by recruitment in the particular area where work was in progress, not least because of the other activities distracting local laborers' attention. The company began to look farther afield for workers. By July 1899, six hundred were en route from the northern region of Tulcán, and additional workers were recruited from the Cayambe region in Pichincha province during this period. A substantial setback occurred in February and March 1900, however, when the majority of the work completed to date was destroyed by flooding and landslides during the rainy season, resulting in a modification of the route to follow the valley of the Chanchán River. This difficulty provoked a renewed attempt to recruit labor from as many sources as possible. In July and August 1900 the company increased its efforts to recruit Ecuadorian labor and to contract foreign workers.

Ecuadorian labor was recruited through a reorganized system of *enganchadores*. The company compensated parish-level political and police authorities for each worker they helped to enlist. Local authorities appointed work group leaders from among the laborers enlisted, for whose conduct the parish authorities were responsible from the time they were recruited until they were registered in the provincial capital. Each leader, who received a daily wage of 2 sucres, was responsible for delivering fifty peons to the construction site and ensuring that they fulfilled their duties, as well as acting as the peons' representative before the company. Travel time for leaders and workers was to be paid at the rate of 20 centavos per day. While on the job, laborers were to be paid daily wages of 1.20 sucres for nine hours of work, payable each fortnight. The company also offered to make cash advances to workers when appropriate guarantees were offered.

While the wages offered to railway laborers appear to be high, in fact the situation outlined above did not always come to be. In fact, local labor recruiters received a certain amount of money for each worker provided, even when the worker was obtained at a lower wage. The high wages that the company offered, therefore, did not necessarily reach the workers themselves. Rather than 1.20 sucres per day, the majority of day laborers on the railway line received from 50 to 65 centavos. The remainder of their wages was distributed among a series of intermediary links in the labor recruitment chain, including local authorities and the recruiter himself. In addition, some large landowners may have sent their peasant laborers to work on the line and pocketed the wages.[32]

Despite these problems, there is no question that many workers took advantage of the availability of well-paid labor in the area, once the construction had moved out of the tropical zone and when it did not interfere with their agricultural tasks. For instance, in 1899, in Alausí canton, most of the peons from

Chunchi parish had gone off to work on the rail line; in 1901–02 the peons of Sibambe were all at work on the line; and in Tixán in 1901 villagers took their children out of school to help them with their work on the line. That wages were higher on the line provided a powerful justification for refusing to work on local projects, and railway construction caused a shortage of labor for the municipal public works system as well as for repairs on the telegraph line. The attraction of railway work became stronger as the job sites moved farther up the mountain and closer to Alausí.

Despite the efforts to increase the number of Ecuadorian workers on the line, labor shortages continued. The MacDonald Company should have had six thousand laborers at work on the line in 1900 but had only been able to obtain fifteen hundred after an intense campaign. Meanwhile, large quantities of materials were en route; and if they could not be used quickly, they would have to be stored, risking damage, through the following rainy season. This would set the construction schedule back even further. As a railway company agent explained, "Vigorous and able laborers abound in this country who can carry to completion the project . . . and it would be unjust, unpatriotic and of little profit, to resort to workers from other countries, existing as there are many thousands of indigent Indians who lie around in a constant and punishable idleness."[33] However, given that "our hopes have been dashed so many times in regard to the workers of this Republic,"[34] it was determined that the construction up to the highlands could be completed only with foreign laborers. In relation to the great public works projects of nineteenth-century Latin America, there was a perception that certain "natural labor reserves" existed. These reserves included indentured Chinese laborers and the populations of some Caribbean islands.

When Marcus Kelly had run into labor problems in 1888, he had requested permission from the Ecuadorian government to contract Chinese workers. Not only was this request denied, but a prohibition on all further Chinese immigration also was made law in September 1889.[35] The Chinese who did live in Ecuador—who either had arrived before the 1889 prohibition or had entered the country clandestinely from neighboring Peru—were primarily merchants.[36] In Guayaquil they ran several large import-export firms (exporting Ecuadorian agricultural products and importing silks and fine fabrics) and were closely associated with China-based companies that dominated the trade between Ecuador and Asia. In the coastal zones of Yaguachi, Babahoyo, and Vinces, Chinese residents were the owners of small- to medium-size agricultural properties, but the vast majority of the Chinese who lived in other towns on the coast were involved in commerce. Their businesses, which sold general merchandise and bought local agricultural products for export, were often the largest commercial establishments in those areas. In every town where there were Chinese merchants (with only one exception), the average capital of their enterprises was significantly higher than the average capital of other commercial enterprises. It is clear that the competition that Chinese merchants posed to Ecuadorian merchants on the coast underlay anti-Chinese policies. As the British consul in Quito pointed out when the original prohibition against Chinese immigration was passed in 1889, "Great stress is laid on the demoralizing influence of their race. This is a mere pretence, the reason which determined the adoption of this high-handed measure being the well-known grievance of those who fear Chinese competition: the great intelligence displayed by the celestials in commercial pursuits, and the cheapness of their labor."[37]

In 1900, James MacDonald met with the Chinese government's representatives in New York to discuss the possibility of contracting five thousand coolies, who would be transported from Hong Kong to Guayaquil at the cost of the MacDonald Company and be returned to China once the railway was completed to Palmira, at the apex of the western cordillera. The MacDonald Company offered the Ecuadorian government a guarantee that it would remove from the country any surviving Chinese once the railway reached Palmira or would pay a compensation of $100 in gold for each coolie who remained. As Archer Harman explained to Eloy Alfaro, "In all of the great railways of the United States, Mexico and South America, it has been necessary to employ Chinese labor; without which it would have taken long years to finish the lines, in the mentioned countries just as in Ecuador." He insisted that without the contracting of four to five thousand Chinese laborers, the company could not complete the railway in a timely manner because it was "clearly impossible to rely on Ecuadorian workers" for the ascent to the highlands.[38]

Despite the liberal rhetoric emphasizing the importance of the free movement of labor and goods, the Ecuadorian government refused to approve the contracting of Chinese laborers and went on to uphold and strengthen the restrictions against the

Chinese already resident in Ecuador. These restrictions included constraints on their movement around the national territory. Although the coastal elite, who supported the liberal governments and the free movement of goods and people, were usually eager to gain access to additional labor, they found that the presence of Chinese undermined their own commercial interests both in Guayaquil and in the company stores on their plantations. Restrictive policies on Chinese represented a clear contradiction in liberal policy, but the paradox was resolved by invoking racial danger. The Chinese were accused of spreading vices such as opium smoking, prostitution, and gambling and thus causing the degeneration of Ecuadorian workers. It was also argued that liberal principles of free trade did not apply to the Chinese because they themselves were unfair traders: they limited their own living expenses to such an extent that they undercut merchants who operated under more "natural" conditions.

Instead of contracting Chinese coolies, then, James MacDonald traveled to Jamaica to contract several thousand workers. Blacks were considered to be better suited to heavy construction work than local Indians due to both the nature of the work and the tropical climate. The British colonial government in Kingston had instituted an elaborate system for supplying Jamaican laborers for the construction of large-scale infrastructure projects such as the Panama Railroad as well as for the protection of such workers' rights outside of Jamaica.[39] MacDonald himself had served as the labor contractor for the construction of the Port Antonio extension of the Jamaica Railway, so he was familiar with Jamaican labor, and apparently he had a good reputation among them as an employer. Given the scarcity of well-remunerated work on the island at the time, MacDonald found no difficulty in procuring the four thousand laborers he sought, both among the skilled workers employed on the Jamaica Railway and among unskilled laborers. The contract that MacDonald signed with the British Colonial Office provided for the appointment of an inspector to watch over the interests of the laborers and ensured that while the Jamaicans were at work, a fund would be accumulating in the Banco del Ecuador to guarantee their return passage home and to provide them with savings at the end of the contract.

Soon after the arrival of the Jamaican laborers in Ecuador in November 1900, however, complaints began to be sent back to Jamaica about their treatment; these complaints appeared in the press and were passed on to the government by the workers' friends and relatives. A Mr. Leach was dispatched to investigate the conditions of Jamaicans employed in Ecuador, and he reported that armed police and soldiers were being used to bring back deserters from the line and to keep them, as he characterized it, at forced labor in convict camps. It was later reported that "there is no doubt that during the first few months of their contract many of the men were cruelly treated by some of their contractors and their foremen but after Mr. Leach's report . . . their treatment was considerably improved. There were always, however, occurring incidents of unpleasant character, springing from American prejudice against the negro, in which it was very difficult, sometimes impossible, to obtain anything like justice for the latter."[40] The result was that desertions on the line were common, so much so that the railway police lay in wait every day at the Durán terminus of the line to capture runaways, who could easily find work in Guayaquil or on the plantations of the zone.

By September 1902 the work that the Jamaicans had been hired for had been completed, with the inauguration of the railway in Alausí. The ascent had required enormous labor in cutting through rock, for which the Jamaicans were considered especially adept. From Alausí onward, however, the railway would use Indians for what was considered to be lighter work through the sandy soil. The majority of the Jamaicans who had not broken their contracts left the country under the original agreement with the MacDonald Company. Approximately three hundred remained, many of them settling in Bucay and finding work on the sugar estates of the zone.

Once the railway was completed to Alausí, Ecuadorian labor was again recruited through mechanisms of *enganche*. The remainder of the rail line was built with local labor, and the working conditions were considered to be good, particularly in comparison with the labor regime organized for road construction by García Moreno in the 1860s and 1870s. An elderly indigenous man who worked on railway construction during the liberal period compared his own experiences with those of his father under García Moreno. In his father's case:

> The priest and the political lieutenant, along with the *alcaldes ordinarios* [indigenous authorities], forced all of the adult Indians to work in public works for the municipality, for the province, on other *haciendas*, and also on the properties of these

officials. They used to capture them on Sundays when they came down for Mass and keep them overnight in jail, like animals. That was to make them work in road construction without any pay. García Moreno used to carry them off to the *chaco* [public works labor], seizing them by force, putting them in jail and then sending them to work on the roads and other projects. They used to tie them together by the waist and make them march in line like animals and take them off to work tied up like that, and guarded by military troops. But then Alfaro arrived to do us the favor of building the railway, and that did pay, one sucre a day, five sucres per week. I worked on the line. I never actually met Alfaro, but I served him in the great work of the railway, which was good, not like García Moreno who used to take people away all tied up, as happened to my father.[41]

Although the railway to Quito was completed in 1908, new work opportunities became available after 1915, when construction began on the two extensions of the line from Sibambe to Cuenca and from Quito to Ibarra. Again, many people offered to work on the extensions, including hundreds from the Alausí area (causing labor shortages for other local projects). In the parish of Guasuntos alone, which had a very small population, fifty workers volunteered in a single month in 1919. In addition to day wages of 1 sucre, the company also provided housing, canteens selling inexpensive provisions to workers (particularly important because food was so expensive on the line that some workers would not otherwise have been able to afford to work on the railway), a paid cook for each work group, and transportation costs for all those who worked at least three fortnights. Local political and police authorities continued to be paid by the company for recruiting laborers, as is evident from the number of conflicts in which Indians claimed to have been fined by local authorities for not voluntarily going to work on "the line of sacrifice and progress."

The process of labor recruitment and treatment on railway construction reveals some of the contradictions of liberalism. One principle underlying the liberal project was a conception of all individuals as being equal before the state. In this sense, the discourse of the liberal state was a universalizing one. Nonetheless, it was clear to many liberal politicians and ideologues that all Ecuadorians were not equal. President Plaza, during his first administration, recognized that it would be difficult to graft liberal principles of equality onto the diversity of Ecuadorian reality:

> Our people, the sum of all of the inhabitants disseminated across our national territory, is a heterogeneous entity because of the diversity of its origins and tendencies. Thus it is divided in classes little less than antagonistic, each one of which has its peculiar customs and occupations, which seldom allows them to come into contact with each other except in very rare cases and circumstances. This notably retards the social perfection and advance of the whole; and, as a result, the Public Powers should attempt to procure the mixture and assimilation of classes in order to obtain a compact unit. *Until this happens, in addition to the existing differences, it is difficult to apply the same law to everyone, rendering the activity of authorities over citizens unequal, and making equal demands by the state on all discordant.* Liberty cannot exist except on the foundation of Equality; and where that is lacking, Liberty rests directly on the ground, and is in danger of being trampled.[42]

During the colonial period, Indians had been constituted and governed as a separate "republic" from Ecuadorians of Spanish descent. The colonial separation of castes was based in part on notions of distinct lines of descent. But Plaza and other liberals had fundamentally different concerns: they proposed not racial separation but assimilation for Indians, in accordance with the liberal ideology of the equality of individuals. Yet, paradoxically, this ideology was associated with continued inequality. This contradiction could be justified, however, where the biological differences of individuals was perceived as scientific "fact." Concern thus emerged in many countries in the nineteenth and early twentieth centuries with quantifying biological differences.

During the Ecuadorian liberal period, this concern was particularly evident in regard to Chinese immigrants, who made up a significant community on the coast despite the prohibitions on additional immigration. Chinese were measured alongside criminals in the police anthropometry office in Guayaquil and were required to carry an identity card detailing not only their name, address, and occupation but also their height, weight, the shape of their nose and mouth, hair texture, and so on. There was less interest in measuring biological differences in relation to Indians. Instead, Indians were considered incapable of participating fully in the nation because of their history—a history of oppression by the Catholic Church, by highland landowners, and, in some cases, by local officials. Thus, liberal discourse about the Indian focused on the need to free him from abuse and transform him into a being capable of participating in national life. Liberal emphasis on the redemption of the Indian was often articulated in relation to labor issues. As the minister of justice formulated the problem in 1897: "It is shocking to see the lamentable situation of the Republic's most unfortunate group—the Indians. Their complete ignorance and the lack of cultivation of their intelligence does not allow them to manage their commitments with discernment, resulting in their perpetual slavery, the endless accumulation of their labor obligations. Thus it is necessary that the officials of the liberal government make an effort to rescue this neglected race from its prostration and barbarousness."[43]

The process of working for wages and contracting freely, rather than remain submerged in colonial relations of peonage and oppression, would thus transform the indigenous peasant into a more modern, moralized worker, capable of participating fully in the national economy and polity.[44] The railway was central to this goal because "surely the project of the trans-Andean Railway is the scalpel that will cut out the cancer and cast into the sewer the infectious cause that produces it, because the colossal enterprise will give work to thousands of laborers, today inert or debilitated by vice and abjection."[45] More broadly too, the railway would help break the bonds that tied labor to the highlands.

The Railway and the Labor Market

There was great demand for labor on the coast in three general areas: urban work, or agricultural work on either cocoa or sugar plantations.[46] The urban growth of Guayaquil, associated with the export boom, generated considerable work opportunities. The docks and import-export companies provided jobs for day laborers, and one niche for recently arrived migrants from the highlands was in the police service. After a massive fire swept through Guayaquil in 1896, the reconstruction of the city required twenty-five hundred day laborers, who were paid 2 sucres per day, through 1897.[47] With this help, within four years the customs house, three banks, two schools, four churches, and 527 houses (122 of which had three stories) had been constructed.[48] These were in addition to the homes of the poor, which were built without paid labor.

The labor needs of the cocoa plantations increased from fifteen thousand workers in 1900 to thirty-five thousand in 1920.[49] The coastal sugar plantations and mills needed at least twice as many workers at harvest and milling time as at other moments.[50] These enterprises expanded significantly with the crisis of the First World War. The war undermined Ecuadorian cocoa production, but it also disrupted sugar beet production in Europe, creating an opening for expanded sugar cane production. The result was an expansion in both the production and the processing of sugar in Ecuador, in which there was a transfer via banks of cocoa capital toward the sugar sector, a release of labor from cocoa plantations, and an abandonment of land previously cultivated with cocoa. While the processing of sugar was quickly industrialized, the expansion of production into new territories and the increased harvest of cane relied entirely on additional labor, much of which was temporary. This labor was attracted through the high day wages paid, reaching 1.60 to 2 sucres in the harvest and milling period (higher than the wages paid on cocoa plantations). As already discussed, the actual mechanism for obtaining labor from the highlands was the *enganchador*, usually a plantation foreman, who himself received payment for each worker he obtained. The *enganchador* visited population centers in the highlands to recruit workers for three- to four-month periods, offering to pay their transport to and from the plantations.[51]

In 1918 the elimination of coercive means to control labor through *concertaje* (debt peonage), coinciding with the rise of the sugar agro-industrial elite, represented the culmination of previous measures to undermine highland control over labor, further contributing to the creation of a free labor market. Nonetheless, Jorge Trujillo has argued that the actions of the railway constructors may have been more effective in ending *concertaje* than these laws, given the high wages they paid on infrastructure projects and their extensive use of *enganchadores*.[52] The railway stimulated the labor market in three important ways.[53] First, it employed indigenous labor at significantly higher wages than those available in local agriculture or municipal public works. In 1915, after the completion of the Guayaquil-Quito Railway, work on the railways from Sibambe to Cuenca and from Quito to Ibarra began. These lines used a great deal of indigenous labor, mobilizing peasants who had been subject to the hacienda system. After deductions for commissions paid to labor recruiters and local authorities, the daily pay for railway construction work at this time was 60 to 65 centavos, while on highland haciendas the pay was 10 to 20 centavos and in municipal public works, 20 centavos. In 1918, when the railway to Cuenca was under construction in the Alausí area, the police chief raised wages on municipal projects to 40 centavos per day in an effort to attract workers, with little success.

Second, the railway indirectly stimulated labor migrations in various ways. It encouraged agricultural modernization in the highlands, which in some cases involved either the release of workers from haciendas with the mechanization of production or hacienda incursions into indigenous lands. In addition, in Bolívar province, which had been on the main route to the highlands prior to construction of the railway through Chimborazo province, mule driving declined, prompting former muleteers to migrate from Bolívar to coastal plantations, particularly to those in Los Ríos province.

Third, the railway offered workers an efficient and rapid form of transportation. In many cases, their trips were paid for by *enganchadores*. In other cases, workers did not travel by train but walked along the line, which was still a relatively rapid way of traveling from the central highlands to the sugar zone of Milagro. These migrations, which took advantage of the railway, were often undertaken by peasants whose poverty was not caused directly by the railway, unlike those peasants driven out by agricultural modernization. For instance, in areas where haciendas had a rigid monopoly over land or where erosion of peasant plots had occurred, demographic pressure often led peasants to engage in seasonal migrations. Monopolistic control of land by large landowners was especially common in the north-central highlands. The provinces of Imbabura, Pichincha, and Cotopaxi provided workers for railway construction (on the Guayaquil-Quito and Quito-Ibarra lines), while Cotopaxi also provided migrants for coastal plantations. In Tungurahua province, where peasants had access to *minifundia*, limited access to water led to their impoverishment and availability for seasonal work in other areas. Peasants in the central highlands found an easy route to the coast along the rail line. In addition, erosion and demographic pressure especially affected Azuay and to a somewhat lesser extent Cañar. In these southern provinces the hacienda system had already been undermined by erosion and by the fact that local peasants had access to resources to obtain land from mule driving or from the artisanal production of

Panama hats. This sector of *minifundista* peasants also engaged in seasonal migrations to supplement their income.

Under these conditions, both the coastal plantations and large-scale infrastructure projects such as railway and road construction gained access to sufficient labor reserves to cover the cyclical needs of periods of greater work. It is generally agreed that until the 1930s or 1940s the majority of migrants from the highlands to the coast were white and mestizo.[54] But there were also more indigenous peasant migrations over this period. In regions that achieved privileged proximity to the coast with railway construction, this migration process may have been stimulated somewhat earlier. For instance, there were seasonal migrations of indigenous peasants from Alausí canton dating from 1917 and continuing throughout the 1920s.

The language of movement and connection articulated around the railway thus was brought to fruition in the formation of a labor market, which was dear to the hearts and pocketbooks of coastal liberals. In a sense, this represented a triumph for the interests of the coastal elite against those of highland landowners. However, the highland elite were interested in taking advantage of a different aspect of movement and connection: the possibility of forging an internal market by supplying basic foods to the coast and even exporting agricultural and livestock products. Their interests too would be promoted by the railway.

Notes

1. Deler, *Ecuador*, 63.
2. Ibid., 173–74.
3. Trujillo, *La hacienda serrana*, 109–10.
4. Ronn F. Pineo, "Guayaquil y su región en el segundo boom cacaotero (1870–1925)," in *Historia y región en el Ecuador: 1830–1930*, edited by Juan Maiguashca (Quito: CERLAC, FLACSO, and IFEA, 1994), 260.
5. Ibid., 258.
6. Trujillo, *La hacienda serrana*, 111.
7. Deler, *Ecuador*, 211–12.
8. W. George Lovell, "Surviving Conquest: The Maya of Guatemala in Historical Perspective," *Latin American Research Review* 23, no. 2 (1988): 25–57; Carol A. Smith, "Origins of the National Question in Guatemala: A Hypothesis," in *Guatemalan Indians and the State, 1540 to 1988*, edited by Carol A. Smith (Austin: University of Texas Press, 1990), 72–95.
9. See the essays in William Roseberry, Lowell Gudmundson, and Mario Samper Kutschbach, eds., *Coffee, Society, and Power in Latin America* (Baltimore: Johns Hopkins University Press, 1995).

10. For the classic statement of the difference between haciendas and plantations in Latin America see Eric R. Wolf and Sidney Mintz, "Haciendas and Plantations in Middle America and the Antilles," *Social and Economic Studies* 6 (1957): 386–412.

11. Partha Chatterjee, *The Nation and Its Fragments: Colonial and Postcolonial Histories* (Princeton: Princeton University Press, 1993), 211; Gramsci, *Selections from the Prison Notebooks*, 44–120.

12. See Andrés Guerrero, "Una imagen ventrílocua: El discurso liberal de la 'desgraciada raza indígena,' " in *Imágenes e imagineros: Representaciones de los indígenas ecuatorianos, siglos XIX y XX*, edited by Blanca Muratorio (Quito: FLACSO, 1994), 197–252; idem, *La semántica de la dominación: El concertaje de indios* (Quito: Libri Mundi, 1991); Joseph B. Casagrande and Arthur R. Piper, "La transformación estructural de una parroquia rural en las tierras altas del Ecuador," *América Indígena* 29 (1969): 1039–64. For a fictional account of the collusion of local landowner, priest, and political lieutenant against indigenous peasants see Jorge Icaza, *Huasipungo* (1934; reprint ed., Bogotá: Editorial Oveja Negra, 1985), Ecuador's most important indigenist novel.

13. Samuel Ackerman, "The 'Trabajo Subsidiario': Compulsory Labor and Taxation in Nineteenth-Century Ecuador" (Ph.D. diss., New York University, 1977).

14. Hernán Ibarra, *"Nos encontramos amenazados por todita la indiada":*
El levantamiento de Daquilema (Chimborazo, 1871) (Quito: CEDIS, 1993).

15. For a description of labor recruitment for municipal public works and the struggles that resulted see A. Kim Clark, "Indians, the State and Law: Public Works and the Struggle to Control Labor in Liberal Ecuador," *Journal of Historical Sociology* 7, no. 1 (1994): 49–72.

16. Trujillo, *La hacienda serrana*, 111.

17. More ambiguous were the results of the 1897 and 1906 constitutions, which stated that no one who had a contract to work for someone else could be required to work on municipal projects. In at least some cases, this provision led to an increase in debt peonage contracts on haciendas, which became areas of refuge from state labor demands. See Chap. 6, this volume; and Clark, "Indians, the State and Law."

18. Clark, "Indians, the State and Law," 55–56.

19. Regidor of Linge to the political lieutenant of Sibambe, Sibambe, March 1, 1898, AJPA 1898.

20. Ministerio de Previsión Social y Trabajo, *Informe que el ministro de previsión social y trabajo, Dr. Carlos Andrade Marín, presenta a la nación* (Quito: Talleres Gráficos de Educación, 1941), 103.

21. John A. Harman, "The Guayaquil and Quito Railway in Ecuador, South America," *Engineering News* 52, no. 6 (1904): 119.

22. C. Lockhart, "Opening the Riches of the Andes," *The World's Work* 2, no. 6 (1901): 1271–77.

23. Manuel Sarasti, "El Consejo de Estado y el depósito de los dos millones," in *Ferrocarril del sur: Juicios imparciales* (Guayaquil: Imprenta de "El Tiempo," 1892), 73.

24. A. Cartwright to the British Foreign Office, Guayaquil, October 1, 1901, 25/107, BCR/FO AHBC-Q.

25. Harman, "Guayaquil and Quito Railway."

26. Maldonado Obregón, *Historia del ferrocarril*, 75. See also Eloy Alfaro, "Historia del ferrocarril de Guayaquil a Quito," 1911, reprinted in *Narraciones Históricas* (Quito: Corporación Editora Nacional, 1983), 395.

27. Alfaro, "Historia del ferrocarril," 399; Hans Meyer, *En los altos Andes del Ecuador: Viajes y estudios* (1907; reprint ed., Quito: Universidad Central, 1940), 471–72.

28. Ministro de lo Interior, Policía y Beneficencia, etc., *Informe . . . 1902*, 27.

29. Harman, "Guayaquil and Quito Railway," 117.

30. López was one of the first graduates of the Polytechnic School established in Quito by President García Moreno in the 1870s, as part of the latter's effort to create a national technical elite.

31. The constitution stipulated that laborers could be made to work only if they had voluntarily agreed to do so in a contract, or if their services were required by law. Paradoxically, the services required by law were often ambiguous. Thus, the fines imposed for labor evasions were justified not for the infraction of a specific labor-related law but rather for disobedience to the order of a superior.

32. Andrés Guerrero, verbal communication, Quito, March 30, 1990.

33. Leaflet by Guayaquil and Quito Railway Company agent G. L. Percovich, enclosed in governor of Chimborazo to political administrator of Alausí, Riobamba, August 18, 1900, AJPA 1900.

34. Archer Harman to Eloy Alfaro, Quito, September 7, 1900, in Ministro de lo Interior y Policía, Beneficencia, etc., *Anexos al informe del ministro de lo interior y policía, beneficencia, etc. al congreso ordinario de 1900* (Quito: Imprenta Nacional, 1900), 23–24.

35. See Antonio Flores Jijón, *Derecho público: Inmigración china* (Quito: Imprenta del Gobierno, 1889).

36. Ecuador did not contract Chinese laborers in the nineteenth century, as was done in Peru, Panama, and Cuba. Compare Anita Bradley, *Trans-Pacific Relations of Latin America* (New York: Institute of Pacific Relations, 1942); Eugenio Chang Rodríguez, "Chinese Labor Migration into Latin America in the Nineteenth Century," *Revista de Historia de América* (Mexico) 46 (1958): 375–97; Michael J. Gonzales, "Chinese Plantation Workers and Social Conflict in Peru in the Late Nineteenth Century," *Journal of Latin American Studies* 21 (1989): 385–424; Humberto Rodríguez Pastor, *Hijos del celeste imperio en el Perú (1850–1900)* (Lima: Instituto de Apoyo Agrario, 1989); and idem, "El inmigrante chino en el mercado laboral peruano, 1850–1930," *HISLA* 13–14 (1989): 93–147. Instead, the majority of Chinese in Ecuador were merchants who had entered the country from Peru. The Ecuadorian case was more like the situation in Mexico, where Chinese merchants migrated from the United States, where they had been contracted as railway construction workers, to northern Mexico, where they established themselves as merchants. Compare Kennett Cott, "Mexican Diplomacy and the Chinese Issue, 1876–1910," *Hispanic American Historical Review* 67, no. 1 (1987): 63–85; Evelyn Hu-DeHart, "Immigrants to a Developing Society: The Chinese in Northern Mexico, 1875–1932," *Journal of Arizona History* 21, no. 3 (1980): 49–86; Leo M. Jacques, "Have Quick More Money Than Mandarins: The Chinese in Sonora," *Journal of Arizona History* 17, no. 2 (1976): 201–18.

37. Alfred St. John to the British Foreign Office, Quito, September 26, 1889, 25/85, BCR/FO AHBC-Q.

38. See note 34.

39. The following discussion of Jamaican laborers in Ecuador is based on governor of Jamaica to the Colonial Office, Kingston, April 9, 1901, No. 188, 25/107, BCR/FO AHBC-Q.

40. Reverend D. W. Bland (inspector of Jamaican laborers) to the colonial secretary, November 7, 1902, 25/110, BCR/FO AHBC-Q.

41. Hugo Burgos Guevara, *Relaciones interétnicas en Riobamba: Dominio y dependencia en una región indígena ecuatoriana* (Mexico: Instituto Indigenista Interamericano, 1970), 172.

42. Leonidas Plaza, address to congress, August 10, 1904, in Noboa, *Recopilación de mensajes*, 213 (emphasis added).

43. Reproduced in circular no. 11 from the governor of Chimborazo to the political administrator of Alausí, Riobamba, February 23, 1897, AJPA 1897.

44. Labor on railway construction was not always a source of morality, however. As one labor contractor reported, "an element of disorder" had been introduced into the construction camps by *cantineros*, ambulant vendors of aguardiente, and prostitutes, who together caused "the intellectual and physical demoralization of the workers, and especially of the Indian peons." Gambling was a particular danger to labor discipline, because it involved "people who stay sleeping all day and never work, rob the others, and live from the worker." In addition, "the property of the railway is also destroyed, wood, ties, supplies, etc. are stolen by this class of idlers who follow the camps and live from those who construct the line." James MacDonald to the political administrator of Alausí, April 19, 1902, AJPA 1902. See also Meyer, *En los altos Andes*, 471–72.

45. Annual report of the Quito police chief, in Ministro de lo Interior y Policía, Beneficencia, etc., *Informe del ministro de lo interior y policía, beneficencia, etc. al congreso de 1899* (Quito: Imprenta Nacional, 1899), n.p.

46. The following paragraphs draw on the discussions of the conformation of a labor market and labor migrations from the highlands to the coast in Trujillo, *La hacienda serrana*, chap. 4; Ibarra, "Ambato"; and idem, *Indios y cholos: Orígenes de la clase trabajadora ecuatoriana* (Quito: El Conejo, 1992).

47. Ibarra, *Indios y cholos*, 9–10.

48. Mena Villamar, *Ecuador*, 29. The reconstruction of Guayaquil was accomplished quickly, in part due to the resources from customs receipts, but also with the assistance of a decree requiring all municipalities to contribute 10 percent of their revenues in 1897 and 1898 to the rebuilding of the port city.

49. Ibarra, *Indios y cholos*, 10.

50. For instance, on May 28, 1923, the sugar plantation and mill Ingenio Valdez in Milagro advertised in the Quito newspaper *El Comercio* that it needed 2,000 seasonal workers as of June 15, when the milling season would begin. It offered to pay wages of 1.6 to 2 sucres daily or, for work by task, up to a possibile 6 sucres per day. It should be noted that this advertising in the highlands for additional workers came when the crisis affecting cocoa plantations was already well under way, involving a significant release of labor, which was still clearly inadequate.

51. Trujillo, *La hacienda serrana*, 113.

52. Ibid., 114.

53. Ibid., chap. 5.

54. Ibarra, *Indios y cholos*, 13; Carola Lentz, "Los 'Pilamungas' en San Carlos: Un estudio de caso sobre la inserción de migrantes serranos como trabajadores eventuals en un ingenio azucarero de la costa ecuatoriana," *HISLA* 7 (1986): 45–63.

5

Movement from the
Perspective of the Highlands

The Politics of the Internal Market

Some of the basic components of the liberal project were expressed through the development of a language of movement and connection, a language that had multiple meanings and uses. For coastal plantation owners this language was associated with the project of forming a labor market, and it could be extended to undermine the economic and political power of the Catholic Church. In the highlands, too, this language had its uses, particularly for those landowners who wanted to modernize and expand their production to gain access to the coastal market for basic food products. The shared nature of this discourse masks the fact that in some ways these goals could not be pursued simultaneously: for instance, the intensification of production for the internal market depended in some cases precisely on increased control over labor.

In the development of the liberal discourse of movement and connection, the highland region was defined as dormant, stagnant, traditional, backward, and disconnected internally as well as closed to external influence. Despite the dominance of these images in liberal discourse, however, only in the mid-1910s did the state begin to pay sustained attention to the highlands in terms of "awakening" the productive potential of this region.

An examination of railway traffic indicates that in the 1910s and 1920s there was a significant increase in the circulation of highland agricultural and livestock products in Ecuador's internal market. This growth was stimulated by the First World War, which had multiple and far-reaching ramifications not only for the country's exports but also in relation to the production of goods for internal consumption. Indeed, the scramble to deal with the ensuing crisis crystallized into a focus on the need to expand and modernize highland agriculture in order to provision the internal market. However, neither the existence of transport links alone, nor the changing international context, can be seen as directly causing the growth of the internal market. Rather, these two factors changed the terrain on which social groups made decisions and organized to promote their class interests: in the first decades of this century a group of modernizing highland landowners mobilized to present an image of highland agriculture as essential to national well-being, and of the highlands themselves as a central component of the national community. The sense of urgency generated by the altered international context provided what railway construction alone had not, that is, the opportunity for certain sectors of the highland landowning elite to organize in order to promote their interests successfully.

The Internal Market and the Railway

At the turn of the century, the Ecuadorian economy relied overwhelmingly on the export of cocoa, the country's *pepa de oro* (golden seed). The coastal agro-export region was strongly integrated into the international market. Not only was the coast the center of export-oriented production, but also the majority of the basic food products consumed on the coast were imported. Prior to the cocoa boom the region had been supplied with basic foods by the haciendas of the zone. However, as the cocoa plantations expanded, the production of basic food products on haciendas began to be displaced, especially because the plantations absorbed the scarce labor force of the zone. The plantations allowed workers some subsistence food production (especially of manioc and plantain, which were grown as shade to protect the cocoa plants), but the majority of the subsistence needs of the plantation workers were provided through the purchase of food, particularly in company stores. The displacement of basic food production on haciendas by the plantation system, and the rapid growth of the population of Guayaquil and the province of Guayas, meant that food staples had to be brought from elsewhere. Given that it imported not only luxury goods but also large quantities of staple foods, Ecuador was unusual for an agricultural country. According to President Eloy Alfaro, this anomaly had a variety of causes:

> The scarcity of labor, the elevated type of interest on capital that is employed in the Republic, the rudimentary nature of our agriculture, the meteorological phenomena that themselves provoke food shortages, the difficulties of transport, the almost nonexistent use of mechanical force applied to field labors, etc., are immense obstacles for national production. Hence the price of our products results excessively high in comparison with the costs of foreign producers in the same situation. For instance, grains produced in California, even given the cost of transport to Guayaquil, can be sold at a lower price there than the same product grown in this country.[1]

At the beginning of the liberal period the highland region was unable to provision the coastal market, but highland agriculture continued to be oriented primarily to local markets within the thirteen intermont basins. While there was some increase in interprovincial integration after 1870, this was primarily in livestock products. With the improvement of the Vía Flores passing through Guaranda at the end of the 1880s, traffic between the highlands and coast intensified, with some limited transportation of agricultural products of the central and southern highlands (Chimborazo, Bolívar, and Azuay) and of livestock from Tungurahua, Cotopaxi, and Pichincha. Even so, because of the difficulties of transport, the movement of live cattle over large distances was severely limited, and it was impossible to export them, given the rigors of travel: "No matter how fat they are when they leave the pastures of Quito and Machachi, they arrive weak, skinny, and crippled at the ports of embarkation, after an arduous trek of fifteen days."[2]

The transport of basic agricultural products was even more limited. In 1897 the lack of good routes between highland provinces raised the cost of shipping agricultural products so much that in one province there might be great scarcity while in a neighboring province the abundance of grains might lead to prices too low for the grower to make a profit. According to one Tungurahua hacendado, novelist and politician Luis A. Martínez, abundant harvests paradoxically led to ruin because prices were driven well below production costs. As a consequence, agriculturalists were discouraged from expanding production. With better transportation routes, a balance could be achieved between supply and demand; in their absence, the prices of agricultural products swung between extremes. Martínez gave examples from the early 1890s:

> There are some years, such as 1890–91, when agricultural prod-
> ucts in the central highland provinces sell at excessively low
> prices. In that year, a quintal of barley was worth forty centa-
> vos, one of potatoes, thirty centavos, and so on. This was be-
> cause there was an overabundance of these products, well
> beyond local necessities. The granaries overflowed, and it was
> impossible to send these products to distant provinces where
> there was scarcity, because of the cost of transport. But then in
> the year 1893–94 the price of these same articles increased five-
> fold, followed the next year by a fall in price to the level of
> 1890–91. . . . If they were connected by good roads, however,
> the diverse production zones of Ecuador would be liberated
> from these repeated swings. Then if a harvest declined in one
> province, products could be sent there from a province where
> they were abundant, and a balance would be established.[3]

The underlying problem was the exorbitant cost of transportation. For instance, Martínez stated that between Ambato and
Quito (which were linked by the best road in the country), transport by mule cost at least 1 centavo per quintal per kilometer in
this era, over the 125-kilometer distance. For the quintal of
potatoes worth 30 centavos in 1891, this added a minimum of
125 centavos to its sale price in Quito, and Martínez estimated
that in fact more often the cost of transport between these two
points was closer to 160 centavos. In contrast, in the United States
at this time, products transported by train paid the equivalent
of 1 centavo per quintal per 10 kilometers. Even worse, the cost
per quintal to transport wheat from Chile or Australia to Europe was less than it cost to transport the same product from
Quito to Guayaquil.[4] When the Ecuadorian railway was inaugurated in 1908, the cost of transport for 1 quintal of agricultural produce over the entire 444 kilometers from Quito to
Guayaquil was 82 centavos[5]—twice the going rate in the United
States, but only one-fifth (or less) the previous cost of transport
by muleteers. As another highland hacendado and agronomist
commented in 1912, an efficient transportation route is to the
national territory what the circulatory system is to the human
organism.[6] Hence the importance of the railway as the principal
"artery" of national transportation and communications.

What then was the effect of the railway on the possibilities
of expanding production and consolidating the internal market? Already in the period from 1903 to 1908 there was a notice-
able decline in the volume of potatoes imported, from 70,602 kilos
costing 4,871 sucres to 11,009 kilos at a cost of 992 sucres.[7] Even

though Ecuadorian flour mills in the north-central highlands were increasing their production for the consumption of the lower classes, imports of wheat flour had increased significantly. Imported flour was of higher quality than domestic flour and was used in more refined baked goods. Although imports of legumes (beans, lentils, and peas) rose, the increase was minor; meanwhile, consumption had expanded greatly, with the difference being supplied by national production. The amount of butter imported increased only slightly (from 60,995 to 67,269 kilos), but its price rose notably (from 37,117 sucres to 60,371 sucres, for the respective volumes imported). National production of butter was identified as having the potential to displace imports, given that it was beginning to be made by modern means in the highlands. In the 1910s and 1920s the imported products that competed with and displaced local ones were those that were industrialized elsewhere lard and wheat flour, for instance—thus lowering their cost relative to Ecuadorian production. The highland products that could potentially compete with imported goods were those not subject to industrialization, such as potatoes, onions, corn, and beef.

It is difficult to assess the growth of Ecuador's internal market; detailed statistics were not kept on this movement, unlike the careful measurements made of imports and exports for taxation purposes. Nonetheless, one way to evaluate the success of efforts to expand agricultural production for the internal market is to examine railway traffic. The Guayaquil-Quito Railway, unlike many railways elsewhere in Latin America, was not dedicated principally to the transport of export products. Ecuadorian export production was overwhelmingly centered in the coastal region, which was served by a system of steamboats that plied the extensive network of rivers making up the Guayas basin. Without the necessity of an expensive infrastructure, Guayaquil was in direct contact with the principal economic zones of the Guayas basin: the Daule region, with its plantations growing tobacco destined for the urban market; the zone of the "upriver" cocoas of Los Ríos province, around Babahoyo and Vinces; the zone of "downriver" cocoas, between Naranjal and Machala; and the expanding zone of sugarcane cultivation around Milagro.[8]

Rather than coastal export products, staple foods grown in the highlands made up a much more important proportion of train cargo in the late 1910s and the 1920s. Table 2 compares the importance of selected products originating in the highlands and on the coast in terms of quantities exported and quantities moved by rail in 1921. Products from the highlands, which represented only a tiny part of the country's exports, fed a significant internal traffic of more than 26,000 metric tons on the railway line. The important export products of cocoa and coffee, totaling 55 percent (by weight) of the country's exports in 1921, made up only 1.5 percent of the railway traffic in the same year. In addition, to appreciate the role of agricultural production in the national market, it should be noted that the tonnage of agricultural, livestock-related, and forest products transported by the rail line in 1921 totaled 76,253 metric tons. This figure was clearly superior to the exported volumes of cocoa and coffee.[9]

Table 2. Agriculture: Exports and Railway Traffic, 1921 (Selected Highland Products Compared to Coastal Ones)

Product	Exportation		Railway Traffic	
	Weight (tonnes)	Value (sucres)	Weight (tonnes)	Value (sucres)
Highlands				
Potatoes	109.15	15,062	12,995	1,793,200
Cereals	106.39	13,858	10,018	2,717,600
Dairy products	34.07	58,600	2,375	3,556,400
Meats	4.48	5,631	404	507,500
Hides	407.85	239,722	594	349,100
Totals	661.94	332,873	26,386	8,923,800
Coast				
Cocoa	42,858.83	20,363,000	1,078	512,200
Coffee	6,112.42	3,209,500	542	284,600
Totals	48,971.25	23,572,500	1,620	796,800
Total products				
Highlands	902	775,300	—	—
Coast	88,765	32,952,200	—	—
Totals	89,667	33,727,500	108,853	—

Source: Deler, *Ecuador*, 222.

To examine the growth of production for the internal market over time, Table 3 illustrates the evolution in railway traffic of selected products from 1910 to 1927. By weight, the most important transported by train was potatoes: total average annual tonnage almost doubled from 8,671.0 from 1910 to 1914 to 15,210.6 from 1920 to 1924. Wheat and barley transported by train increased significantly in annual tonnage from 1,396.2 to 4,916.4 during the same period. Various grain flours and meals similarly increased from 1,402.2 to 4,200.6 in annual tonnage.

Table 3. Merchandise Transported by Rail, 1910–1927 (Average Annual Tonnage Transported Each Period)

Product	1910–1914	1915–1919	1920–1924	1925–1927
Agricultural Products				
Temperate grains[a]	1,396.2	3,030.2	4,916.4	4,569.7
Potatoes	8,671.0	12,601.8	15,210.6	14,383.3
Rice	2,143.2	3,983.6	4,764.8	5,158.7
Bananas	1,232.0	3,425.4	7,007.4	13,911.0
Cotton	522.4	357.8	958.0	698.0
Cocoa	646.8	782.4	879.2	990.3
Flours	1,402.2	3,298.6	4,200.6	5,209.0
Sugar	6,588.2	7,673.2	10,123.8	15,210.3
Other	4,909.0	8,625.0	12,647.0	15,340.0
Totals	27,511.0	43,778.0	60,707.8	75,470.3
Livestock-Related Products				
Cattle	5,074.2	5,931.6	7,056.8	7,147.0
Other livestock	1,415.8	1,773.2	1,510.0	1,278.7
Dairy products[b]	352.4	937.0	1,873.8	2,201.0
Other	672.2	1,802.0	2,520.6	3,268.7
Totals	7,514.6	10,443.8	12,961.2	13,895.4
Forest Products				
Totals[c]	1,499.4	2,752.8	5,490.8	5,016.7
Heavy Products				
Salt	4,511.2	4,867.4	6,259.8	7,107.3
Construction materials	2,937.6	2,489.8	7,042.0	6,427.0
Petroleum products	357.8	673.6	1,278.0	2,084.7
Other	2,138.0	435.8	282.0	581.7
Totals	9,944.6	8,466.6	14,861.8	16,200.7
Industrial Products				
Equipment	711.8	734.6	2,577.4	4,330.3
Beverages[d]	1,429.8	1,763.8	2,467.8	2,919.7
Other	8,680.6	8,165.2	14,617.0	20,820.7
Totals	10,822.2	10,663.6	19,662.2	28,070.7
Total merchandise	**57,291.8**	**76,104.8**	**113,683.8**	**138,653.8**
Merchandise transported free of charge for the government	16,186.2	14,863.0	17,381.0	20,825.0

Sources: Deler, *Ecuador*, 224, with additional data from Coverdale and Colpitts, Consulting Engineers, *Report on the Guayaquil and Quito Railway Co. of Ecuador* (Quito: Guayaquil & Quito Railway Co. Printing Department, 1930), 24.
aWheat and barley.
bMilk, butter, and cheese.
cLumber, charcoal, bamboo, rubber, etc.
dWine, liquor, beer, etc.

And dairy products experienced a spectacular increase in annual tonnage, from 352.4 to 1,873.8 during this period.

When railway traffic was disrupted in mid-1925 by the destruction of a long section of track between Alausí and Bucay during the rainy season, it became possible to estimate the increase in commerce. "Our best calculations fix the annual volume of commercial exchange between the highlands and the coast at seven thousand mule loads, prior to the construction of the railway. We now know, however, due to the recent interruption in railway traffic, that 2,500 mules are needed for the transport of the cargo of a single train. From this we can deduce that the volume of merchandise moved in one week is now three times greater than that of an entire year prior to 1908."[10] By March 1919 it was claimed in the magazine of the Sociedad Nacional de Agricultura, a group of modernizing highland agriculturalists, that "whether due to the increase in the population, its subsequent necessities, the relative facility of transport, the greater cultivation of land, or, especially, the improved techniques employed, it is evident that the agricultural production of Ecuador has doubled in the last twenty years. We do not believe that we are mistaken in this, and to prove our point, it is enough to consider that the livestock, cereals, tubers, and vegetables produced in the highlands used to be consumed only in the interior provinces, while today they also provision those of the coast."[11] While there were frequent complaints by agriculturalists and merchants about poor railway service and high tariffs, without doubt highland agricultural products were being marketed far beyond their zones of origin by the 1920s.

The railway stimulated the internal market by improving transportation in three ways. First, it allowed rapid transportation, which facilitated the commercialization of fresh vegetables and dairy products in coastal cities and towns. Second, the railway made it possible to transport heavy or bulky products such as onions, potatoes, grains, and corn. Third, the reduced cost of transportation permitted an increase in the profit margins for certain products destined for the internal market: livestock, dairy products, and some legumes (especially lentils and peas). In contrast, transport by mule had been restricted to products that were not highly perishable or easily damaged by the rigors of travel. That transport had also included the cost of mule drivers and shipment by river. There were also advantages for highland products transported by rail compared to some goods imported by sea, which faced problems of storage, preservation, and port and customs fees.[12]

The Crisis of World War I

Existing studies tell us how the crisis in Ecuador provoked by the First World War affected the coastal region and cocoa exports,[13] but it also affected the highlands. However, the immediate impact on the Ecuadorian economy of the declaration of war in Europe in August 1914 was minimal. The principal commercial houses had large stocks of previously imported goods on hand, so despite the difficulty in ordering additional merchandise, for the moment sufficient goods were available to satisfy the country's needs. The decrease in imports did cause an immediate decline of approximately 20 percent in the nation's customs revenues in 1914 (customs revenues making up the largest part of the national government's budget at this time). Still, given the warring nations' need to provision their armies, the abundant crop of cocoa in 1914 found a ready market, and prices were high.

The same could not be said for other coastal export products, most notably *tagua*, or vegetable ivory. *Tagua* conspicuously illustrates the vulnerability of the Ecuadorian export economy, since it depended overwhelmingly on the vagaries of the European fashion industry. The fruit of the *tagua* palm contains six to nine seeds the size of small potatoes, of hard, white, fine-grained composition, closely resembling tusk or dentine ivory. This vegetable ivory was used primarily to manufacture buttons, with smaller quantities made into umbrella handles, chessmen, and poker chips. Not only was *tagua* not an essential product, but also the center of the vegetable ivory trade was, unfortunately, Hamburg, Germany. Prior to the war, *tagua* was Ecuador's second most important export. In 1913 it made up 15.6 percent of total export value, following cocoa, which provided 63.2 percent of export value. In 1914 exports of *tagua* dropped to 3.5 percent of total export value, which represented a decrease from 31,684 kilos exported to 8,583 kilos, with a value of 4,399,000 sucres in 1913 and only 944,000 sucres in 1914.[14] By January 1915, Ecuadorian producers were unable to find a market for their *tagua* in either Germany or the United States. Large quantities of *tagua* nuts were destined to remain in Guayaquil warehouses during the war, to be destroyed by weevils.

In early 1916 the export crisis intensified with the increasing diversion for Admiralty purposes of the British-owned Pacific Steam Navigation Company's merchant steamers (the company that dominated trade along the Pacific coast of South America prior to the war). This heralded problems not only for Ecuadorian export interests but also for the shipping monopoly of the British themselves. Such problems were particularly evident when American shippers W. R. Grace and Company and the Johnson line sent steamers to Ecuadorian ports in February and received full cargos. Even when the Pacific Steam Navigation Company was able to transport Ecuadorian cargo as far as Panama, by May 1916 only 25 percent of the cargo reaching the Panamanian port of Colón found passage on other British steamship lines to Europe. Moreover, in mid-1916 exports of jute from British India to Ecuador were severely restricted—another blow to the Ecuadorian export economy, since imported jute had been manufactured into burlap sacks in Guayaquil for the transport of cocoa (in one of cocoa's few forward linkages) and other coastal agro-export products.

On February 23, 1917, King George's Importation Prohibition No. 14 threw the Ecuadorian economy into a downward spiral. A wide variety of articles were prohibited from import into the United Kingdom, including raw and refined cocoa. Repeated petitions were made by the Ecuadorian government for this measure to be either repealed or modified; all such petitions were denied. The only significant market that remained open for cocoa was the United States. The most immediate consequence was a steady decline in the price, given the glut on the U.S. market. In 1917 the United States was able to absorb one-half of the world's cocoa production, importing nearly the entire Ecuadorian crop that year. But as the months passed, the situation worsened. In November 1917 total shipments of Ecuadorian cocoa to the United States amounted to a mere 5,784 sacks, compared to 34,730 sacks in November of the previous year. In 1918 the situation deteriorated even more. To guarantee the supply of sugar for their European allies, the U.S. government ordered that the amount of sugar that could be made available to chocolate manufacturers in 1918 be reduced by 50 percent as compared to 1917. Only at this point did the large stocks of cocoa warehoused in the United States begin to cause concern there. Because Ecuadorian stocks on hand were greater than those of any other country, further imports of Ecuadorian cocoa into the United States were prohibited.

The Ecuadorian import-export crisis was not merely a temporary problem related to the First World War. Cocoa exports never fully recovered. However, the end of the cocoa boom had been foreshadowed during the first decade of the century, when Africa's Gold Coast surpassed Ecuador as the world's largest producer. The existing crisis was intensified in 1920–21 by a plunge in the price of cocoa on the world market: while it reached a high of 26.75 cents per pound in New York in March 1920, in 1921 the corresponding price was only 12 cents. As a result, Ecuador's cocoa exports in 1921 were worth only 49.8 percent of what they had been worth in 1920, and by 1923 were worth only 38.8 percent of their 1920 value.[15] In addition, during the war, diseases began to spread through the plantations, causing their worst damage after 1923. Thus, the falling price of cocoa could not be compensated for by increased production; rather, the reduction of export earnings due to falling prices was further aggravated by a decline in the volume of cocoa produced, from 865,010 quintals in 1920 to 447,111 in 1926. The latter was the lowest level of production since 1900. Ecuador's largest plantation, Tenguel, had 23,000 cocoa trees in production in 1918, but by the end of 1924 it had fewer than 1,000.[16] Ecuadorian cocoa sales were soon to enter an additional crisis with the shrinkage in world demand during the depression. Moreover, new techniques for refining cocoa allowed chocolate manufacturers to use lower-quality raw material, further undermining Ecuador's position, which had been based on the high quality of its cocoa. Another boom product would not be found until after the Second World War with banana production.

From the beginning of the crisis in the coastal export economy, it was clear that the possibility of importing goods was also affected. In memos to the Foreign Office in London, British diplomats in Quito pointed out that if the United Kingdom did not import Ecuadorian cocoa, Ecuador would not be able to continue to buy the majority of its own imported goods from Britain. As a British merchant in Guayaquil reported to the Foreign Office in December 1917:

> I am selling British goods in Ecuador to local merchants who pay me in local currency: said local currency must be converted in some way into pounds sterling so that I may pay my principals in London for the goods they send me. One method of converting currency into sterling is to buy drafts from the local Banks, but this way is practically denied to me because the

export of cocoa to Great Britain and elsewhere is greatly restricted. Another method is to buy cocoa with the currency and ship it to London where it is sold for sterling; this way is absolutely denied to me because no cocoa may be shipped from here to England.

At the present moment, exchange of cocoa for General Merchandise from England is prohibited and trading is greatly restricted thereby; in my opinion, the condition of exchange of one material for another is essential to promotion of trade between Great Britain and Ecuador, and until there is a freer exchange between the countries nothing very much can be done.[17]

The British consul in Quito noted at this time that already, given the difficulty in obtaining British goods, Ecuadorian merchants were looking to the United States for many articles that they had previously purchased in the United Kingdom.[18] For Ecuadorians, the balance of trade problem affected not only imports from Great Britain but all imports, especially in light of the scarcity of foreign currency as the cocoa crisis deepened. The difficulty of importing goods provoked a serious situation, given the need to import basic food products for coastal consumption. If the war revealed the vulnerability of an export economy based on nonessential products such as cocoa and *tagua* (rather than on manufactures, mining, or staple foods), it revealed too the danger of not producing enough food to satisfy the internal market.

The Politics of Transforming Highland Agriculture

The railway was seen as central to the project of stimulating the economy of the highlands. Even before the railway was built, however, there were already incipient efforts being made by certain highland *terratenientes* (large landowners) to expand and modernize their production, especially through the adoption of new cultivation methods such as crop rotation.[19] With railway construction, the expectations of highland *terratenientes* mounted considerably. In 1899 the minister of the interior warned: "Until the locomotive puts us into direct communication with the ocean, agriculture will not awaken from the secular lethargy in which it lies. But in order for the railway to bring all of the benefits that we expect, we urge agriculture especially to prepare itself in anticipation to receive the railway. With the current production, scarcely sufficient for the needs of each zone, the movement that commerce promises us appears illusory."[20]

Highland hacendados would have to prepare themselves in a number of ways if they wanted to take advantage of the opportunities that the railway might offer. For instance, highland landowners needed a credit and banking system of their own. All of the existing banks had their main offices in Guayaquil. At the beginning of the century, Quito had neither deposit institutions (there was only a branch office of the Banco Comercial y Agrícola) nor strongboxes. The methods for safeguarding money were old-fashioned: coins and jewels were placed in trunks, buried in walls or floors, or simply hidden inside mattresses, which took capital out of circulation. No institutionalized system of credit existed in the highlands.[21] Two earlier banks—the Banco de Quito, established in 1862, and the Banco de la Unión, founded in 1880—closed in 1885 and 1895, respectively. The primary activity of these banks had been the negotiation of credits to the central government to finance public works, with the funds coming from profits from highland agriculture and some commerce.[22]

In the early twentieth century, motivated by the need for an adequate financial system, the Banco del Pichincha was established in Quito in 1906.[23] The bank's capital came from a group of large landowners and from the Catholic Church, which sold some of its estates in an attempt to protect itself from a possible nationalization of its properties (which indeed occurred in 1908). In addition, at the end of 1907 the Compañía de Crédito Agrícola e Industrial was established in Quito to provide credit to encourage the development of highland agriculture, livestock raising, and industry as well as to define "rational" commercialization channels. Finally, just prior to the arrival of the railway in the capital, the Bolsa de Comercio was created within the Compañía de Crédito Agrícola e Industrial aimed both at commercializing and distributing coastal products in the highlands and distributing highland products on the coast.[24] As the region's agriculture and commerce expanded during and after the war, the highlands experienced a further development of banking. From 1915 to 1925 local banks were established: the Banco de Tungurahua in Ambato and the Banco de los Andes and the Sociedad de Chimborazo in Riobamba, as well as branches of Quito and Guayaquil banks in Latacunga and Ambato. By the end of the 1920s, Quito had caught up to Guayaquil both in the number of banking establishments and the amount of capital circulating in them (not taking into account the establishment of the Banco Central in Quito in 1927).[25]

The founding of the Banco del Pichincha with the participation of highland landowners and the Catholic Church raises the question of the relationship between these two groups. While highland landowners were in many ways more socially and politically conservative than coastal elites, they were not necessarily economically conservative. Indeed, they were quite willing to transform their properties into profit-making enterprises by expanding production. Because it caused the church to sell some of its properties, the anticlericalism of the liberals, against which many highland landowners protested, was precisely part of what generated the availability of capital for investment in highland production. The subsequent nationalization of the remaining properties of religious communities in 1908 also provided large landowners in the highlands with new opportunities to profit. These landowners went on to lease these nationalized properties from the Junta Central de Asistencia Pública, which used the proceeds to support urban public welfare institutions such as hospitals and orphanages and child welfare projects. But because the leases were for eight years, and holders were never assured of having the leases renewed, this system did not encourage leaseholders to invest in modernizing these properties. The system did, however, funnel a significant flow of capital into the hands of the leaseholders, who paid set rents to the Junta de Asistencia Pública rather than a proportion of their profits.

The anticlericalism of the liberals liberated highland landowners from a subordinate position vis-à-vis the Catholic Church, which had been the largest highland landowner in the nineteenth century and one of the only sources of capital for productive activities in the region. While these changes led to a certain economic liberation of highland landowners from the church, noneconomic pressures were brought to bear on those who attempted to take advantage of new opportunities generated by liberal policies. Some of those Ecuadorians who took on leases of nationalized properties soon after passage of the Ley de Beneficencia were threatened with excommunication by the church, just as were those who registered their children in the new secular schools established during this period. As their own modernizing bent was consolidated during the first three decades of the twentieth century, however, some highland hacen-dados were instrumental in transforming the axis of debate over how the nation would be modernized. Increasingly, as the liberal period matured, the emphasis on the church-state conflict was displaced by priority placed on economic and technical transformations of the country, by elites of all political persuasions.[26]

Returning to a consideration of highland elites' efforts to prepare themselves for the new opportunities that the railway might present, even prior to the arrival of the railway, some of them had begun to import new livestock breeds. In 1906, before the railway reached Quito, José María Fernández Salvador imported the first purebred Holstein-Friesian dairy cows, from the U.S. breeding houses of Carnation Farms, for his hacienda in Machachi, south of Quito. The expansion of the dairy products industry required rapid transportation facilities. But as the example just cited shows, agricultural expansion was in progress among certain highland landowning sectors concurrent with and in some cases prior to railway construction. Although the railway was a powerful symbol of the transformative possibilities of technology for the highlands, it was inserted into a context in which certain groups had already started to modernize. The highlands, and highland landowners, were not as dormant as they seemed.

With the construction of the railway, large landowners of the highlands were able to set their sights on capturing the staple food market of the coast and even on exporting their products. As already stated, most of the food consumed on the coast was not produced there because most of the land under cultivation was dedicated to export agriculture. The demand for food increased with the dramatic growth of Guayaquil during the late nineteenth and early twentieth centuries. From thirty thousand inhabitants at the beginning of the 1880s, Guayaquil's population had doubled by 1899, had reached ninety thousand by 1920, and by 1930 was well over one hundred thousand.

Despite the high expectations entertained by some highland *terratenientes* of access to new markets with the construction of the railway, there is no evidence that during the immediate postconstruction period these hopes were fulfilled. The coast continued to import the majority of foodstuffs consumed there, and the highlands continued to supply primarily local markets because of both limited production and the cost of transportation to the coast. On the horizon, however, was World War I. Isolated efforts at the beginning of the war to expand highland production of basic foods gathered steam only with the advent of the full crisis in 1917–18. There had been suggestions since 1915 that an agricultural development office be established to coordinate agricultural policy and disseminate information about agronomic science. With the deepening of the crisis by 1917, the need to reform highland agriculture began to gain momentum. After years of growing demands from highland agriculturalists dating from at least 1884, government officials finally recognized that the state should be involved in promoting highland agriculture.[27] Finally, on October 6, 1917, the Dirección Nacional de Agricultura was created within the Ministry of Education. In addition, in December 1917 an eight-member government committee was formed to study measures to improve national commerce and agriculture.

By the end of the decade, government officials were referring to highland agriculture as "the means and factor of national improvement."[28] As President Alfredo Baquerizo Moreno argued in 1918, "If we offer what others need, they will easily give us in return what we need. We will have ships and commerce, if we offer grains, potatoes, minerals, etc. With only cocoa, without anyone attempting to benefit the country or establish an industry with it . . . nothing will be achieved, except as a favor, and a scanty favor at that. The world's gold is destined today to war. It is obvious that it will not flow to us if we do not offer in exchange something of value to it."[29] Those valuable products would result from the intensification and expansion of agriculture and the associated industry of textile production.[30]

In October 1918 the Ecuadorian congress passed the Ley de Fomento Agrícola e Industrial (Law of Agricultural and Industrial Development). Despite its name, this law was overwhelmingly concerned with agriculture and livestock production. The industrial development in question was rooted in agriculture. The Ley de Fomento Agrícola represented the first attempt to organize and promote agriculture and stock raising at the national level. In every canton in the highlands, local agricultural committees were established to administer agricultural policy. In accordance with the emphasis on connection, these local juntas sought to construct and repair paths and mule trails so as to facilitate the movement of agricultural products. Imports of agricultural machinery and improved seeds and livestock breeds were declared free of customs duties. The law also mandated the distribution of information about modern agricultural techniques and the investigation and control of crop and livestock diseases. Given the high rates of failure of imported seeds, the Dirección Nacional de Agricultura established experimental farms to determine how to adapt imported species to local conditions. The Ley de Fomento Agrícola was clearly an effort to carry liberal reforms into the countryside and to centrally organize agricultural policy. The results were rapid. By 1921 it could be claimed that:

> in the coast and in the highlands, in the east and in the west, an enthusiastic movement in favor of agriculture can be observed. Every day modern machinery and farm implements are introduced into the country, valuable seeds are imported of every kind of food and fodder plants, and people are talking, everywhere people are talking about agriculture, not only among landowners but also in the press and in official sectors. All of this leads one to expect better days for the Republic, since agricultural production and industrial production, which is its consequence, are the only positive and true sources of the advance of peoples.[31]

The Ley de Fomento Agrícola was a key component of the attempt to find a long-term solution to the problem of provisioning the domestic market.

The Ley de Fomento Agrícola also encouraged industry directly related to agriculture, such as the production of textiles. At the turn of the century, there were four textile factories in the highlands. By 1930 there were twenty-one, most of them founded after the First World War (see Table 4).[32] These highland factories represented more than 90 percent of the textile industry in the country. Between 1914 and 1930 the majority of factories were established in the north-central highlands in the corridor between Ibarra and Riobamba. By 1928, 1,300 people were employed in large-scale textile production in and around Quito with an additional 1,200 employed elsewhere in north-central highland textile factories.[33] Increased textile production represented a modest import-substitution effort that was not capable of satisfying the coastal market but did provision the highland region and southern Colombia. Textile manufacturing expanded significantly after 1930, aimed principally at production for the internal market. Also associated with the Ley de Fomento Agrícola were three other kinds of "industrial" development rooted in agriculture: the establishment of food-processing industries such as dairy production, especially in the north-central highlands; the establishment and expansion of leather tanneries; and the expansion of sugar processing in the coastal area around Milagro. All took advantage of the Ley de Fomento Agrícola. None could have expanded without the railway, for,

as had been recognized in 1892, "the manufacturing business of
Ecuador is far from the development of which it is capable. . . .
due principally to the lack of good roads, and the consequent
difficulties in the transportation of machinery and other articles
of great weight or volume."[34]

Table 4. Textile Factories in the Highlands, 1840–1930

Year Est.	Location	Name of Factory	Owner
1840	Quito (Amaguaña)	San Francisco	J. Jijón y Caamaño
1845	Quito	La Victoria	Nicanor Palacios
1900	Quito (Amaguaña)	San Jacinto	J. Jijón y Caamaño
1900	Otavalo	San Pedro	Alfonso Pérez P.
1914	Otavalo	La Joya	Alarcón Hnos.
1916	Quito (Sangolquí)	San Juan-Chillo	—
1917	Riobamba	El Prado	Carlos Cordovez
1919	Quito	La Bretaña	Fernando Pérez P.
1919	Ambato	El Peral	J. Jijón y Caamaño
1919	Tambillo	La Inca	—
1920	Ambato	La Industria Algodonera	Sociedad Anónima
1921	Quito	La América	Daniel Hidalgo
1924	Atuntaqui	Imbabura	Sociedad Anónima
1924	Quito	La Internacional	Sociedad Anónima
1924	Quito (Amaguaña)	La Dolorosa del Colegio	J. Jijón y Caamaño
1925	Otavalo	San Miguel	Pinto Hnos.
1927	Quito	Luz de América	Abusaid Dassum
1928	Ambato	La Florida	Camilo Haffar
1928	Riobamba	Fábrica Hilados	J. Elias Castillo
1928	Cuenca	Textil Azuaya	Viver y Cía.
1930	Ambato	La Sultana	Alvarez Hnos.

Source: González, "Breves notas sobre la industria textil," 37–38.

The construction of the railway did not fulfill all of the expectations of modernizing landowners, who were particularly
active in lobbying for lower transport tariffs. Nonetheless, the
period of the late 1910s through the 1920s did see significant
transformations in highland agriculture. With increased access
to markets, including the urban markets of Quito and Guayaquil, and some export possibilities came a great expansion in
the scale of cultivation and livestock raising in the highlands.
According to a 1927 study evaluating highland agriculture by
Ramón Ojeda, an agronomist and a large highland landholder,
the access to new markets stimulated the clearing of new fields
for an enormous expansion in potato and grain cultivation.
Massive irrigation works were constructed to double or triple

the areas under cultivation. Many new kinds of seeds were imported to enhance the quality of pastures. Similarly, great improvements in the quality of livestock resulted from increased attention to the selective breeding of local livestock as well as interbreeding with imported cattle, sheep, and horses. Better sheep meant a higher quality of wool for the local textile industry, and better cows meant that more milk could be produced for an expanded dairy products industry. And, for the first time, there were extensive imports of foreign machinery and farm implements of all kinds.[35] While Ojeda attributes these changes directly to the railway, these processes were also the result of political struggles such as those that had led to passage of the Ley de Fomento Agrícola.

The new policies of agricultural development were promoted by the state as part of a long-term solution to the crisis, given government recognition that Ecuador had suffered so severely during the war because of a lack of foresight and planning. In the short term, however, something had to be done about the rise in food prices throughout the country. Scarcity and the consequent price increases were caused by speculation and by the fact that basic food products were at a premium in the international market. It was reported in April 1917 that "the wholesale purchase by the British government of potatoes as well as of the coming crop has caused great discontent with the government of Ecuador and among the poorer population on account of the large rise in prices."[36] As a result, several executive decrees were passed, beginning in February 1917, which temporarily suspended the exportation of many staple food products. By March 1918 there were export prohibitions on all of the following necessities: peas, rice, sugar, barley, broad beans, flours and meals of every kind, lentils, corn, beans, chickpeas, suet, lard, white corn, potatoes, plantain, wheat, butter, and "other cereals and vegetables." The result was a decline in food prices. In addition, the Junta de Subsistencias y Abastos was formed in March 1918 to supply basic food products to the inhabitants of the capital at prices below commercial rates. All of these measures were taken just until the "natural" law of supply and demand had a chance to reassert itself. Indeed, "only the special circumstances of the moment could convince the Executive to restrict exportation. The wealth of a people is based on the greater quantity of products that can be sold in the exterior in exchange for the gold that is sent in payment. To limit exportation is to drive away wealth."[37]

Highland agriculturalists lobbied congress and the president to have the export prohibitions removed. Although these restrictions were not lifted unreservedly until 1921, the president reduced them in January 1919 and again in July 1920 to permit the export of limited quantities of potatoes, corn, and butter. That highland agriculturalists had a strong lobby by this time is clear from these events and in debates in congress. The Sociedad Nacional de Agricultura (SNA), representing a modernizing highland agricultural elite, was formed in 1913 but became much more active in 1918.[38] In its early years, the SNA limited itself as an organization to the occasional exhibition of agricultural products in Quito. Individual members were nonetheless very active. By 1915, Enrique Gangotena Jijón (the SNA's first president) was the owner of "splendid dairy installations"; other members, such as Víctor Eastman Cox, had imported "fine pasture seeds"; and José María Fernández Salvador had imported bulls that were credited with "the improvement of national livestock."[39] In early 1918, however, the organization began to increase its activities. Over several days, the SNA held meetings in the halls of the Banco del Pichincha to carry out a reorganization of the association. Collaboration and monthly financial contributions were solicited from highland *terratenientes* to assist in the promotion of their interests before the government and the nation. In August, following a July general meeting, the association's office was established and opened to the public for six hours per day. In September the SNA founded a regular magazine and appointed a permanent commission to advise the government's director of agricultural development.

The members of the SNA were not simply responding to the government's initiatives, nor did the international context create their interest in expanding and modernizing highland agriculture. As we have seen, some members had been attempting to expand their operations since the turn of the century, and they had made agricultural improvements during the construction of the Guayaquil-Quito Railway in the hope of gaining access to new markets. The crisis of the First World War did make the government aware of the need to expand highland agricultural production. Yet despite liberal rhetoric about the need to transform the highlands, the specific initiatives for doing so were developed not by the government, but by the group of north-central highland hacendados organized in the SNA. They were the lobbying force behind both the passage of the Ley de

Fomento Agrícola and the resumption of food exports. In fact, the Ley de Fomento Agrícola was first developed in meetings of the organization and then presented to the minister of agriculture, who in turn submitted it to congress. Official recognition of the importance of the SNA's activities for national economic stability was indicated when, on November 7, 1920, congress voted to establish a special tax to support the association. The tax amounted to 2 sucres on agricultural properties with values from 10,000 to 30,000 sucres, 5 sucres for those worth 30,000 to 50,000 sucres, 10 sucres for those worth 50,000 to 100,000 sucres, and 30 sucres for properties with higher values. This tax was to be applied in all of the central and northern highland provinces —Carchi, Imbabura, Pichincha, León (later Cotopaxi), Tungurahua, Chimborazo, and Bolívar—with the rationale that the "Sociedad Nacional de Agricultura of Quito cooperates effectively in the development of national agriculture and lends valuable support to the State."[40] Highland agriculture had finally found its place in conceptualizations of national prosperity.

Who belonged to the SNA? The organization principally reflected the concerns of large agriculturalists from the north-central highlands, the region most affected by the railway, as well as where the large haciendas were consolidated in the late nineteenth century. Many SNA members and directors held other influential positions in Quito during and after the liberal period (see Table 5). Some of the early leaders of the organization were hacendados whose modernizing activities focused on the dairy industry for the growing urban market, first of Quito, then of Guayaquil, and later, for the export market. This group was perhaps best exemplified by Enrique Gangotena Jijón, who owned property in Guaytacama in Cotopaxi province, along the railway line. The railway's proximity saved hacendados in the Guaytacama area from having to make expensive investments in infrastructure; they could invest instead in other variables that further augmented their competitiveness, such as imported machinery, pasture seeds, and livestock breeds.[41] In 1919, Gangotena imported the first machinery for the manufacture of butter, thus initiating the industrialization, a year later, of dairy production in Ecuador. Much later, in 1936–37, his hacienda would be the site of the first manufacture of powdered milk. Gangotena prospered with this innovation until the end of World War II, when cheaper powdered milk from the United States displaced his product in the internal market.[42]

Table 5. Selected SNA Members and Their Other Positions

Name	Position in SNA	Other Positions
Neptalí Bonifaz A.	vice president, 1927	president of the Banco Central, president-elect (1932)
Luis Calisto M.	director, 1919	member of the Junta Monetaria, councillor of state, senator and congressman in various governments
Francisco Chiriboga B.	director, 1927–1930	president of Quito's municipal council
Carlos Freire Larrea	director, 1919	president of Quito's municipal council, president of the Guayaquil and Quito Railway Company, minister of public works
Jacinto Jijón y Caamaño	member	mayor of Quito, president of Quito's municipal council, congressman
Modesto Larrea Jijón	director, 1919	minister of government, president of Quito's municipal council, vice president of congress, president of the Guayaquil and Quito Railway Company, minister of foreign relations (1931), diplomat
Víctor M. Peñaherrera	member	minister of state, president of the Supreme Court
Leonidas Plaza Gutiérrez	member	president (1901–1905 and 1912–1916)
N. Clemente Ponce	president, 1927–1930	minister of foreign relations, diplomat, vice president of the Banco Central (1929)

Sources: Arcos, "El espíritu del progreso," 119; *El libro de la ciudad de San Francisco de Quito hasta 1950–51* (Quito: Ediciones CEGAN, 1951); B. Pérez Marchant, *Diccionario biográfico del Ecuador* (Quito: Escuela de Artes y Oficios, 1928); *Revista de la Sociedad Nacional de Agricultura*, 1918–1930. The dates of the political positions held have been included when available.

The growing market for dairy products could not be fulfilled by the existing practice of grazing local breeds on natural pastures because of the low amounts of milk yielded by these cows, further reduced by the poor quality of their diet. The expansion of dairy production generated an increased interest among landowners in controlling the most ecologically favorable lands for the development and maintenance of artificial pastures, the need to control resources such as irrigation water, and concern with ensuring proximity to markets and consumption centers. The introduction of artificial pastures and rotation of pastures promoted efficient production on relatively small parcels (100 to 800 hectares). Thus, the modernization of production in these areas stimulated a market in land and the decomposition of large properties.

Some dairy producers became "modern" in other ways as well. They began to facilitate the purchase of small plots of hacienda land by indigenous peasants, who thus became independent property owners. Because of the restricted size of these plots, however, which did not provide for the full subsistence of the peasant household, some members of these families continued to work seasonally for hacendados in exchange for cash. Haciendas became smaller but more efficient, ensured of a stable labor force available for seasonal work without having to institutionalize relations with these workers, with the mutual responsibilities that this would have implied. Even though the SNA opposed the abolition of debt peonage, some members (usually those who specialized in dairy production) had already voluntarily abolished or reduced it on their own properties. Dairy hacendados such as Enrique Gangotena, who dominated the SNA, were best situated to use their political clout to present their own interests as being in the general interest, and to push through laws that would serve those interests at the national level.

In addition, some members of the SNA in the north-central highlands engaged in an important expansion of cattle ranching for meat and hides. Cattle ranching had begun to expand in the late nineteenth century, and hides in particular reached international markets in the early twentieth century. Prices for leather and shoe soles in the international market doubled between 1921 and 1925. Toward the end of the 1920s, especially in 1927–28, the export of leather and soles grew both in value and in volume. In 1929 and 1930, in contrast, the export of these items decreased, but the export of finished shoes rose, suggesting an important increase in the capacity of leather tanners and shoe manufacturers.[43] The introduction of imported breeds of beef cattle (Shorthorn) and of dairy cows (Holstein and Normanda) also enabled the owners of large haciendas to crossbreed cattle for sale to other agriculturalists, which provided them with significant profits.

Other forms of agricultural modernization were also undertaken. In Tungurahua province, fruit production was modernized and expanded through the introduction of new species. Fruit cultivation required increased control over water, especially through the construction of irrigation works, rather than control over the extensive tracts of land. Smallholding peasants in Tungurahua thus continued to have access to land, although without access to water. Many of these peasants engaged in wage labor in fruit orchards and, perhaps even more important, on the construction of irrigation works. Throughout the north-central highlands there were other kinds of agricultural expansion, as Ojeda indicated. This expansion was also encouraged by modest price increases in international markets for potatoes and barley, and by a significant, steady rise in international prices for lentils throughout the 1920s, with exports to Colombia and beyond.

Although there had always been a perception among liberals that the highlands required transformation, and there had also been efforts by individual landowners to modernize and expand production, particularly in the context of railway construction, only with the mid-1910s crisis was a sense of urgency provoked that facilitated the passage of legislation favorable to the interests of modernizing highland agriculturalists. Whereas Ecuador had always considered itself an "essentially agricultural country," early liberal references to this characteristic focused on tropical export agriculture. With the economic crisis of the 1910s and 1920s, the expanded production of staple foods in the highlands also began to be perceived as a source of national prosperity and stability.[44] The new images of highland agriculture underline the extent to which the conceptualization of the highlands explored in Chapter 3 framed the region in terms of a series of problems and absences. The highland region was seen as the passive recipient of changes that would come to it from beyond its Andean barriers, via liberal state policies such as the development of transportation and communications, which would introduce new ideas and new forces of modernity from the coast and abroad. The crisis of World War I and the reconcept-ualization of the highlands as central to the country's well-being marked the emergence of a perception of the region as a much more active component of the national community. This perception was not a "natural" or an inevitable result of the crisis, but rather was one of the central struggles that the SNA undertook in its activities and magazine.

The changing fortunes of highland landowners must be seen, too, in the context of the shifting national political conjunctures. Already between 1903 and 1905, before the railway had been completed, there was something of a decline in the volume of some basic agricultural imports such as potatoes and peas. This tendency was reduced in 1907, however, when Alfaro's second administration exonerated basic food products from import taxes. Alfaro's policy was in response to a drought in parts of the highlands in 1906 and to pressure by the coastal import-export elite (acting because of high food prices). Policies that favored imports over national production concentrated money in the hands of the commercial import-export elite of the coast. This revenue would otherwise have been channeled into the hands of highland landowners.[45] The result was that incipient interregional commerce in basic food products was displaced by imports, which hurt highland landowners. However, after 1911, and in general during the second Plaza administration, a situation of compromise between the coastal and highland elites emerged, in which several highland products, including onions, corn, potatoes, and wheat, began to displace imported ones. This was to be further stimulated by the war.

Finally, let us reflect for a moment more on the SNA and the broad project to forge an internal market. There are two ways to create an internal market: one is to provision another region, and the other is to create additional consumers. The SNA was concerned with both of these issues. Its concern with the first has just been explored. Its concern with the second was demonstrated at its Primer Congreso de Agricultores (First Agriculturalists' Congress), held in Quito in August 1922. The program for the conference included, in addition to discussions about exporting products and importing machinery, livestock, and seeds, the following proposals: to design legislation to dissolve indigenous communities (by distributing communal lands among their members); to reduce Indian drinking; to reduce vagrancy; to educate the Indian; and to promote the spirit of savings (*el espíritu de ahorro*) among indigenous peasants. Although stated in general terms, the latter point also included various specific proposals, such as:

> To ensure that in religious festivals it is prohibited to name Indians as *priostes* [sponsors], who consume in such events not only all of their own assets but also those of their companions, indebting themselves in amounts well beyond their economic situation.

> To similarly obtain the absolute prohibition that Civil au-
> thorities give permission for bullfights in the villages and for
> the fiestas called *danzantes*, which require of the Indians very
> high expenditures and are the cause of abuses on the part of
> local authorities.[46]

These issues were closely tied to the control of peasant drinking, a problem debated in the Agriculturalists' Congress and, in
1925, discussed at length in a letter to the national police commissioner from a prominent member of the SNA.[47] Along with
the problems of disciplining the work force that underlay these
proposals was concern that indigenous peasants frittered away
their earnings in nonproductive ways. Altogether, this reveals
the beginning of a new view of the indigenous peasant on the
part of the large agriculturalists of the highlands. What stimulated this?

In October 1918 modernizing agriculturalists of the highlands achieved a major victory with the passage of the Ley de
Fomento Agrícola. In the same month, however, they suffered a
major defeat with the elimination of debt peonage. On the coast
at this time, the cocoa export crisis was undermining the prosperity of the agro-export elite, while the agro-industrial and
banking elites (especially those involved with sugar production)
were strengthened by new export opportunities. Not only did
sugar planters gain access to the financial resources to expand
production, but they also gained access to the land and labor to
do so. They required new labor arrangements, particularly large
contingents of seasonal labor. It was in this context that debt
peonage was abolished by the government of Baquerizo Moreno,
associated with this emerging elite sector. But the abolition of
debt peonage undermined the highland *terratenientes'* access to
labor just when they wanted to expand production. Nevertheless, through the Ley de Fomento Agrícola, they were able to
push through other measures that promoted their interests in
expanding and modernizing production. Thus, this era was a
contradictory one for highland landowners, and they could impose their interests at the national level only partially. On the
one hand, the expansion of production in the highlands to provision the coastal market required labor. On the other hand, the
growth of the internal market after the war in part depended on
the migrations of peasants to the coast to work on plantations
—peasants who had to buy food. At some level, the Ley de
Fomento Agrícola may have represented a compromise with

the agro-industrial elite of the coast, who also needed to import machinery.

The issue of the highland landowners' relation to labor also raises the question of to what extent the machinery imported into the country saved labor. Alfaro's government had encouraged the introduction of machinery, for use in both agriculture and industry, by a decree issued on July 26, 1906, which freed these articles from import duties. Nonetheless, in the following decade the proportion of agricultural machinery within the total imported machinery was relatively low (in 1915 only 0.4 percent). This percentage changed considerably after the war: by the end of the 1920s, the proportion of imported machinery made up by agricultural machinery was 25.1 percent in 1929, and 40.2 percent in 1930 (although these figures no doubt also included machinery for coastal production).[48]

Imported machinery did allow a reduction in the labor force. However, agricultural development policies also encouraged the importation of farm implements, such as hoes and machetes. Unlike machinery, farm implements did not necessarily save labor. In many cases they simply allowed for the optimal utilization of traditional forms of labor. Investments in farm implements rather than in machinery were also more accessible to many landowners. The value of imported farm implements was significantly higher than that of imported farm machinery both during and after the war, despite the much higher cost per unit of the latter. Between 1913 and 1930, this difference ranged from two and one-half to thirteen times greater.[49] Also, the imports of farm machinery in 1919 (after both the end of the war and the passage of the Ley de Fomento Agrícola) were more than eight times the weight of such imports in 1911 and more than eighteen times their value in sucres. Thus, while the Ley de Fomento Agrícola clearly encouraged the importation of farm implements and machinery, the result was not necessarily a reduction in labor needs on highland haciendas, and large landowners did not easily acquiesce to policies weakening their control over labor.

It is clear that the legislation ending debt peonage undermined, to some extent, traditional forms of domination. (The regional effects of the abolition of debt peonage will be studied in Chapter 6.) Within this context emerged a new attitude toward indigenous peasants on the part of at least some highland hacendados, reflected in a new concern with both moralizing agricultural workers and transforming them into small individual property owners, who would then also be limited consumers.

This project was much further developed after the period considered here, especially in the 1930s, with the expansion of textile production for the internal market and with increased concern with developing the indigenous population as consumers. This was also associated with new ways of imagining the national community with the consolidation of a national ideology of *mestizaje*.[50] But in the early 1920s, in contrast, the moral reform language used tended to be associated with the landowners' desire to exert tighter control over peasants, given the abolition of debt peonage, stimulating a series of indigenous uprisings.

The formation of Ecuador's internal market, through the expansion of production in the highlands and the movement of products to the coast, was facilitated by the railway. However, the existence of the railway was not in itself enough to ensure this project. Rather, modernizing highland landowners succeeded in pushing through a project in their own interests because of changing political openings at the national level and an altered international context. Most important, though, their success depended on their capacity to take advantage of a moment of crisis by organizing sufficiently to achieve this project.

Notes

1. President Eloy Alfaro, special address to congress, January 9, 1907, in Noboa, *Recopilación de mensajes*, 384.
2. T. Wolf, *Geografía y geología*, 515.
3. Luis A. Martínez, *La agricultura del interior: Causas de su atraso y modos de impulsarla* (Quito: Imprenta La Novedad, 1897), 12–13.
4. Ibid., 14.
5. Maldonado Obregón, *Historia del ferrocarril*, 190.
6. Ramón Ojeda, *La agricultura y el estado: Carta agrícola al Sr. Dn. Emilio Estrada* (Quito: Imprenta de Julio Sáenz R., 1912), 8.
7. Compañía Guía Comercial y Agrícola, *El Ecuador: Guía comercial, agrícola e industrial de la república* (Guayaquil: Talleres de Artes Gráficos de E. Rodenas, 1909), 943.
8. Deler, *Ecuador*, 194.
9. Ibid., 221.
10. Abelardo Moncayo Andrade, "El problema del ferrocarril del sur y la compra del control," 1925, reprinted in *Pensamiento económico de Abelardo Moncayo Andrade* (Guayaquil: Archivo Histórico del Guayas and Universidad de Guayaquil, 1981), 11.
11. J. M. Larrea Jijón, "Nuestra situación agrícola-económica," *Revista de la Sociedad Nacional de Agricultura* 1 (1919): 365.
12. Trujillo, *La hacienda serrana*, 73.

13. See especially Chiriboga Vega, *Jornaleros y gran propietarios*; and Crawford de Roberts, *El Ecuador en la época cacaotera*.

14. Rodríguez, *The Search for Public Policy*, 178–79, 198. Prior to the First World War, the sucre had a fairly stable value of approximately two sucres per dollar and ten sucres per pound sterling.

15. José Samaniego Ponce, *Crisis económica del Ecuador: Análisis comparativo de dos períodos históricos (1929–1933)-(1980–1984)* (Quito: Banco Central, 1988), 74–79.

16. Oscar Efrén Reyes, *Los últimos siete años* (Quito: Talleres Gráficos Nacionales, 1933), 40.

17. In H. W. Wilson to the British Foreign Office, Quito, December 26, 1917, no. 24192, 368/1898, BCR/FO AHBC-Q. Note that this merchant traveled to Ecuador as an employee of the J. G. White Company, the British engineering firm that directed the sanitation of Guayaquil. It was common practice for visiting foreign experts to become involved in economic ventures during their sojourns in Ecuador.

18. Ibid., December 17, 1917, no. 21049, 368/1898, BCR/FO AHBC-Q. While imports from the United States and the United Kingdom were roughly even at the beginning of the war, by 1927 imports from the United States made up 48 percent by volume of all imports to Ecuador, while those from the United Kingdom made up only 18 percent. Total imports in 1927 amounted to 57,050,437 sucres, with the United States accounting for 27,608,081 sucres and the United Kingdom following with 9,120,325 sucres. In 1928, Ecuadorian exports amounted to 98,379,028 sucres, with the United States receiving 34,966,879 sucres worth of goods, and the United Kingdom (now following France, Colombia, Germany, and Spain) taking goods valued at only 7,250,877 sucres (see R. M. Kohan to the Foreign Office, Quito, January 18, 1930, no. A2502/2502/54, 371/14224 BCR/FO AHBC-Q).

19. Carlos Arcos, "El espíritu de progreso: Los hacendados en el Ecuador del 900," *Cultura* 19 (1984): 121–22.

20. Ministro de lo Interior y Policía, Beneficencia, etc., *Informe . . . 1899,* 31.

21. Banco del Pichincha, *Banco del Pichincha: 80 años, abril 1906–1986* (Quito: Banco del Pichincha, 1986).

22. Trujillo, *La hacienda serrana*, 49.

23. Ignacio Fernández Salvador, one of the most dynamic hacendados of this era, was the first president of the Banco del Pichincha.

24. Roque Espinosa, "Hacienda, concertaje y comunidad en el Ecuador," *Cultura* 19 (1984): 187–89.

25. Deler, *Ecuador*, 229–30.

26. Arcos, "El espíritu del progreso."

27. Ojeda, *La agricultura y el estado*.

28. Alfredo Baquerizo Moreno, *Mensaje del presidente de la república al congreso nacional de 1918* (Quito: Imprenta Nacional, 1918), 38.

29. Ministro de Instrucción Pública, Justicia, Beneficencia, etc., *Informe que el ministro de instrucción pública, justicia, beneficencia, etc., presenta a la nación, 1919* (Quito: Imprenta y Encuadernación Nacionales, 1919), 78.

30. Ministro de Instrucción Pública, *Informe . . . 1921,* 101.

31. Ibid., 121–22.

32. José Luis González A., "Breves notas sobre la industria textil en el Ecuador," *Boletín del Ministerio de Previsión Social, Trabajo, Agricultura e Industrias* 4 (1937): 37–45. See also Guillermo Bustos Lozano, "La identidad 'clase obrera' a revisión: Una lectura sobre las representaciones del Congreso Obrero de Ambato de 1938," *Procesos* (Quito) 2 (1992): 73–104; Ibarra, "Ambato"; idem, *Indios y cholos.*

33. Quito went on to become Ecuador's most industrialized city in the following decade: in 1939, Quito had 62 percent of the electrical capacity of the country, with another 14.2 percent in the rest of the north-central highlands. See Bustos Lozano, "La identidad 'clase obrera.' "

34. Bureau of the American Republics, *Ecuador*, 71.

35. Ramón Ojeda, "Efectos del ferrocarril en la agricultura y la ganadería," 1927, reprinted in *Pensamiento agrario ecuatoriano*, edited by Carlos Marchán (Quito: Banco Central, 1986), 647–56.

36. Report on economic conditions in Ecuador, London, April 18, 1917, no. 84088, 368/1718 BCR/FO AHBC-Q.

37. Ministro de Hacienda, *Informe que el ministro de hacienda presenta a la nación en 1918* (Quito: Imprenta y Encuadernación Nacionales, 1918), n.p.

38. See Arcos, "El espíritu del progreso," for an analysis of this organization.

39. Ministro de Instrucción Pública, Bellas Artes, Correos, Telégrafos, etc., *Informe que el ministro de instrucción pública, bellas artes, correos, telégrafos, etc., presenta a la nación en 1916* (Quito: Imprenta y Encuadernación Nacionales, 1916), n.p.

40. *Registro Oficial*, November 30, 1920.

41. Carlos Arcos and Carlos Marchán, "Apuntes para una discusión sobre los cambios en la estructura agraria serrana," *Revista Ciencias Sociales* 2, no. 5 (1978): 13–51.

42. Osvaldo Barsky and Gustavo Cosse, *Tecnología y cambio social: Las haciendas lecheras del Ecuador* (Quito: FLACSO, 1981), 67.

43. Trujillo, *La hacienda serrana*, 172.

44. For instance, see Luciano Andrade Marín, *Nuevos aspectos agrícolas: ¿Qué haremos de nuestros páramos?* (Quito: Sociedad Nacional de Agricultura and Tipografía y Encuadernación de la "Prensa Católica," 1925).

45. Trujillo, *La hacienda serrana*, 67.

46. Sociedad Nacional de Agricultura, *Primer Congreso de Agricultores: Programa* (Quito: Tipografía y Encuadernación de la "Prensa Católica," 1922), 9.

47. Reproduced as "El alcoholismo en los campos," in *Revista de la Sociedad Nacional de Agricultura* 50 (1925): 125–27.

48. Trujillo, *La hacienda serrana*, 144.

49. Ibid., 220–23.

50. A. Kim Clark, "Indigenous Ecuadorians and Imagined Political Communities during Two Economic Crises," paper presented at the meetings of the Canadian Association of Latin American and Caribbean Studies, Toronto, November 1996.

6

The Contradictions of Redemption

The Uneven Development of Alausí

One of the regions that was transformed through the movement and connection associated with the railway was the canton of Alausí, in the central highland province of Chimborazo.[1] The Spanish town of Alausí was founded in 1534 by Sebastian de Benalcázar. During the colonial period this region was the site of important textile workshops that drew on indigenous labor drafts. The focus on textile production was associated with sheep raising for wool. This specialization may have also inhibited the formation of large grain-producing haciendas in this region during the early colonial period, because of the constant labor requirements of the textile workshops.[2] In 1699 an earthquake and the eruption of Carihuairazo caused the destruction of these workshops and the deaths of many indigenous laborers. The colonial town of Alausí itself was seriously damaged in 1797 by the earthquake that also destroyed Riobamba, dealing the final blow to textile manufacturing in the zone.

The inter-Andean zone is divided into numerous intermont basins that are separated from each other by mountain ridges that traverse the long corridor formed by the two ranges of the Ecuadorian Andes. During the nineteenth century, the highland economy contracted from a more integrated system to more restricted local agricultural economies within each basin (see Chapters 2 and 5). The majority of these valleys form the basis for political divisions as well. In most cases there is now one province per intermont basin, but in the case of Tungurahua and Cotopaxi there are two provinces in a single intermont basin. The basin of Alausí is an exception in that, although characterized by a separate regional economy, it was and continues to be politically part of the province of Chimborazo, whose

administrative center is Riobamba.[3] To the north, the canton of
Alausí is separated from the rest of Chimborazo province by
the Tiocajas mountain ridge. To the south, Alausí is divided from
the province of Azuay by the Azuay ridge.

In 1895, as the liberal period began, the canton of Alausí was
divided into the urban *parroquia* (civil parish) of Alausí, the cantonal seat, and seven rural parishes: Achupallas, Chunchi, Gonzól, Guasuntos, Pumallacta, Sibambe, and Tixán (see Map 2).
Two other settlements were raised to the status of civil parish
during the period of this study: Huigra, which achieved administrative independence from Sibambe in 1905; and Sevilla, which
was severed from Gonzól in 1915. The town of Alausí was located at an altitude of 2,395 meters above sea level. Some twelve
kilometers northeast of the cantonal seat was the village of Tixán
(center of the parish of the same name), located at 2,925 meters
altitude. Southeast of the town of Alausí were the villages of Guasuntos, at 5 kilometers distance and at an altitude of 2,940 meters;
Pumallacta, at 10 kilometers distance and 2,937 meters altitude;
and Achupallas, 20 kilometers away and 3,317 meters above sea
level. Ten kilometers to the south of the cantonal seat was the
village of Gonzól at 2,228 meters altitude. To the southwest of
the town of Alausí were the villages of Chunchi, at 20 kilometers distance and 2,273 meters altitude; Sibambe, at 10 kilometers distance and 2,419 meters altitude; and Huigra, at
22 kilometers distance and 1,215 meters altitude.

The cantonal seat was the political, economic, social, and
religious center of the canton. Political administrative offices,
the jail, schools, and the marketing center of the region were all
located there. The locally elected municipal council had its offices in the town of Alausí, as did the *jefe político* appointed by
the national government as its regional representative. Alausí
was the focal point for the flow of products to market and of
labor from the rural areas to the town to construct public works.
People from outlying areas also traveled there for numerous
administrative or legal matters, and often for access to artisans.
Each of the rural parishes of Alausí contained a parish seat (the
town after which the parish was usually named), indigenous
anejos (communities), and *caseríos*, or small hamlets with some
white inhabitants (the latter two categories were not always
clearly distinguished). The parish seat had the office of the
teniente político (political lieutenant, the central state's most local representative), a church, and often a small number of traders and artisans. In principle it would have separate primary

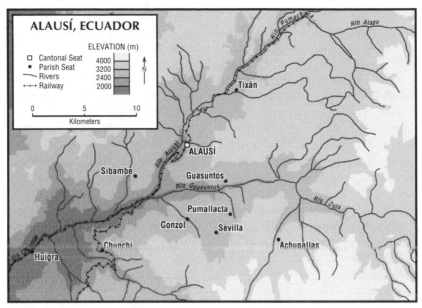

Map 2. The Canton of Alausí

schools for boys and girls and a jail. While these rarely existed in parishes at the beginning of the liberal period, by 1910 they had been established in most parishes. Their construction was facilitated by the fact that after 1906, political lieutenants were able to recruit labor from the outlying areas for local public works projects in the parish seat. In addition, each parish was entitled to half of the municipal taxes collected there, which went to fund such construction (previously, local public works were built only in the cantonal seat).[4]

While the inhabitants of *anejos* or *caseríos* tended to be involved almost exclusively in agricultural pursuits, those living in the parish seats occasionally had additional roles as small merchants or artisans. Nevertheless, larger merchants, artisans, and professionals were overwhelmingly concentrated in the town of Alausí itself. Political authorities at the cantonal level, including the political administrator, members of the municipal council, and the employees they appointed (such as the police chief), came from the ranks of merchants, medium landowners, professionals, and master artisans. In most cases, they belonged to at least two of these categories. At the parish level, the positions of local authorities such as political lieutenants or civil judges circulated among a very restricted group of small to medium landowners, merchants, and artisans. The largest landowners of the zone were not directly involved in local politics. Instead, these elites participated in much wider circles of power at the regional and national levels. Julio Teodoro Salem, for instance, heir to the largest hacienda in the canton, was politically active in Riobamba as political administrator of the Riobamba canton in the late 1920s (therefore also replacing the governor on occasion), and later in Quito, where he served as a congressman and cabinet minister. While he may not have held local political posts, his influence over local affairs was strong. Indeed, in 1930, in regard to the problem of finding a new political lieutenant for Tixán, the political administrator reported to the governor that "it is difficult to find someone truly impartial in that parish, because of the domination that Sr. Julio T. Salem exercises, since almost everyone ultimately depends on him for their livelihood."[5] Another landowner who traveled in wider regional economic circles was Manuel Puyol, owner of the Chimba-Guataxi hacienda in Chunchi and a prosperous merchant in Riobamba.

Topographically the canton is mountainous and uneven, with deep gorges cut by rivers and a wide variety of altitudes and climatic zones. Toward its eastern portion there are *páramos*, or high-altitude grasslands, especially in Tixán and Achupallas. Altitudes decrease as one moves closer to the rivers that drain the basin toward the coast, the most important of which are the Ríos Alausí and Guasuntos, affluents of the Río Chanchán. In the western part of the canton, the gorge that the Río Chanchán cuts through the western cordillera marks the entryway of the rail line from the coast. The railway crosses this river twenty-six times between Bucay and Alausí. The tracks rise nearly six hundred meters in altitude in the short distance between the stations of Sibambe and Alausí, via the double switchback built around Nariz del Diablo.

Alausí was a heavily agricultural zone, whose products varied by altitude, topography, and climate. The high-altitude *páramos* lent themselves to livestock pasturing, with potato cultivation at slightly lower altitudes. The upper limit for the cultivation of cold-resistant crops such as barley and wheat at this latitude was approximately 3,300 meters. These crops were grown especially between 3,000 and 3,300 meters, while at slightly lower altitudes, peas, broad beans, beans, and lentils were cultivated. At still lower altitudes, corn was cultivated as well as temperate-zone fruits and vegetables. In the lowest altitudes of the canton, 2,000 meters and below, tropical crops such as coffee, cocoa, sugarcane, and tropical fruits were grown. Sugarcane and the aguardiente distilled from it were particularly important products of the haciendas in Sibambe and Huigra. The high-altitude zones of Tixán and Achupallas were cold and humid; Chunchi was also relatively humid. The medium-altitude zones of the canton tended to be somewhat drier and were characterized in many places by steeply sloping grades. On traveling through this region in 1906, British geographer Reginald Enock was particularly impressed by the extensive terracing of these slopes required for their cultivation.[6]

Alausí was a primarily grain-producing agricultural region with important extensions of livestock raising in those haciendas with access to high-altitude *páramos*. The parishes with substantial *páramos* were Tixán, Achupallas, and Chunchi, and the haciendas especially in the first two parishes were the largest in the canton during the period of study (see Table 6). Those haciendas undertook livestock raising as well as some grain production. Other parishes at slightly lower altitudes had smaller haciendas focusing more on agriculture than livestock. The parishes of Gonzól and Pumallacta had no haciendas and were characterized instead by the division of the land into much smaller properties among both indigenous and white landholders. In Gonzól, Indians owned some two-thirds of the land, while in Pumallacta they held just under half of it. In Guasuntos there were no large haciendas either, but the land was held primarily in medium-size properties rather than being extensively subdivided into small plots. The parishes of Gonzól, Pumallacta, Guasuntos, and Sevilla also had limited areas of communal lands, used by the inhabitants primarily for pasture and to collect firewood and straw.

Table 6. Large Haciendas in Alausí Canton, by Parish, 1928

Hacienda (Owner)	Hectares
Alausí	
Llactapamba (heirs of Camilo Ricuarte)	500
Conventillo, Cochapamba, and Guñag chiquito (Virginia Fiallo)	300
Chibatus and Danas (Víctor Manuel Toledo)	600
Tixán	
Moyocancha (Julio C. Salem)	40,000
Tipín (Ricardo Borja)	250–300
Pachag (Miguel León and Floresmilo Herrera)	300

Huigra

Joyaczhi (Manuel María Chiriboga)	500
Paccha (Rosario Mancheno)	300
Lugmas (Ernesto Vásquez)	260
Sulchán (Enrique Bahamonde)	370
Pazán (Virgilio Vásquez Molo and brothers)	600
Licay (Eduardo Morley)	250
Tilange (Miguel Calle and Federico Nicholls)	250

Sibambe

Pistichi (Silverio Torres)	250
Guallag (Daniel Barragán)	300
Zhablud (Angel María Paredes)	255
Alpachaca (Virginia Fiallo)	300
Gulag (Manuel Roldán)	350
Chol (Lorenzo León)	250
Chipche (Rosa Larrea)	350
Citado (Luis Cruz)	400
Yalanca and Pagma (Federico and Carlos Nicholls)	700

Chunchi

Chimba-Guataxi (heirs of Manuel F. Puyol)	300
Seteleg (Leopoldo Espinoza, Nelson Velasco, and heirs of Manuel Valdivieso)	340
Laonac (Emeterio Bermeo, Alejandrina Vásquez, and Nelson Velasco)	500
Magnag (Teofilo Saenz, Leopoldo and Antonio Murillo)	400

Achupallas

Ozogoche (Curia de Riobamba)	2,600
Zula (Curia de Riobamba)	2,500
Pomacocho (Odelina Bamonde v. de Ricaurte)	700
Pubal (E. Bermeo)	6,000
Chitanló (Francisca Andrade and heirs of Virgilio Andrade)	900

Sources: Various memorandums from the political lieutenants of Alausí's parishes to the political administrator of Alausí, listing the haciendas larger than 250 hectares, AJPA 1928.
Note: There were no haciendas larger than 250 hectares in Guasuntos, Gonzól, Sevilla, or Pumallacta. In fact, it was estimated that there were none larger than 50 hectares in Guasuntos, and no properties larger than 10 hectares in the latter three parishes.

On its route inland from the coast, the railway passed through Huigra (altitude 1,355 meters above sea level), Sibambe (1,834 meters),[7] up around the Nariz del Diablo to the town of Alausí (2,395 meters), and on to the village of Tixán (2,708 meters). If any settlement was truly created by the railway, it was the tropical village of Huigra, located at the lowest altitudes of the canton. In the 1890s, Huigra was not an important settlement. But then Eduardo Morley, the English engineer and economist who had accompanied Harman on his first trip to Ecuador in 1897, and who then became the railway company's first treasurer, bought a large cattle ranch in Huigra, settled there permanently with his Ecuadorian wife, and built a hotel. He also surveyed and promoted a new, more direct route between Huigra and the southern highlands and was thus instrumental in assuring the commercial growth of the village.[8] The railway company established its headquarters and company hospital in Huigra, on land donated by Morley, and Archer Harman constructed a house that became famous for its fountains and gardens. By 1905, Huigra had become so dynamic that it was elevated to the status of parish (at which point Morley contributed the land for the village's market square). During the early liberal period, the train trip to Quito from Guayaquil took two days, with an overnight stop in Riobamba. On the first day's journey, Huigra was the midpoint where the train paused so that passengers could buy their lunch. It also became the entrepôt for goods and people traveling south to Cuenca. In this context, Huigra rapidly became a bustling commercial town with more than a hint of a lawless frontier post about it, according to documentation from the early liberal period. This was an internal frontier, attesting to the marginality of the link between Alausí and the coast at the turn of the century. However, it was a frontier that would dissolve as the liberal period progressed.

With the construction of the railway (inaugurated in the town of Alausí in September 1902), there was widespread agreement that Alausí was transformed. By 1903 the governor of Chimborazo could report to the minister of the interior that "following the arrival of the railway in Alausí, that has been justly called a redemptive work, a current of well-being was felt, born in the love of work, infecting all social classes, banishing idleness, awakening the stimulus of activity, and providing facility for prosperity."[9] As a resident of Alausí put it, "The railway that crosses this extensive and fertile territory has offered a powerful incentive to agriculture: work, like an electric current, has put into growing activity all of the social classes."[10] By 1930 it could be said that "before the construction of the railway from Guayaquil to Quito, agriculture, commerce, industries, and other activities were stagnant; but once the monster of progress announced with the locomotive's whistle its arrival to those lonely mountainsides of the Andes, the people of the Alausí canton developed their energies in work, and today, it is one of the most commercial, industrious, and rich cantons of the province."[11]

The growth of Alausí after the construction of the railway can be seen in a wide variety of indicators. For instance, the population of the canton grew significantly over the period studied. In 1909 the canton's population was estimated at 16,050, distributed among the parishes as follows: in Alausí 4,000 people, in Tixán 1,500, in Guasuntos 1,000, in Pumallacta 400, in Achupallas 2,800, in Gonzól 550, in Chunchi 2,800, in Sibambe 2,500, and in Huigra 500. By 1914 the population of the canton was 22,000, and by 1930 it had reached 26,743.[12] And while in 1909 the population of this canton made up 11 percent of the province's total population, by 1930 this figure had reached 15 percent. This meant that Alausí canton in 1909 was home to 20 percent of the province's population that lived outside of Riobamba; by 1930 this figure had risen to 30 percent.

Perhaps more significant from the perspective of the white townspeople, the numbers of literate white/mestizos increased during the liberal period. Table 7 has two purposes. The first two columns compare the number of adult male Indians in 1895 with the number of literate adult men registered in the voters' lists of 1896. Most of these voters would have been white/mestizos, simply because few Indians were literate at the time (literacy was a precondition for voting rights and full citizenship until the 1979 constitution).[13] The rest of the columns compare the number of registered voters in each parish over a twenty-five-year period as a rough indicator of the increase in the literate white/mestizo population. The number of eligible voters could increase in three ways: when young men came of voting age, when new literate citizens moved into the area, and when illiterate inhabitants learned to read and write. It should be kept in mind that these figures refer only to adult male inhabitants; women were not granted the vote until 1929, and taxes were paid by indigenous men, not by women. Nonetheless, treated cautiously, these figures do serve a comparative purpose.

It is clear from Table 7, first, that in most cases, at least among adult males, there were about twice as many indigenous men as their literate white counterparts at the beginning of the liberal period. High-altitude zones tended to be associated with indigenous communities, and in areas such as Tixán and Achupallas, the proportions of Indians are significantly higher than elsewhere. Second, the literate population increased rapidly over the period studied, probably due both to the expansion of liberal institutions such as primary schools and to the arrival of new merchants, artisans, and other literate inhabitants. In addi-

Table 7. Adult Male Population in Alausí Canton, by Parish, 1895–1920

Parish	Adult Male Indians 1895	Registered Voters									
		1896	1897	1898	1899	1900	1903	1913	1915	1916	1920
Alausí	297	150	175	199	214	260	235	321	483	425	544
Sibambe	181	161	186	192	233	281	350	392	443	419	530
Tixán	398	151	158	212	217	248	231	229	274	250	294
Chunchi	197	122	190	173	212	207	217	378	489	527	569
Guasuntos	285	154	181	197	216	280	248	n/a	334	304	326
Achupallas	442	63	63	128	119	132	145	185	248	220	292
Gonzól	167	60	100	85	88	95	106	177	119	122	124
Pumallacta	102	64	83	81	78	89	84	112	123	122	127
Huigra								274	631	614	532
Sevilla									100	105	79
Totals	2,069	925	1,136	1,267	1,377	1,592	1,616	n/a	3,244	3,108	3,417

Sources: Catástro de uno por mil. AJPA 1895; Registros de electores, various years, ACMA.
Note: Huigra was part of Sibambe until 1905, while Sevilla was part of Gonzól until 1915.

tion, the literate population increased more quickly in those parishes crossed by the railway—Alausí itself, Sibambe, Tixán, and Huigra—than in those parishes more distant from the line. Chunchi appears to be an exception, but by the mid-1910s it was the site of construction of the railway from Sibambe to Cuenca.

Additional information about increasing occupational differentiation bears out these general conclusions. At the beginning of the period under consideration, artisans were so scarce in Alausí that the municipality paid the tuition of local students to study in the Salesian trades school in Riobamba. Once their studies were completed, they were provided with free workshop space in Alausí in exchange for training local apprentices over a four-year period. In 1907 several artisans from the southern highlands applied to the municipal council for free workshop space in order to settle in Alausí. The municipality did not approve these petitions because "then we would have to make the same concession to other artisans, and there just is not enough space."[14] Even without free space, however, these artisans decided to move to Alausí and set up shop. By 1909 the master artisans in the cantonal seat included six carpenters and cabinetmakers, three blacksmiths, one pyrotechnist, two tinsmiths, two silversmiths, five tailors, and four shoemakers.[15] By 1930 these numbers had risen to ten tailors, fourteen carpenters and cabinetmakers, sixteen shoemakers, two electricians, two mechanics, ten stonemasons, two stonecutters, twelve potters, three tinsmiths, three cigar makers, and eight barbers.[16] The growing number of artisans indicates an increase not only in the variety of services available to the town population but also in the townspeople's ability to pay for those services.

There was also an increase in the number of professionals in Alausí over this period. In 1909 there were five lawyers, one physician, and two notaries in the cantonal seat; by 1930 there were eight lawyers, four physicians, and one professional midwife (trained in the Universidad Central in Quito). Four pharmacies took turns offering all-night service. By 1909 three hotels were open in Huigra, and by the mid-1910s there were another two in Alausí. There were also a small number of "factories" (meaning enterprises that used any kind of machinery), many of them established in the 1920s (see Table 8). It is surely not a coincidence that almost all of the factories were in parishes through which either the Guayaquil-Quito Railway or the Sibambe-Cuenca rail line passed. (The three exceptions were also among the four factories with the smallest capital investment—those in Gonzól and Guasuntos.)

Another measure of economic growth can be seen in the increase in municipal tax revenues, based on such variables as the

Table 8. Factories in Alausí Canton, by Parish, 1928

Year Est.	Name of Owner and/or Factory	Capital Invested (sucres)	Goods Produced	Number of Machines	Motive Power	Number of Employees	Daily Wage[a]
Alausí							
1904	Molinos	1,800	flours[b]	1	hydraulic	2	60
1908	Prensadora	1,500	forage	1	animal	2	80
1917	Molinas	1,000	flours	1	hydraulic	1	60
1925	Molino	6,000	flours	1	hydraulic	1	80
1925	La Fama	250	soda	1	manual	4	50–80
1926	La Eléctrica	70,000	light	1	hydraulic	2	266
1927	La Minervita	1,500	soda	1	manual	1	150
1927	Guerrero	5,429	candles	1	manual	4	90–100
1927	Romero	500	soda	1	manual	1	60
1928	La Perla	1,200	soda	1	manual	1	45
Sibambe							
1906	Esperanza	500	soda	1	manual	1	60
1925	Minerva	400	soda	1	manual	1	60
Tixán							
1923	El Progreso	30,000	flours	2	hydraulic	2	130
Gonzól							
1927	T. Lara	300	soda	1	manual	1	50
Guasuntos							
1919	E. Campos	300	soda	1	manual	1	80
1922	J. M. Orellano	300	soda	1	manual	1	80
1924	T. Montalvo	300	soda	1	manual	1	80
Huigra							
1924	La Minerba	600	soda	1	manual	0	n/a
1926	La Eléctrica	5,000	light	1	gasoline	1	150
1926	La Eléctrica E. Morley	3,000	light	1	gasoline	1	150
1926	La Eléctrica N. Dobbie	3,000	light	1	gasoline	1	150
1927	La Perla	500	soda	1	manual	1	80
1927	La Corona	500	soda	1	manual	1	s/20[c]

Source: Cuadro de fábricas en Alausí, March 1928, AJPA 1928.
There were no factories in Chunchi or Achupallas.
[a]In centavos.
[b]Flours and meals ground from a variety of grains and legumes, including wheat, barley, lentils, corn, and peas.
[c]Twenty sucres per month.

value of properties, the value of capital investments and merchandise in stores, and the value of merchandise and alcoholic
beverages introduced into the canton.[17] These revenues rose
from 8,322.33 sucres in 1898, to 12,008.32 sucres in 1900, to
24,882.10 sucres three years later in 1903, when the railway was
inaugurated in the cantonal seat. Between 1903 and 1918 revenues remained fairly stable, with a tendency toward gradual
growth, usually fluctuating by two to three thousand sucres
annually, between a low of 18,604.25 in 1906 and a high of
27,529.80 in 1918. In 1919 revenues rose to 47,261.01, and by 1930
municipal revenues had reached 76,149.24 sucres. These rising
municipal revenues were generated by the growing dynamism
of commerce in the canton. This commercial growth is also suggested by the increase in the number of merchants in Alausí,
who both introduced new goods into the canton, including
manufactured goods and domestic and imported liquor, and sold
agricultural products from the zone to merchants in other regions. Not only did the number of merchants in this canton rise
considerably after the railway was inaugurated, but commerce
grew more here than it did in other parts of Chimborazo province, or even in most of the other central highland towns and
cities. This region also began to provision other areas with food
staples such as grains and potatoes, and lentils from this zone
were exported to other countries by at least 1924.[18] By 1919 wool,
meat, and hides were being marketed well beyond the boundaries of the canton.

One result of the increase in municipal revenues and, more
broadly, of local prosperity was a greater capacity to create what
was considered to be civilized town life in the cantonal seat. For
instance, in 1904 the municipal council of Alausí spent some of
its revenues on the manufacture of plaques with street names,
as well as on numbering and identifying the houses in town with
smaller plaques. Besides being a matter of civic pride, the
council's action also reflected the fact that more strangers, who
could not locate places by conventional means, were passing
through town. In addition, in 1904 a public clock was purchased
and installed on the tower of the municipal building then under
construction. This was a powerful symbol of the town's integration into national space and time with the passage of the railway, whose trains ran on a schedule.

This integration into national space was also indicated by
the fact that Alausí became a vacation and convalescence spot
for residents of Guayaquil, which was threatened by tropical

diseases, especially from January to March. During these months, Guayaquil was hot, humid, and rainy, providing the perfect conditions for the proliferation of mosquitoes and therefore of yellow fever and malaria. Indeed, in 1912 the mortality rate in Guayaquil was 23 percent higher than its birth rate.[19] The port was notorious for its unhealthiness. As a result, foreign governments had problems maintaining diplomats in Guayaquil, and steamship companies sometimes refused to stop there for fear that their ships would consequently be quarantined at other ports.[20]

With the construction of the Guayaquil-Quito Railway, distances and space were reorganized, bringing Alausí—the first highland station on the route inland—rather abruptly into close proximity to Guayaquil. Alausí began to be considered the threshold of the highlands. While previously it had been difficult to reach this town from the port during the rainy season, with the construction of the railway Alausí was a simple six-hour train journey from Guayaquil, a journey into both a different region and an entirely different climate.

Almost immediately after the 1902 inauguration of the railway in Alausí, people began to speak of the area's healthy climate and proximity to the coast. An important seasonal flow of visitors from Guayaquil was established by 1907. These visitors were attracted by Alausí's "unsurpassable climate," and they settled in the cantonal seat and the town of Huigra for several months at a time, usually from January to March. While Alausí's rainy season coincided with that of Guayaquil, because of the altitude of the zone no threat to health was associated with this season. By 1915 the seasonal migrations from the coast had become considerable: "The enthusiasm manifested by coastal residents this year is greater even than in previous years and now we see many of them constructing pretty houses and elegant chalets in the center and on the edges of town. In no time our town will become the preferred vacation area in the nation, and our relations with our brothers of the coast will be cemented ever more strongly."[21]

By 1930 three hundred families from the Guayaquil area regularly wintered in Alausí.[22] In those cases when Guayaquileño businessmen sent their families to Alausí for the rainy season, they could easily visit on weekends and return to Guayaquil during the week, since the train from the port arrived in Alausí at one in the afternoon and left the following day at eleven in the morning, as local officials were pleased to point out. In addition, in 1906 the Franciscan nuns who directed the girls' school in Alausí began to take in boarding students of delicate health who were threatened by the coastal climate. In 1915 they also established a "vacation colony" in Alausí on a charitable basis for poor girls ages seven to twelve who were considered at risk from the tropical rainy season. This colony served the social welfare societies of Guayaquil, which sent it some of their wards. The nuns' success with their boarding school led another local teacher in October 1915 to expand his own small private school for boys to offer a limited amount of boarding for coastal students.

The presence of visitors from the port stimulated not only projects of civic pride but also new forms of social life in Alausí during this period. A municipal band was formed in 1914, and the band director also began to offer music lessons to a group of young ladies in town. By the mid-1920s the band was offering regular Sunday concerts. In 1915 a public library was also inaugurated in the town. In 1923, during the rainy season, Alausí was entertained by movie shows and a visiting theater company, both from the coast, and by 1928 movies were being offered regularly by a local impresario. The early 1920s also saw the establishment among the town's "distinguished and patriotic youth" of a variety of local clubs and social circles dedicated to music, sports, and the "improvement of the town." Another social event occurred outside of the season of Guayaquileño visits: in 1916, Alausí began to hold civic festivities on November 13, the anniversary of the town's founding, during which Alauseños represented to themselves their position in the Ecuadorian nation.

Alausí appears on maps as rather central geographically, located between Ecuador's three principal cities of Quito, Guayaquil, and Cuenca. However, despite this seeming centrality, Alausí was not fully integrated into the national space at the beginning of the liberal period. Although Alausí was on the weekly mail route from Quito south to Cuenca (passing through Pumallacta), there was only limited movement of other goods and people through this canton. It was also marginal in many other ways. Alausí had few schools and teachers, and there were no maps or books in those schools. Local jails were in such disrepair that prisoners regularly escaped over the crumbling walls. For that matter, except for some funds for sanitation in the mid-1910s, no monies were dedicated to Alausí in the central state budget prior to the reorganization of national finances following the 1925 July Revolution. In contrast, especially during the first half of the liberal period, Alausí was expected to contribute a set percentage of its annual municipal revenues to everything from the construction of monuments in Quito, Guayaquil, and Riobamba, to maintenance of the lepers' hospital in Quito, to educational facilities and the installation of electric lighting in Riobamba. Although it did not receive significant state investment, with the inauguration of the railway Alausí did become incorporated in other ways.

Bubonic Plague and Resistance to the Sanitation Campaign

Given the emergence of Alausí as a vacation and convalescence spot, it is ironic that one of the first major conflicts associated with the region's incorporation into national space occurred because of an epidemic of bubonic plague brought by train. The bubonic plague, widely accepted as having been the cause of the Black Death that killed one-third or more of the population of medieval Europe, is transmitted to humans by the bites of fleas that have fed upon infected rats or other rodents. The disease is characterized by the enlargement of the lymphatic glands and may lead to pneumonia, high fever, shock, delirium, coma, and death. Bubonic plague first appeared in Guayaquil in 1908. The Ecuadorian Public Health Service (Servicio de Sanidad Pública)—the earliest health and sanitation service organized on a national level in Ecuador—was established in that year largely as a response to this threat. The same year also saw passage of the first Law of Public Health. During the following years the plague spread to other coastal areas, but in 1913 it appeared for the first time in a highland town, Alausí, the gateway to the Andes. It was destined to be a seasonal visitor there for the next several years.

As early as 1908, a Special Commission for the Hygiene and Sanitation of the Railway was organized, with jurisdiction between Durán (the coastal rail terminal across the Guayas River from Guayaquil) and Alausí. One of the first measures it took in 1908 to prevent the spread of plague to the interior was to temporarily suspend train service between Huigra and Alausí. With the subsequent outbreak of plague in the town of Alausí, the central government mobilized resources to prevent the disease from reaching farther into the interior of the country. Regional Public Health offices were created in both Riobamba and Quito (the national office was in Guayaquil), while an additional commission was formed in Quito to decide on the actions needed to prevent the inland spread of the disease. These measures included the requirement that all baggage and cargo that passed through Alausí be disinfected before proceeding. Nevertheless, plague reached Ambato in 1916–17, provoking panic that the capital city would be next. The first case in Ambato was traced back to Alausí.

The importance of the railway for understanding bubonic plague in Ecuador lies not only in its role in making Alausí the gateway to the highlands but also in its being the preferred mode of transport for the germs themselves. The trains literally carried plague to the highlands on the infected rats that traveled in the baggage cars. Some efforts to eliminate the disease therefore focused on the daily disinfection of railway cars in Durán as well as in Riobamba, where trains stopped for the night. In addition, efforts were made to regulate the passengers traveling to the interior, who, during outbreaks of the epidemic, were required to show certificates verifying that they had been vaccinated.

Although bubonic plague had previously affected the tropical village of Huigra, within the canton of Alausí, its appearance in the higher altitude cantonal seat was unprecedented. At the end of March 1913, dead rats began to appear in the town. A Guayaquil-based public health inspector arrived on the evening of April 8, and early the next morning he discovered the first case of bubonic plague in the eight-year-old son of the train station chief. To "avoid the propagation of the scourge toward the interior of the Republic," he immediately and indefinitely placed the town under absolute quarantine.[23] In light of the alarm caused by the quarantine measures, the inspector requested the assistance of armed troops. "The presence of the plague caused panic in not a few inhabitants of Alausí; but due to the disbelief of many and the ignorance, bad will, or damaged intentions of others, it was difficult . . . to convince the public to effectively support the measures adopted in such critical circumstances."[24] With the assistance of the troops and police, who ensured that the sanitation measures were carried out, the plague was under control by May 5, and the interior cities were safe.

The appearance of bubonic plague had provoked great alarm among the townspeople of Alausí, and on the night of April 10, local notables gathered outside the municipal offices to propose the immediate construction of a quarantine station.[25] Some townspeople offered to provide the necessary materials, for which they were later reimbursed with central government funds. Construction of the quarantine station was completed in less than two weeks. Funds for its construction and subsequent operation, for other sanitation works, and for the provision of antiplague vaccine came from the budgets of the municipal council and the central government. In 1913, Alausí was the only highland town that received monies for sanitation from the national budget.[26]

In March 1914 bubonic plague struck again in Alausí, with such force that a special cemetery was created for its victims. On July 20 the governor of Chimborazo sent a memorandum to the political administrator of Alausí:

> This authority has received news that the lower classes of Alausí, stirred up by certain individuals who today as in the past exploit their ignorance to provoke them to nefarious ends, are currently concocting a plot against the sanitation employees of that canton.
>
> The sanitation institution is deemed in any civilized country to be the most beneficial of all institutions, and therefore the people who comprise it are esteemed and respected. The very fact that there has been hostility shown to these employees reflects very poorly on the culture of that town.
>
> It is imperative, therefore, that the authorities of Alausí use their influence to prevent the occurrence of acts that, filling us with disgrace, would shame us before the civilized world.[27]

The precise activities involved in this "plot" were not detailed. Instead, dark comments were made about opposition by subordinate groups to the sanitation commission, which had been sent from Guayaquil to prevent bubonic plague from spreading to the inter-Andean cities. There was resistance to both the sanitation measures undertaken and the obligatory vaccination program against plague. If threats were being made against certain sanitation employees, the questions then arise of who these employees were and what they did. In addition to the public health inspector sent to Alausí from Guayaquil and the locally funded municipal doctor, the municipal police were charged with responsibility for sanitation as well as for a wide range of other duties, such as the regulation of commerce, local public works construction, and generally ensuring compliance with municipal by-laws.[28]

The campaign against bubonic plague in Alausí was fought on two fronts: the elimination of sources of infection and the vaccination of healthy people. Because of the role of rats and other flea-ridden animals in spreading plague, the extermination of rodents was the cornerstone of the sanitation campaign. The railway station was disinfected with creosote, and double walls were destroyed because they provided spaces in between for rat nests. A rat-hunting team was set up, equipped with 100 traps sent from Guayaquil (1,445 rats were killed in the town of Alausí in April 1913 alone), followed by the chemical disinfection of streets and houses where infected rats were discovered. House-by-house visits were made to inspect hygiene conditions, and again double-wall constructions were destroyed. In an indigenous settlement outside of Alausí, the straw roofs of houses were burned because they were considered unhygienic. "As the largest number of sick appeared in a hacienda close to town in the huts inhabited by Indians, we had to resort to the painful but necessary measure of incinerating the straw roofs, given that no other means was effective in those miserable dwellings whose hygienic conditions are disastrous, and where any work of sanitation is impossible. No recourse but fire was available to save the lives of the inhabitants."[29] The burning of houses that had sheltered plague victims was considered the only effective means of eliminating the microbe.

In addition, the cohabitation of people and animals was prohibited, and small livestock were driven out of the town limits. In the village of Huigra, which had also been attacked by the plague, the political lieutenant reported: "I have ordered death for pigs, *cuyes* (guinea pigs), cats, rabbits, etc., who can serve for the shelter and development of the loathsome coccus bacillus. Against dogs I have decreed strangulation since I do not have the eliminating poison that is usually administered, and I must beg you to order that I be granted the necessary materials as soon as possible, since today as never before, I must declare war to the death against the canine race."[30] A later document demonstrates that the inspection of animals became an opportunity for officials to appropriate healthy livestock for their own use. In 1927 it became notorious that the "Sr. Rat Inspector" was collecting "guinea pigs and rabbits that, taken on the pretext of examining them, end up being eaten on outings or in the house of said Inspector."[31] There is no evidence that any compensation was offered to owners either for the animals killed or the houses burned; if such compensation had been provided, it would have appeared in municipal records. Other activities to eliminate foci of plague involved the collection and disposal of waste and spreading lime throughout affected areas. Altogether, many of the measures taken involved the policing of private as well as public hygiene, that is, state officials entering private homes to regulate waste disposal, to ensure that animals did not inhabit domestic areas, and so on.

The vaccination program undertaken was compulsory and was carried out by the health inspection team with the assistance of the municipal police. During April 1913 alone, 1,032 people were vaccinated in the town of Alausí. In the cantonal seat, people were required to appear at the police headquarters to be vaccinated. In outlying areas, either the police went to houses or people were ordered to go to the offices of the political lieutenants. It was an accepted, if regrettable, fact that sometimes coercion had to be used in obligatory vaccination programs.[32] The calls for armed troops whenever the epidemic broke out demonstrates that force was integral to the overall sanitation efforts. But beyond their use of force, the involvement of the municipal police in sanitation and vaccination efforts in Alausí must be considered in more specific terms.

One of the most important duties of the municipal police—certainly the duty that brought them most often in contact with Indians in outlying areas of the canton—was the recruitment of indigenous labor for municipal public works construction.[33] And much of the sanitation campaign involved efforts to clean up Alausí, work that was undertaken through this same labor regime. Thus, a large proportion of the work detailed earlier—including fumigation, disinfection, rat catching, and the removal of garbage—was carried out by day laborers. In general, labor recruitment for public works was often resisted because of such common abuses as nonpayment for the work done, the use of force in recruitment, and the use of recruited workers in private rather than public enterprises (all of which were against the law). During the mid-1910s, however, a series of advances had been achieved by indigenous workers in their resistance to this labor regime, and central state authorities sent several widely publicized communications to local authorities upholding the rights of workers.

The sole area in which new labor requirements were added in the mid-1910s was in the sanitation of the town of Alausí, because the public health campaign there was considered crucial to the health and safety of the entire highland region.

Resistance to this project was reflected indirectly by the frequent complaints of Guayaquil-based public health employees that local authorities in Alausí were not cooperating in the sanitation efforts (meaning that they were having problems recruiting the labor demanded by health officials). These complaints culminated in requests for the dismissal of the police chief and other local authorities. But superior political authorities had little patience for petitions from Indian laborers or complaints about abuses during labor recruitment, even when these were based on constitutional arguments. Even if these new labor demands had not been made, it is unlikely that indigenous peasants would have welcomed agents of a broader forced-labor regime into their homes or been willing to present themselves at the municipal police office. The distaste that peasants showed for appearing at the police office for vaccination is even more understandable. They had to balance any protection they might receive from the vaccine against the possibility that they would be recruited to work in precisely the most infected areas.

To understand the differential effects of these campaigns on social groups, it is important to recognize that sanitation measures were not undertaken evenly throughout the canton. While the funds supplied by the central state for sanitation campaigns in the towns of Alausí and Huigra in 1913–14 helped to control plague in these areas, the disease continued to strike other areas of the canton throughout the 1920s. Sometimes this occurred in indigenous communities that were not crossed by the railway. Provincial authorities did order the municipal physician to be sent to these communities but provided no money for supplies or medicines to fight the plague.[34] He resigned his post in frustration in 1920 because "the simple presence of the physician is of little comfort to the afflicted, if he arrives without disinfectant or vaccine."[35] When indigenous day laborers were forcibly recruited for sanitation campaigns, they usually had to travel into an infected zone to carry out this work; when their own communities were afflicted, the townspeople of Alausí did not, of course, return the favor by traveling out to assist them. It is not clear which was worse for indigenous peasants: to live far from the rail line and receive no assistance when plague struck, or to live close to the line and have their huts burned down and guinea pigs taken.

In 1921 the sanitation service was moved from the responsibility of the Ministry of the Interior, Police, and Public Works to the Ministry of Education. This administrative change reflects a transformation of the field from one concerned with the construction of public works to prevent the spread of disease to one that emphasized the reform of "bad habits." The state's priority shifted from sanitation to hygiene, that is, from an effort to change the environment in which people lived to a concern with changing how people lived in that environment.[36] Thus, in Ecuador during the 1920s, reports about public health issues revealed an increasing interest in problems such as venereal disease, alcoholism, and personal and domestic cleanliness.[37] In regard to plague, a series of instructions sent out in 1927 by Dr. Pablo Arturo Suárez, the general director of public health, illustrates this shift. His orders, meant to represent a more "permanent campaign" against the tenacious bubonic plague, began with two programs involving vigilance over the cargo and passengers traveling on trains as well as the public health conditions of the towns through which the trains passed, followed by a third program involving scientific research on rodents. The final two points merit quotation, in light of the concern with reforming people's behavior:

> 4. Local measures related to the personal hygiene of Indians in villages that have been infected, and the cleanliness of homes and public streets.
>
> 5. Special measures dealing with indigenous housing, with emphasis on the following. First, to prohibit Indians from sleeping directly on the floor. They should sleep on a platform at least fifty centimeters from the ground, to decrease their proximity to fleas that multiply on the ground and to rats that enter the huts at night and come into intimate contact with the inhabitants. And second, to obligate them not to construct guinea pig corrals in their sleeping quarters but rather in other rooms, and to surround these corrals with a secure barrier eighty centimeters high, so that there is less promiscuity between man and these rodents, who are very susceptible to the plague and serve as a means of contagion.[38]

This excerpt demonstrates rather clearly where the blame for plague was seen to lie: not in the state's lack of investment in services for this region and these communities, but in the "uncivilized" behavior of Indians, focusing on cohabitation with guinea pigs, a highly symbolic practice in Andean life.[39]

The conflict over the 1913–14 sanitation campaigns reveals how the interests of social groups within Alausí differed in relation to the processes of incorporation associated with the railway. The townspeople of Alausí—merchants, professionals, medium landowners, and artisans—did not participate in municipal labor calls, which were limited to indigenous peasants. The townspeople were clearly much more supportive of the sanitation efforts than were the local Indians, who were considered to be either ignorant of or superstitious about the benefits being offered them. Besides the danger that the plague posed to health in Alausí—and Indians may have been at much greater risk than whites, given the lack of resources to protect their communities—it represented quite a different kind of threat to white townspeople than it did to indigenous peasants. The townspeople saw their commercial interests threatened by the suspension of train traffic, which prevented the shipment of goods and jeopardized the flow of seasonal visitors from Guayaquil. For the Indians, in contrast, it was the campaign itself that posed a threat, whether through forced labor recruitment or through such actions as the burning of houses and killing of small livestock.

Agrarian Conflicts and the Challenges of Agricultural Development

Together with the new agricultural development policies discussed in Chapter 5 were other conflicts that occurred in the rural areas of the canton in the 1920s, especially in the relations between indigenous communities and haciendas. The new policies were not "caused" by the railway, but they were nonetheless associated with it. No attempt to increase production to provision the internal market would have been possible without facilities for the transport of goods. The opportunities offered by access to new markets, however, could not be effortlessly acted on by hacendados at the local level. Rather, in addition to the conjuncture of national and international processes already delineated, local, historically constituted social relations also intervened in how agricultural expansion and modernization efforts were carried out.

A conflict between the Hacienda Moyocancha and the indigenous peasants of Pizhillig, in the parish of Tixán, is revealing. Moyocancha was by far the largest hacienda in the canton of Alausí (see Table 6). It had close relations with the peasants of Pizhillig, many of whom were debt peons on the hacienda, while others worked there periodically without becoming permanently indebted. In 1922 the Indians of Pizhillig complained to the nation's president about the abusive behavior of the hacendado of Moyocancha, Julio Salem. The immediate result was that the national police chief was sent from the town of Alausí to investigate. He reported:

> In the Hacienda Moyocancha I first interviewed Sr. Julio Salem, who, informed of my purpose in being there, manifested to me his best good will to arrive at an agreement with the Indians of Pizhillig. He explained the two principal bases of such an agreement, which are: the obligation to work four days a week for the hacendado; and the obligation, also, to pay him two sucres annually for each head of cattle and ten centavos for each sheep, for the use of pasturage on his hacienda.
>
> Scarcely had I arrived in the *anejo* of Pizhillig, when twenty-five Indians responded to my summons, to whom I manifested the objective of my presence there and the bases of the agreement proposed by their *patrón* Sr. Salem, tending, wisely, to calm the excitation that they exhibited from the beginning, as they described their claims against the conduct of Sr. Salem's agents and employees. They complain of oppression and harsh treatment at the hands of these agents, whose abuses and constant attacks led them to solicit protection and shelter for their persons and goods; that their livestock is seized by force and without paying them a cent, and they have no right to make reclamations; that at the moment they are blocked or enclosed within their community by the employees of Sr. Salem, who gave the order, requiring them to pay *derechos de sitiaje* for the use of the meadows and natural pasturage of the hacienda. The Indians are intransigent, inexorable in their intention to leave the hacienda. They have resolved to neither work nor provide any service whatsoever to the hacienda, nor to use anything from it. As a result they have started to feed their own crops to their herds, and now only ask to be given free passage to leave with their families and belongings, in order to establish themselves elsewhere. Sr. Salem opposes this, as I had the chance to hear from him and from the Indians of the *anejo*; for which effect, he has established the blockade that I mentioned.
>
> Having returned to speak with Sr. Julio Salem, and informing him of the result of my efforts, he insisted on his resolution not to permit the departure of the Indians of the above-mentioned community, until they pay for the use of pasturage on the hacienda.[40]

Additional evidence from May 1922 indicates that Salem's employees had seized peasants' sheep when they were encountered within Moyocancha. The police chief ordered them to return the livestock to Pizhillig (a similar incident occurred in 1924).

In June several Indians from Pizhillig presented a new complaint to the provincial governor that Salem had closed a path that they had traditionally used to reach the public road. The following week, the national police chief reported that while investigating this complaint, he had encountered two hacienda employees guarding the estate's border closest to Pizhillig, "in order to prevent persons unrelated to the hacienda from entering to collect straw or water, or to herd animals into the pastures or fields."[41] In July, Pedro Morocho took his complaint that Salem had closed down seven paths, isolating Pizhillig from other villages, directly to the nation's president. In August, Marcial Aucacama was accused of stealing livestock from Moyocancha's *páramos*. Given that hacienda employees had seized peasant livestock when they found it within Moyocancha, this accusation may have been an effort to recover sheep belonging to the Indians of Pizhillig.

In the previous decade the relationship between Pizhillig and Moyocancha had been peaceful and mutually beneficial. How can the eruption of this conflict be explained? A clue appears in an earlier complaint to the political administrator of Alausí, filed by the community members (*comuneros*) of Pizhillig in 1919: Sr. Julio Teodoro Salem, Jr., "operates in a way contrary to that of his Señor father Julio Salem, in whom we encountered goodness, consideration, and gratitude since we served him willingly, and who, to our misfortune, retired to Riobamba, leaving the care of the hacienda in the hands of his Señor son."[42] Julio Jr. took over the administration of the property in 1917 or 1918 and immediately attempted to raise the customary pasturage payments, which were duly paid in November 1918. In early 1919 the *comuneros* approached Salem to complain about this increase, with the result that, "resentful, . . . [he] deprives us of occupying a single inch" of his hacienda. Salem sent his dogs among the peasants' herds to drive them out of the pastures, in the process maiming and killing several animals. The peasants' request to the political administrator for protection went unheeded, and by 1922 the conflict had escalated on both sides. The *comuneros* of Pizhillig took their complaint to the president; they may also have turned to livestock rustling. And Julio Salem, in addition to making further monetary demands on the peasants, began to close down local paths. In doing so, he not only cut off Pizhillig, but, perhaps more important, he also restricted public access to his own property.

It is useful to place this dispute in the context of other serious conflicts between peasants and hacendados in Alausí during the early 1920s. There are three elements common to all of these cases. First, the haciendas on which conflicts occurred were those that had access to high *páramos* rather than those that were limited to the steep slopes typical of the Alauseño countryside. As a result, these haciendas—Zula in Achupallas, Susnia and Chimba-Guataxi in Chunchi, and Moyocancha in Tixán—engaged in extensive livestock pasturage as well as in potato and grain cultivation. Second, the majority of the landowners involved in these conflicts were part of a new generation in estate management, whether as sons, as administrators, or as new tenants. Thus, Zula was rented from the Curia de Riobamba by Vicente Guevara, and the other three haciendas were run by the owners' sons: Susnia by Ezequiel Bermeo, son of Isaac; Chimba-Guataxi by Wilfrido Puyol, son of Manuel; and Moyocancha by Julio Salem, Jr. Third, the administrators of these haciendas were all accused of ignoring customary rights-of-way on local roads and often other forms of enclosure. They consistently responded that they had the legal right to protect their property and goods. As Wilfrido Puyol of Chimba-Guataxi argued, "I will proceed to close as many paths as necessary for my own right and in virtue of the obligation to conserve the rented property in good condition and without detriment."[43] Ezequiel Bermeo of Susnia contended that people did not use the path that crossed his hacienda to reach any particular destination, but because "it serves them for provisioning themselves with firewood in abundance and with fodder for their animals, firewood and fodder of my hacienda. The complainants do not use the path to travel its full extension, but rather to go where it is convenient for them."[44]

In addition to closing down paths, these landowners simultaneously attempted to expand hacienda territories. They often presented titles to lands that had been traditionally occupied by indigenous communities and attempted to enclose such properties by force. In 1923 the indigenous community of Cobzhe, whose lands were situated between the Haciendas Zula and Moyocancha, suffered attempts at expropriation from both estates. Vicente Guevara, the administrator of Zula, also clashed with the community of Totoras, in Achupallas parish, when he produced a property title to lands possessed by the community,

which countered with its own title dating to 1658. These conflicts resulted in thefts of livestock, beatings of Indians by hacienda employees, and, in at least two cases, the disappearance of
Indians from their respective communities, leading other *comuneros* to conclude that they had been killed. In the example of
the Hacienda Susnia, which bordered smaller properties rather
than indigenous communities, Ezequiel Bermeo engaged in a
vigorous process of buying up neighboring plots. When he was
accused of closing paths, he explained that while the paths had
previously served a purpose by connecting numerous small
properties, now he had incorporated those lands into his hacienda, and the paths were therefore private, internal ones rather
than public roads. In every instance cited here hacendados had
tried to consolidate their estates and assert more control over
land.

How can we account for the emergence of agrarian conflicts
in this particular conjuncture? The evidence indicates that efforts to expand production on these haciendas underlay such
conflicts. As already demonstrated, the late 1910s was a time of
economic crisis that drew elite attention to new marketing possibilities and state attention to the need to expand highland agricultural production. In Alausí, the most serious conflicts
occurred with the expansion of livestock raising. By 1919 wool
and hides from Alausí were being marketed beyond the canton.
Throughout the 1920s, there were also an increasing number of
complaints about the poor quality of meat sold in local markets
in Alausí, which may indicate that the higher quality meat was
being shipped out to more distant urban markets. By 1927 the
canton had at least nine major livestock enterprises and six large
butcher establishments. Ezequiel Bermeo alone had 12,000 sucres
invested in his livestock. And by 1930 the quality of Julio Salem's
"cattle, sheep, and horses of pure and mixed lineage [*fina y me-
dia sangre*]" merited special mention in a monograph on Chimborazo province.[45]

The expansion of livestock raising implied both the need for
more land under use and the possibility of eliminating unnec-
essary and unproductive labor.[46] Debt peonage relations (*concertaje*) were convenient for hacendados if their goal was to
maintain a stable resident labor force, but the inflexibility of the
system constrained the employer as well as the worker.[47] Agriculture, in contrast to livestock raising, was more labor inten-
sive and therefore less likely to involve the expulsion of workers.
Moreover, although the modernization policies under the Ley

de Fomento Agrícola allowed the importation of improved breeds of livestock, such investments were worth making only if they were protected. As Gavin Smith has argued for the Peruvian context, the practice of allowing peasants to pasture their herds among those of the hacienda made it impossible to maintain the quality of improved breeds.[48]

In Alausí, the specific nature of these conflicts suggests that the kind of livestock production under expansion involved sheep farming for wool and cattle ranching for meat and hides. When ranching was modernized instead for dairy production (as occurred in the highlands around Quito), it involved a reduction in the need for land because of the importation of better livestock breeds, seeds for improved pasture, and machinery for processing milk.[49] Hacendados thus could reduce the amount of land they used, concentrating their production on the more fertile valley floors, and sell off small plots on the mountainsides to peasants to create a stable labor reserve. In contrast, the expansion of sheep and cattle raising for wool, hides, and meat was associated with increased control over high-altitude *páramo* pastures and often with an extension of the land under hacienda control.

Conflict between a hacienda and its neighboring indigenous communities was particularly likely to occur whenever the ownership or management of an estate changed.[50] The question then becomes why the management of so many haciendas changed hands in the late 1910s and early 1920s, not only in Alausí but throughout the north-central highlands.[51] The marketing possibilities created by the crisis of the First World War, the opening of the coastal market, and the new government policies favoring expansion of agricultural and textile production were constrained by existing relations of reciprocity between hacendados and their peasant workers.

Even though the peasants, in their complaints to political authorities about hacendado abuses in the early 1920s, used language that suggested the rupture of a timeless pact, it should be noted that these relations were not static ones.[52] For instance, many indigenous peasants from Pizhillig became debt peons on Moyocancha. This was not a long-standing traditional pact, but rather a relationship created within the recent experience of many of the Indians involved in these conflicts. These hacienda-community relations were forged in a context of intensified municipal demands for indigenous labor to construct public works in the town of Alausí, which took peasants away from their own agricultural plots for a fortnight at a time. Frequently, public works laborers were recruited at moments of peak agricultural activity. In this context, some haciendas became zones of refuge from state labor demands, because debt peons (or anyone else who had a previous contract to work for someone) could not be recruited for public works projects.[53] Prior to the agrarian conflicts of the 1920s, the owners or administrators of the estates where conflicts subsequently emerged (such as Julio Salem, Sr.) had been able to reach mutually beneficial arrangements with local peasants whereby the peasants worked on the estate and the hacendado protected them from municipal labor recruitment. In at least one instance, when peasants had been rounded up for public works labor in the cantonal seat, the employees of Moyocancha freed them on the trail from Tixán to Alausí.

The evidence suggests that the peasants of Pizhillig were not actual *huasipungueros* on Moyocancha, that is, they did not receive a plot of land (*huasipungo*) for subsistence agriculture in exchange for working on the estate. They had their own subsistence plots in Pizhillig, but they worked on the estate during peak periods and paid a certain amount (*derechos de sitiaje*) for the right to pasture their animals in the *páramos* of the hacienda. In exchange, they gained access not only to pasture but also to firewood, straw, and water. Perhaps their status as debt peons derived from not paying the full amount in any given year, as well as from requesting additional *suplidos* or *socorros* (advances in cash or products) from the hacendado.[54]

Up to this point it has been argued that the hacendados involved in conflicts were attempting to take advantage of the new policies favoring agricultural and livestock development associated with the opening up of the coastal market. In these cases, hacendados expanded livestock raising. However, a closer examination of the documents suggests that large landholders did not have a monopoly over decision making in these processes and may have been compelled to choose this form of expanding production by the actions of peasants.

October 1918 saw two state actions that were highly significant for agrarian relations. One was the passage of the Ley de Fomento Agrícola, and the other was the abolition of debt peonage by dropping the article in the Código de Enjuiciamientos Civiles that sanctioned debt prison. These broader changes to agricultural policies and labor laws help to explain an inconsistency between the 1919 petition to the political administrator from the Indians of Pizhillig and the police chief's report about his visit to Pizhillig and Moyocancha in May 1922. The accounts of the *comuneros* of Pizhillig and hacendado Julio Salem diverged in one crucial way: how each side represented the character of hacienda-peasant relations at the time of the conflict. The Indians of Pizhillig argued that over the years they had paid for pasturage for their animals and had helped out on the estate during peak agricultural periods; in exchange, they had gained access to pasture, water, and straw. These Indians were said to be working as *ayudas* in the Ecuadorian context, and it occurred when *indios libres* (free Indians) were associated with a hacienda. Julio Salem, as well as raising the customary pasturage payments, dictated that the Indians must work four days per week on the estate. This requirement was one of the classic minimal conditions for access to a *huasipungo*. By making this demand, Salem implied that the peasants were not *indios libres* at all, but rather *indios propios* ("owned" Indians) of the hacienda. With the elimination of *concertaje*, the conversion of debt peons into *huasipungueros* was among the surest ways, from a large landowner's perspective, to guarantee a stable resident labor force. Julio Salem's claim to four days' work can be read in precisely this way. In addition, the movement to expand the land under estate control during this period—and hence to force peasants to become *huasipungueros* to gain access to land for subsistence production—can similarly be read as an effort to tie workers to the hacienda under the changed labor conditions.

These maneuvers were strongly resisted by peasants. As the police chief explained to the political administrator in July 1922, "given the Indians' refusal to work, Sr. Salem in the same manner does not allow them to use straw, water, or the pastures belonging to his hacienda."[55] It was also as a result of the Indians' refusal to work on Moyocancha that Salem began to limit their access to his property by closing paths. The peasants of Pizhillig not only refused to work four days per week on the estate, but they began to feed their own crops to their livestock. They claimed they were prepared to pack up their families and possessions and move from the area rather than capitulate (although there is no evidence that they actually did so). Thus, it was the peasants' refusal to acquiesce that led hacendados to take advantage of the opportunities to provision the internal market in the way that they did, by expanding livestock production (requiring relatively less labor) rather than labor-intensive grain production. Their refusal carried a high price for indigenous peasants, but then surely submission would have also.

In summary, the economic crisis brought on by World War I and the new policies promoting agricultural expansion and associated access to new domestic markets caused some hacendados to turn the management of their properties over to their sons or to new administrators. With the addition of the abolition of debt peonage, large landholders attempted to assure themselves of a stable labor force by converting former *conciertos* (debt peons) into *huasipungueros*. The hacendados escalated their labor demands and tried to expand hacienda territory into indigenous lands. Both of these efforts, facilitated by the change in estate administration, can be seen as rupturing previous hacienda-community relations. Faced with resistance from indigenous peasants that limited the hacendados' abilities to exploit new markets, those large landowners who did have access to high *páramo* pasturelands chose to expand livestock raising rather than agricultural production. Thus, these landholders could not expand production as they might have wished, given favorable market conditions, but were constrained by the social relations of production and peasant resistance. The expansion of livestock raising in turn was consistent with both hacienda encroachment on Indian lands and the expulsion of indigenous labor, actions that not only responded to economic rationality but also took on the appearance of punitive measures.

Before we move on, some comment should be made about the expansion of agriculture during these years. The conflicts just analyzed occurred in haciendas that engaged in extensive livestock raising. Although there were important pockets of livestock raising in Alausí, the region was best known for its agricultural production, particularly of lentils, but also of wheat, barley, corn, peas, and broad beans, as well as potatoes at higher altitudes and, at lower ones, sugarcane. By 1924 lentils had become an export product,[56] and other agricultural products were being marketed in other parts of the republic. By 1930 it could be stated that Chimborazo province's "agricultural . . . products, given their superior quality, provision other regions of the Republic and even the exterior. The commercial exchange with the coast is imponderable."[57]

Yet there is no evidence that agricultural expansion created the kinds of immediate land and labor conflicts that the expansion of livestock raising did, possibly because it did not necessarily involve either the expulsion of workers or the expansion of hacienda territories. In fact, it appears that a wide variety of landowners were able to take advantage of the market for agricultural goods. For instance, in May 1924 it was argued that the Indians of Nisag should repair a road in Gonzól because they had destroyed it "with the continual passage of their heavily laden pack animals."[58] However, while the benefits of agricultural intensification may have been more widely distributed than the benefits of livestock expansion, another kind of conflict did emerge associated with this process—serious and continual disputes over access to water. These occurred in areas where properties were somewhat smaller and were dedicated to grain, vegetable, and fruit cultivation that could best be expanded through the increased use of irrigation. One such conflict broke out in 1919 between the inhabitants of Pumallacta and those of Guasuntos. And between 1921 and 1924 a series of conflicts occurred between the Guasunteños and the indigenous communities of Nisag, Zuñac, San Pablo, Tintilag, Alogucho, and Izuay in Guasuntos and the neighboring parishes of Sevilla, Gonzól, and Achupallas. The people of Gonzól as a group—indigenous and white smallholders and villagers—also confronted Nelson Velasco of Hacienda Bugnag when he attempted to privatize the water of a public spring and stream for the use of his estate and insisted that anyone who wanted access to the water would have to work for him three days per week. The people of Gonzól won back access to this water after taking their petition to the minister of the interior and then to court. Similarly, in 1925–26 in Sibambe, there were several disputes over water use between larger landowners and both indigenous communities and white smallholders.

In all cases, the conflicts resulted from attempts to privatize and monopolize water sources that had customarily been held in common. Water was one of the resources needed to intensify agricultural production, and the Ley de Fomento Agrícola included a clause promoting the construction of irrigation works as a strategy to increase yields. Conflicts over access to water were sometimes violent. In November 1921, for example, it was reported that the people of Guasuntos were "attacking and killing the Indians of Sevilla and Nisag" after the Indians had destroyed an aqueduct that the Guasunteños had constructed to channel water toward their farms and therefore away from indigenous lands.[59] However, smallholders and villagers seem to have often won in their conflicts with larger estates over water access, perhaps because this issue drew so many of them

together in common cause. Clearly, access to water is yet another area in which the advantages for some of agricultural expansion came at a cost to others.

Marketing Conflicts and the Ambiguities of Trade

If the agrarian conflicts were centered in the rural areas of the
canton, another set of confrontations involved the zone's more
urbanized population, the inhabitants of the cantonal seat and,
in some cases, the parish seats. These disputes were provoked
by the increased circulation of staple foods such as grains and
potatoes out of their zones of production for the provisioning of
other areas. The Guayaquil-Quito Railway brought new economic "laws" into operation in Alausí. Railway construction, in
association in the late 1910s with new policies to promote the
movement of agricultural and livestock products to the coast,
created newfound access to more distant markets. These economic processes were experienced and interpreted in distinct
ways by people with different social locations. Historian
Florencia Mallon has argued that in Latin America we know a
fair amount about elite debates over economic liberalism and
free trade, but we know much less about how these processes
were experienced at the local level.[60] Alternate visions of economic incorporation were expressed during conflicts in the town
of Alausí, and between Alausí and Tixán, regarding the sale and
movement of grains and potatoes.

At times there were food shortages in Alausí associated with
the provisioning of staple foods to the coast. As early as 1906
(during a highlands drought), the townspeople of Alausí protested against "those who monopolize every article of subsistence, whether of great or small value. When a poor person seeks
something for the sustenance of his family, everything already
rests in the storerooms of such individuals, waiting to be sent to
the coast."[61] Similar complaints were heard in 1913, but they
became more frequent in the 1920s when the zone had become
more closely integrated into national markets, with state policies designed to expand and modernize production and to promote the increased circulation of staple foods.

In early 1925, just before floods destroyed the railway between Bucay and Alausí, the municipal council president of
Alausí reported:

> provisions in general, and especially potatoes, firewood, char-
> coal, eggs, cheeses, etc., are monopolized at the entrances to

the town by three or four middlemen, thus causing general scarcity for the town's residents; that when it comes to potatoes, their price is excessive, given that they are purchased in advance by merchants who send them to Guayaquil and other coastal towns; and meanwhile for the townspeople their price is elevated, beyond the reach of the majority; that every day the meat offered for sale is of worse quality, from scrawny animals that are probably sick; that the bread is of a thoroughly reduced weight.[62]

By 1926, Alausí's police chief had begun to regulate food prices in the town, fixing the prices of basic foods. As a result, a conflict emerged between the villagers of Tixán and the townspeople of Alausí. The political lieutenant of Tixán was accused by the municipal police chief of preventing the provisioning of food to the cantonal seat. However,

> what actually happened yesterday is the following: that the villagers, discovering that there was nothing to buy in our market, proceeded to the outskirts of town to deter the traders of potatoes, barley meal, etc., from going to the town of Alausí to sell them, instead of provisioning the residents here, who offered to pay higher prices than those assigned by the Sr. Municipal Police Chief in Alausí. Given the peaceful attitude of the people here who found themselves without provisions, I could not intervene since no hostile act was committed. With simple entreaties they convinced the merchants to return to the plaza to alleviate their necessities.[63]

The villagers of Tixán could provision themselves only by offering higher prices than those paid in Alausí. The police chief saw this as something like monopoly, since it prevented goods from reaching the Alausí market. The political lieutenant of Tixán, in contrast, saw this movement of goods as the operation of supply and demand. And surely if the police chief had insisted on goods being sent to Alausí despite the relative prices being offered, this would have been perceived in Tixán as monopoly.

Not only did problems arise between parishes and the cantonal seat, but they also occurred between the canton and other regions. Later in 1926, in response to "public clamor," the municipal police chief protested to the provincial governor that the railway station chief "monopolizes every article of primary necessity, leaving the town in absolute shortage."[64] The governor replied that the minister of the interior had passed along orders to the local authorities that they could not prevent food products from being sent out of Alausí and that "in the future you must abstain from any action that implies an obstacle to the liberty of commerce, leaving vendors and consumers in complete freedom to buy and sell."[65]

Finally, in 1930, the president of the railway company complained to the minister of the interior that the municipal police chief had banned the dispatch of potatoes from the town of Alausí.[66] The general manager of the company refused to obey this order, "given that the railway, by its very nature, is always ready to provide facility of transport to whoever requests it," and so the station chief continued to send potato shipments from Alausí to Guayaquil. The company manager recommended that the police chief be instructed "to abstain from issuing orders such as this, which contravene the most elemental principles of commercial exchange." The municipal police chief replied to the governor, who had demanded an explanation:

> in answer to your letter . . . communicating the complaint raised to the Sr. President of the Railway Company by some merchants of this town, claiming that the undersigned has prohibited the embarkation of potatoes to the Stations to the South, I say to you: That certain merchants on market day monopolize the article in question, depriving the public and moreover paying prices that are beyond the means of the poor, prices that have been arranged in advance, in order to guarantee the transaction. As a result, I prohibited the removal of potatoes from the market to the Station while the people provisioned themselves, after which transactions continued without this control. Hence the prohibition is not absolute, but rather aimed at the monopoly that some merchants have achieved over articles of primary necessity.[67]

Thus, he had simply fulfilled his duty, supported by the section of the Police Code that prohibited monopolies.

Despite the fact that there is no evidence for food riots such as those analyzed by E. P. Thompson and Charles Tilly for Europe,[68] it is clear that the removal of food products from the region provoked "public clamor" and popular "entreaties." These outcries were directed at larger merchants, specifically at those who withdrew food from the market before local people had provisioned themselves. In Chapter 5 the term "internal market" is used as if it were a neutral development; here we see how this market's emergence was experienced at the local level. From a broader perspective—certainly from the viewpoint of the minister of the interior—food-provisioning problems in Alausí reflected the operation of the "natural" economic law of supply and demand. Alausí had been brought into the orbit of such a law by its new proximity to markets, facilitated by the railway. This was not merely a spatial development, but a result of the war and postwar conjuncture of social forces. At the local level, however, the same processes did not seem to involve supply and demand at all; rather, they were experienced as monopoly. This monopolizing was perceived to occur when certain merchants paid elevated prices for agricultural products knowing that the products would draw even higher prices on the coast. That temporary control over trade and prices was legislated at moments of recognized *national* crisis—toward the end of World War I and, briefly, with the destruction of the rail line in 1925— lent credence to some local authorities' perception that this was an acceptable strategy at times of *local* shortage. National authorities did not agree.

The conflict in 1930 was particularly interesting in regard to the differing visions of monopoly and supply and demand. What was interpreted by the station chief as an effort by the police chief to monopolize goods was seen by the police chief in precisely the opposite way. During that conflict the railway company manager's reference to the railway as something like a natural proponent of free trade is also telling. It should be noted, however, that the police chief was immediately aware of something that had not been stated in the original petition: that the complaint was initiated by local merchants, and not because of some higher principle about the economic role of the railway. Staple foods were being drained from the region by certain of the canton's larger merchants, who in some cases negotiated in advance with large landowners to purchase their entire crop, at elevated prices.

To understand these conflicts, it is necessary to explore what had happened to marketing in this region over the period studied. As has already been mentioned, many of the local elites who rotated through the political offices of the canton were both merchants and landowners. For many of them, their sales in the canton of local products and of imports of merchandise and beverages from other regions or abroad were firmly rooted in local needs—at least, in the needs of the townspeople, if not of the surrounding rural population. With the increasing incorporation of this zone into national and even international markets, however, there also began to be certain merchants operating in

Alausí and Huigra who were not rooted in local production and consumption.

As early as the 1906 petition discussed earlier, these *shigreros* were identified as those who monopolized commerce. Historian Hernán Ibarra defines *shigreros* as professional merchants who visited highland markets and haciendas to purchase products that would be sent to the coast.[69] These merchants, who began to intensify the commerce between the highlands and coast after railway construction, initiated large-scale commerce by wholesalers rather than the small-scale trade carried out by muleteers in the nineteenth century. These *shigreros* (who had their origin in the small- and medium-size properties of the central highlands) took advantage of the railway to establish commercial links with Milagro, Yaguachi, and Guayaquil. In Guayaquil they had contacts with the Sociedad de Abastecedores del Mercado, a group that was formed by highland migrants to market agricultural products. Ibarra also identifies this group as representing a challenge to the older commercial capital associated with the landowning elite. This elite was increasingly relegated to commerce in luxury goods, as well as attempting to diversify in industrial production, while the *shigreros* undertook trade in textiles and food for the lower classes and in raw materials for artisans.

During the 1910s, merchants from even farther afield arrived in the canton of Alausí. Immigrant merchants began to settle in the cantonal seat and in the village of Huigra, in some cases establishing branch stores of Guayaquil trading companies. These immigrants included a small number of Italian merchants, a somewhat larger number of Syrians, and Chinese, who founded the largest commercial concern of all in the late 1910s. When the Chinese merchants had first settled in Huigra, in early 1913, they were the victims of nocturnal attacks by the local population. Chinese immigrants to Ecuador were especially resented because they bought and sold goods but did not consume local products.

In a petition to the minister of the interior in 1907 regarding the "imminent danger" of the establishment of Chinese merchants in the capital, the merchants of Quito warned: "Being meager consumers, since they [the Chinese] barely feed and clothe themselves, they require only insignificant amounts in order to satisfy their needs. They take advantage of this to drive down wages, depriving a large portion of the population of work. In the same way in their businesses they restrict costs to such extremes that they prevent the legitimate competition of we who must attend to the subsistence of our families and employees under normal conditions. Thus, wherever the Chinese establish themselves, they ruin commerce and all of the manual trades."[70] Essentially, the Chinese limited the cost of their own living expenses to such an extent that they were able to offer their goods at lower prices than the Ecuadorian merchants and still earn a narrow profit. In particular, groups of single Chinese men often lived on the premises of the stores where they worked. For example, the three Chinese who ran the Tay Hong and Company store in Huigra were all single men who lived in the store. To local observers, the fact that they all lived together rather than establishing separate households, requiring greater expenditures in local markets, seemed to be a clear sign of commerce severed from local production and consumption.

At the end of the First World War, and with the passage of the Ley de Fomento Agrícola, commerce in Alausí grew significantly.[71] Between 1918 and 1919 a great increase in trade was registered (see Table 9). While commerce expanded throughout Chimborazo province, it expanded much more in the canton of Alausí than in other areas of the province (see Table 10). The

Table 9. Merchants in Alausí Canton, 1918–1920

Year	Number of Merchants	Capital (total sucres)	Range of Capital (sucres)	Average Capital (sucres)
1918	82	105,900	250–10,000	1,291.46
1919	145	307,600	300–22,000	2,120.00
1920	137	284,300	300–18,000	2,075.18

Sources: Ministro de Hacienda, *Informe que el ministro de hacienda presenta a la nación en 1919* (Quito: Imprenta y Encuadernación Nacional, 1919), 23–24; idem, *Informe que el ministro de hacienda presenta a la nación en 1920* (Quito: Imprenta y Encuadernación Nacional, 1920), 26.

Table 10. Merchants in Chimborazo Province, by Canton, 1918–19

	1918				1919			
Canton	Number of Merchants	%	Capital (sucres)	%	Number of Merchants	%	Capital (sucres)	%
Riobamba	91	36.6	547,400	73.6	98	33.3	842,000	65.3
Alausí	82	32.9	105,900	14.2	145	49.3	307,600	23.9
Colta	60	24.1	56,150	7.5	35	12.0	95,000	7.4
Guano	16	6.4	34,800	4.7	16	5.4	43,500	3.4
Totals	249	100.0	744,250	100.0	294	100.0	1,288,100	100.0

Source: Ministro de Hacienda, *Informe . . . 1919*, 22–24.

figures for 1919 for total commercial capital in the central highlands place Alausí third among the cantons in Chimborazo,
Tungurahua, Cotopaxi, and Bolívar provinces: in first place is
Ambato, the capital of Tungurahua, with 1,013,100 sucres; second, Riobamba, the capital of Chimborazo, with 842,000 sucres;
third, Alausí, with 307,600 sucres; and following at a distance,
Latacunga, the capital of Cotopaxi, with only 159,050 sucres of
commercial capital in circulation.[72] No other central highland
town had more than 100,000 sucres of commercial capital in circulation. Within Chimborazo province, Alausí had 32.9 percent
of the province's merchants and 14.2 percent of its total capital
in 1918; by 1919 this canton was home to 49.3 percent of the
province's merchants, with 23.9 percent of the province's total
commercial capital.

These figures suggest not only absolute growth in the extent and value of commerce but also improved distribution of
commercial opportunities. While only five merchants who were
in business in Alausí canton in 1918 had gone out of business by
1919, an impressive sixty-eight new commercial enterprises had
been established in that time.[73] It is significant that the majority
of the new merchants started with relatively small investments.
While the smallest new business began with 300 sucres,[74] 47 percent of the new businesses (thirty-two of the sixty-eight) began
with 700 sucres or less, and 87 percent of the new businesses
(fifty-nine out of sixty-eight) with 1,500 sucres or less. In contrast, the largest new merchant (a Syrian, Antonio Zaab) began
with 8,000 sucres. In addition, the majority of businesses from
1918 that continued to exist in 1919 expanded their operations;
many of these were small firms that expanded their capital from
500 to 700 sucres. The two that expanded the most, however,
by an increase of 12,000 sucres over their capital the previous
year, were one owned by an Italian, Jorge Rephani (from 6,000
to 18,000 sucres), and the Chinese enterprise of Tay Hong and
Company (from 10,000 to 22,000 sucres).

Although six of the 1918 merchants went out of business in
1919, no other merchant reduced his inventory and capital. Only
one maintained a stable capital investment from 1918 to 1919.
The remaining seventy-six merchants expanded their operations.
But in 1920, fourteen of these businesses closed down, while
only six new ones were established. In addition, seven businesses
reduced their capital, and the other 123 remained the same. This
was the beginning of a scaling back of operations by many
smaller merchants and an increasing concentration of commerce

in the hands of larger ones. By 1930 the number of merchants and "manufacturers" (those who owned "factories" in Alausí) had decreased to eighty.[75] These figures, and the archival documents in general, give a clear impression of a first, heady period in which many townspeople seemed positioned to benefit from increased commerce, followed by a period in which the advantages of commerce were restricted to a smaller group of larger merchants, some of them from elsewhere.

The displacement of merchant-landowners by foreign merchants and by groups such as the *shigreros* occurred throughout the highlands in these years. Ibarra has argued that after 1850 there were merchant-landowners in the central highlands who transferred their agricultural profits to commerce in imported goods (textiles, agricultural implements, luxury items, and some raw materials for artisans) and who established connections with Guayaquil importers.[76] Investment by large landowners in commerce represented a certain diversification of their economic interests, with some minor efforts also at industrialization. With the railway, merchant-landowners who had dominated trade in imported goods until the early twentieth century began to be challenged by new merchant groups operating in the same market with the same products (especially imported textiles). Early in the century immigrant merchants, especially Arabs, Italians, and Chinese, began to settle in the central highlands. There also emerged a group of Ecuadorian merchants of nonelite origin (the *shigreros*) that sold imported goods, national manufactures, and coastal products such as sugar and rice to the highlands and highland agricultural products and hides to the coast. Between these two groups, the merchant-landowners found themselves displaced from commercial dominance. While Alausí was not an area where there had been extensive import-export trade, this zone nonetheless showed some characteristics of the broader picture.

Thus, by the time the marketing conflicts emerged in Alausí, it may have become more evident to some townspeople and villagers that their own interests were not necessarily being served by this expanded commerce and that local priorities were being displaced. In the disagreement over which economic laws were operating (monopoly or free trade), people who lived in the same town, but who inhabited different social locations, argued for the priority of differently defined "communities": local or national. Indeed, it is only from the perspective of a prioritized national community that the removal of products from local markets seemed to involve supply and demand. The "national" perspective was difficult to challenge, however, given that it was expressed in terms of broad principles, rather than in relation to the competing needs of two specific populations (say, Alausí and Guayaquil). In the dispute over which "community" deserved precedence, each side invoked the liberty to trade. What was freedom for some people was constraint for others.

Finally, the local poor may have been affected in this particular set of conflicts, but the effect was limited by the fact that the majority of the canton's inhabitants were rural people who would not have purchased much of their subsistence on the market. It was medium-size merchants who voiced the defense of the local community against larger merchants from elsewhere. Their invocation of community was a political act: they were making a claim about local needs, based on their own social location. If we keep in mind the other conflicts also occurring during these decades, it is clear that the local merchants' defense of the community against outside encroachments was quite selective. Communities are never completed, fully achieved, and internally homogeneous forms that can be taken as given, but are articulations of social relations that are constituted and reconstituted through the exercise of power.[77]

Rethinking Redemption

During the initial period of railway construction, it was not clear that the line would benefit Alauseños. Initially, the railway appeared to pose more of a problem than an opportunity. Early conflicts occurred when construction crews trampled cultivated fields as they conducted land surveys to determine where the line should be built. The railway company was also slow to expropriate the land necessary to lay the tracks, and it may not have been clear at first that people would be paid for the land they lost. The result was the mysterious disappearance of the survey stakes that identified the future location of the line, much to the chagrin of the engineers. Then a grave problem arose for many of the landowners with medium-sized properties in the environs of the cantonal seat: in 1902 construction crews destroyed the municipally owned aqueduct that supplied many of these properties with irrigation water. This destruction led to extended litigation with the railway company, which finally completed a new irrigation canal only in 1920.[78] During this time, the municipality lost thousands of sucres in water taxes, and the properties of several landowners active in local politics were adversely affected. As one of these landowners declared angrily in 1907 about the railway company's intransigence in the negotiations, "What sarcasm to call this a redemptive work, when in fact for this canton, the railway has been a calamity!"[79]

Despite these early doubts, by the end of the first decade of the twentieth century it had become clear that many of the inhabitants of the canton would benefit from the railway. And there is no question that with the construction of the railway through Alausí, this region became incorporated into the national territory in new ways—economically, politically, and socially. These processes continued after our period of study, during the 1930s and 1940s. The Alausí region flourished as Chimborazo province provided the milk, cheese, grains, and potatoes for the Guayas basin. At the junction of travel routes north to Quito, south to Cuenca, and west to Guayaquil, the town of Alausí became a prosperous entrepôt. Not only did products pass through the town, but Alausí also became a meeting place for people from different regions, most notably when Guayaquileños settled there during the rainy season each year. As one Alauseño reflected in 1970, the railway was "a redemptive work for Alausí, placing it in direct contact with the principal centers of commerce and culture and opening up new possibilities for work, production, commerce, and civilization. The railway inaugurated an era of revitalization, above all for agricultural production, whose fruits go to distant markets, especially in the coast, where they find full and preferential reception. But the railroad also brought new people and new challenges of thought and culture from other parts of the Country, opening a renovative horizon in the life of this town."[80]

A persistent sense of dynamism, growth, and change emerges from archival documents in Alausí covering the period from 1895 through 1930. However, the Alausí encountered during research there in 1991–92 was an area in decline, a perception that was widely shared by Alauseños themselves. Townspeople remembered the seasonal migrations of Guayaquileños as the "good old days," when Alausí was more prosperous and when there was much more social activity in town, such as concerts, dances, and movies. Alauseños date the end of the town's heyday to the early 1970s. In general, in the 1960s and 1970s, Guayaquil's dependence on Chimborazo province for foodstuffs declined for a number of reasons.[81] The national government imposed price ceilings on wheat and began to subsidize wheat imports from the United States, rendering uncompetitive the province's more expensive production of national wheat that had been its mainstay. In addition, changes in technology (especially refrigeration) reduced the dependence of the Guayaquil basin on Chimborazo for milk. Furthermore, private capital was increasingly taken out of agriculture and invested instead in the industrial and financial sectors of the economy during the period of import-substitution industrialization. A severe earthquake in 1968 was another serious blow: "Alausí and other towns in this zone were reduced to piles of rubble. Many families left the area, and even though the towns have been rebuilt, they have not regained their earlier prosperity."[82] Finally, just as transportation routes had facilitated the growth of Alausí in the first place, new transportation networks precipitated its decline. The opening of the Quito-Babahoyo-Guayaquil highway meant that the fastest route from the northern highlands to the coast digressed west from Riobamba, leaving Alausí marginalized once again. Similarly, the main route from Cuenca to Guayaquil now turned west well to the south of Alausí. Although the north-south Panamerican Highway passes through Alausí, it does not have nearly as much traffic as the highland-coast routes.

Associated with these processes, there are now few sources of employment for young people in Alausí other than the scarce jobs in government offices or in much-reduced commercial activities. Young people leave to look for work in Riobamba, Quito, or Guayaquil, and they also must go to these cities to pursue postsecondary education. The economic decline of Alausí has also fueled substantial emigration to the United States, where the majority of Alauseños settle in Newark, New Jersey, with smaller numbers going to Stamford, Connecticut, and to Chicago. Nonetheless, just as the images of growth during the liberal period were examined from other perspectives, the image of subsequent marginality should also be deconstructed to some extent. The commercial decline of the zone might also be read as a recovery of subsistence production. In fact, today, medium landowners in the canton date the end of prosperity to the "damage" done to agricultural production by the agrarian reforms of the 1960s and 1970s, although peasants who benefited from those reforms would surely disagree. In addition, the migration of the white/mestizo population to Riobamba, Quito, and the United States may indicate the indigenization of the countryside, which scholars have found for other regions of the highlands over the last two decades.[83] Recent processes are not the focus of this book;

these comments are made to point toward questions for future research.

Thus, the growth of Alausí not only was uneven across social groups and space, but it also was uneven over time. Incorporation is not a unilineal process, wherein region after region is brought into the mainstream, producing a national territory that is homogenized economically, politically, and socially. Instead, on the one hand, there is a continual reorganization of space, with some places becoming incorporated at the expense of others and sometimes with those places subsequently becoming disconnected again. On the other hand, there is a continual reorganization of social relations, a continual production of difference and inequality. The benefits from national incorporation were not equally shared by all social groups. In regard to Alausí, it has been argued that growth and change affected various groups very differently. The railway and the forms of incorporation it entailed transformed the terrain on which people made decisions, but it was their subsequent actions, rooted in past relations and understandings, that reconstituted their relations with other social groups in the region.

Where, then, should the source of social change be sought? It does not lie in technology: the railway did facilitate modifications in the local economy, but only in combination with new emphases in government policy, which in turn were lobbied for by particular social groups (such as the Sociedad Nacional de Agricultura) in the context of a shifting international situation. There is no question that the railway alone was not enough to create an internal market. And within Alausí itself, the particular form that the expansion of production took was the result of class conflict between peasants and hacendados.

Social activity—of the full range of dominant and subordinate groups—was everywhere evident as people made decisions about how to deal with new situations and then attempted to impose their own projects and interests. In this context, distinctions between structure and agency are not very helpful. The relations that constrained people's activities were clearly produced through activity. But this activity must itself be seen as structured, given that people entered into any of the situations discussed in this chapter with already existing differences in social location that dictated whether they would experience a particular situation as an opportunity or as a problem. These differences were not static, however. This was the case, for instance, when peasants became debt peons to escape labor recruitment for municipal public works, in the process engaging state definitions of who was required to work and allying themselves with local hacendados. This was also the case when long-standing indigenous resistance to forced labor recruitment provided part of the framework through which sanitation efforts during plague epidemics were experienced. Determination lies in past struggles, relations, and experiences that in turn constrain how the present will be understood and acted upon. Thus, the past, forged through social practice, constrains the present, although it does not determine it.

Finally, the forms of incorporation experienced by the people of the Alausí region were not only economic, but they were also political and discursive. In the agrarian and marketing conflicts in particular, social groups in Alausí drew on the discourse of the state and the liberal project in order to resist some of their effects at the local level. These represented efforts to stretch the boundaries of central, elite discourses, although different local social groups attempted to stretch them in different directions. In addition, these conflicts reveal local interpretations of what national laws and discourse mean.[84] The various local uses of discourse emanating from the state and elite groups indicate the strength of the language of contention: its basic concepts were both shared and contested, providing the possibility of incorporating, in a restricted way, the aspirations of a wide range of social groups.

Laws and rhetoric from national sources were appropriated in struggles over the marketing of food products: for instance, when local authorities imposed price limits and attempted to control commerce in situations of local scarcity by drawing on regulations that had been used to deal with national scarcity. They were also appropriated in the agrarian conflicts already discussed, not only when large landowners attempted to expand production in accordance with a redefined "national interest" but also when peasants called on the central government to deal with landowner abuses, and to claim their rights as citizens to move freely and to enjoy constitutional guarantees. Interestingly, one of the legal resources that peasants drew on in resisting hacienda expansion was part of the Ley de Fomento Agrícola, the same law that had encouraged and facilitated such expansion in the first place. Although the Ley de Fomento Agrícola had been passed because of lobbying by large landowners, it could also be used against them. One reason that documentation was produced about these conflicts was that the closure of public paths was made subject to fines under the Ley de Fomento Agrícola, which specifically aimed to promote the circulation of agricultural products. Nonetheless, in practice there was a clear difference—one that was not made in the law—between paths that led *out of* haciendas to markets and paths that passed *through* the estates. It was the latter that large landowners were closing down. Given the emphasis in state policy and liberal discourse on the free movement of goods and labor during this period, the argument made by the Indians of Pizhillig, that Sr. Salem prevented their free transit, was no doubt a powerful way to make a claim before the government.

Not only did local Indians use the idiom of citizenship and the freedom of movement in their petitions to higher authorities, but in the 1920s they actually invited state officials into their communities to mediate in their labor disputes with hacendados, something that was unprecedented. In addition, during the 1920s, Indians periodically sent their own representatives to Riobamba and Quito to complain to higher authorities about the abuses of local officials and landowners. This demonstrates the success of the central state in positioning itself as the protector of indigenous rights against the abuses of local powers. Law was central to this project, and law has a peculiar universalizing character in nation-states: once laws are activated, they become powerful resources that can be used by various social groups in ways that might be different from those intended by the groups who promoted them in the first place. After all, if laws promoted the interests of only one limited group, they would lose the power to persuade others of their legitimacy.[85] It is thus that law can become an arena of class struggle as well as of class rule.[86] Law should be seen, then, both as the result of social struggles and as the setting of terms under which subsequent struggles will be conducted. Given these contradictory processes, fraught with unintended consequences, it is important to try to "bring the state back in" in such a way that the people—the actions of subordinate groups in local contexts—are not left out.[87] As Corrigan and Sayer have argued, the state lives in and through its subjects.[88]

Thus, in a wide variety of ways, local relations are not isolated from national processes, but rather are constituted in relation to them. This occurs not only in broad economic terms, but also as people draw on national discursive resources to deal with immediate problems. "Local" here does not mean "isolated," but "particular." As Michel-Rolph Trouillot has argued, a local context, such as a village or a region, "is not a microcosm of the society but a particular configuration in time and space of the processes that affect the nation. It is a 'conjuncture,' an empirical moment in which those processes merge concretely within the daily existence of specific historical actors."[89]

Notes

1. This chapter draws on two local archives in Alausí: the Archivo de la Jefatura Política de Alausí (AJPA) and the Archivo del Concejo Municipal de Alausí (ACMA). Most of the documentation reviewed consisted of correspondence between political and police authorities at various levels. These documents are loosely grouped by year and are identified here by year only. In the case of the ACMA, the minutes of municipal council meetings (libros de actas, LA) are also transcribed in bound volumes. While the processes discussed in this chapter are always identified by year, specific documents are cited only where direct quotes are used, or where the information is drawn from one or two specific documents, rather than based on an overall reading of many local sources.

2. Cristóbal Landázuri N., "Las sociedades indígenas de las cuencas de los ríos Mira y Chanchán, siglos XVI y XVII: Estudios de caso," *Revista de Historia de América* (Mexico) 106 (1988): 49–106.

3. The campaign of Alauseños in the late 1930s to have the canton elevated to the status of a province (to be called "los Andes") then comes as no surprise (see Víctor Rafael Torres, *Provincia central "Los Andes" cuya capital es Alausí* [Alausí: n.p., 1937]). With Alausí's participation in the popular insurrection of May 1944 (La Revolución Gloriosa) that swept President José María Velasco Ibarra back into power for his second administration, Alausí's aspirations seemed close to fulfillment. Velasco Ibarra agreed to make Alausí a province, and several provincial-level institutions, such as the Juzgado Provincial, Juzgado del Crimen, and Subintendencia de Policía, were created in the cantonal seat. Nonetheless, Alausí still has not achieved provincial status.

4. See Clark, "Indians, the State and Law."

5. Political administrator of Alausí to the governor of Chimborazo, Alausí, December 19, 1930, AJPA 1930.

6. Reginald Enock, *Ecuador: Geografía humana* (1914; reprint ed., Quito: Corporación Editora Nacional, 1980), 317.

7. The Sibambe railway station on the banks of the Río Chanchán was built at some distance from the village of Sibambe, located across the river and farther up the mountain.

8. Orellana, *Guía comercial geográfica*, 93.

9. Annual report of the governor of Chimborazo province, in Ministro de lo Interior y Policía, Obras Públicas, etc., *Informe . . . 1903*, no page.

10. *La Unión* (Alausí), August 30, 1914.

11. Rodolfo Maldonado y Basabe, *Monografía de la provincia de Chimborazo* (Riobamba: Imprenta "Nacional," 1930), 126.

12. The figures for 1909 are drawn from Compañía Guía Comercial y Agrícola, *El Ecuador*, 444–45; for 1914, annual report of the governor of

Chimborazo province, in Ministro de lo Interior, Municipalidades, Policía, Obras Públicas, etc., *Informe que Modesto A. Peñaherrera, ministro de lo interior, municipalidades, policía, obras públicas, etc., presenta a la nación en 1914* (Quito: Imprenta y Encuadernación Nacionales, 1914), no page; for 1930, Maldonado y Basabe, *Monografía*, 27.

13. As late as 1933, after suffrage was extended to literate women, only 3.1 percent of the national population voted. Juan Maiguashca and Liisa North, "Orígenes y significado del velasquismo: Lucha de clases y participación política en el Ecuador, 1920–1972," in *La cuestión regional y el poder*, edited by Rafael Quintero (Quito: Corporación Editora Nacional, 1991), 132.

14. Municipal evaluation of Antonio Marquino's petition, Alausí, January 17, 1907, ACMA 1907.

15. Compañía Guía Comercial y Agrícola, *Ecuador*, 450–52.

16. Maldonado y Basabe, *Monografía*, 127; and president of the Sociedad de Obreros de Alausí to the political administrator of Alausí, Alausí, June 2, 1930, AJPA 1930.

17. Budget figures are drawn from the municipal budgets for various years, in the ACMA, supplemented by the annual reports of the governor of Chimborazo province and/or the political administrator of Alausí to the minister of the interior, published as part of his annual reports to congress.

18. Ministro de Hacienda, *Informe que el ministro de hacienda Dr. Alberto Gómez Jaramillo presenta a la nación y a sus representantes al congreso de 1924* (Quito: Talleres Tipográficos del Ministerio de Hacienda, 1924), 70.

19. In contrast, Quito's birth rate in 1912 was 16 percent higher than its mortality rate. Guayaquil's high mortality rate also suggests that all of its spectacular population increase in the late nineteenth and early twentieth centuries must be attributed to migrations. See Pineo, "Guayaquil y su región," 261.

20. Ronn F. Pineo, "Misery and Death in the Pearl of the Pacific: Health Care in Guayaquil, Ecuador, 1870–1925," *Hispanic American Historical Review* 70, no. 4 (1990): 609–37.

21. *La Unión*, January 24, 1915.

22. Indeed, in 1932, Leonidas Plaza settled temporarily in Huigra for health reasons, and it was there that he died in September of that year (Maldonado Obregón, *Historia del ferrocarril*, 88).

23. Assistant, Public Health Service, to the political administrator of Alausí, Alausí, April 9, 1913, AJPA 1913.

24. Ayudante de la Dirección de Sanidad Pública, "Informe que sobre la campaña sanitaria contra la peste bubónica, en las poblaciones de Huigra y Alausí, presenta el ayudante de la dirección de sanidad pública," in *Informe que Modesto A. Peñaherrera, ministro de lo interior, municipalidades, policía, obras públicas, etc., presenta a la nación en 1913* (Quito: Imprenta y Encuadernación Nacionales, 1913), 298.

25. Municipal council session, April 23, 1913, ACMA LA-1913.

26. And conversely, funds for sanitation were the only funds that Alausí received from the national budget between 1895 and the reorganization of national finances after 1925 (directed by the Princeton economist Edward Kemmerer; for more information, see Paul W. Drake, *The Money Doctor in the Andes: The Kemmerer Missions, 1923–1933* [Durham,

NC: Duke University Press, 1989]). At the end of the 1920s the national budget provided some assistance for the installation of an electricity plant in the cantonal seat and initial funds toward construction of a hospital, which was not completed until a decade later.

27. Governor of Chimborazo to the political administrator of Alausí, Riobamba, July 20, 1914, AJPA 1914.

28. Three separate police forces operated in Ecuador during this period: the municipal police, the national police, and the railway police. The national police were the "order and security police" (*policía de orden y seguridad*), responsible for the investigation of crimes and, generally, for the maintenance of public order. The "ambulant railway police" (*policía ambulante del ferrocarril*) was set up to patrol the rail line through an agreement between the Ecuadorian government and the railway company.

29. Ayudante de la Dirección de Sanidad, *Informe. . . 1913*, 299.

30. Political lieutenant of Huigra to the political administrator of Alausí, Huigra, March 14, 1914, AJPA 1914.

31. Municipal police chief of Alausí to the political administrator of Alausí, Alausí, January 14, 1927, AJPA 1927.

32. This was admitted in regard to smallpox vaccination in 1917; see Director de Sanidad Pública, "Informe de la dirección del servicio de sanidad pública al señor ministro de lo interior y sanidad, 1916–1917," in *Informe que el ministro de lo interior, policía, obras públicas, municipalidades, etc., presenta a la nación, 1917* (Quito: Imprenta y Encuadernación Nacionales, 1917), 463–76. Although little is known about how the vaccination program in Alausí was carried out, a possible clue is offered by Hugo Burgos's description of an obligatory smallpox vaccination program undertaken in 1968 among indigenous peasants in the rural areas around Riobamba. First, vaccinators prepared to enter indigenous communities, having taken the precaution of arranging a signal to warn each other of uprisings: they would fire their guns in the air (making it clear that they were armed). The Indians did resist, so the vaccinators decided to wait outside the parish seat on Sundays, when Indians came down from their communities for Mass. As an informant told Burgos, "They caught the Indians like animals when they came down to Mass and they vaccinated them in the road, hitting and kicking them" (Hugo Burgos Guevara, *Relaciones interétnicas en Riobamba*, 329). We can assume that the program undertaken in Alausí in the 1910s was equally unpleasant.

33. See Clark, "Indians, the State and Law."

34. In 1906 the part-time position of municipal physician was created, with a small salary paid by the municipality, to attend to the poor. Concern with the health of the poor population was particularly evident in the case of contagious diseases that threatened the white townspeople.

35. Municipal physician to the president of the municipal council of Alausí, Alausí, November 3, 1920, ACMA 1920.

36. Alan Sears, " 'To Teach Them How to Live': The Politics of Public Health from Tuberculosis to AIDS," *Journal of Historical Sociology* 5, no. 1 (1992): 61–83.

37. For a further consideration of these issues see A. Kim Clark, "Género, raza y nación: La protección a la infancia en el Ecuador (1915–1945)," in *Palabras del silencio: Las mujeres latinoamericanas y su historia*,

edited by Martha Moscoso (Quito: Abya Yala, DGIS-Holanda and UNICEF, 1995), 219–56.

38. Director, Public Health Service, to the political administrator of Alausí, Quito, April 28, 1927, AJPA 1927. It should be noted that this project, in principle, went far beyond the mere entrance of the state into the private sphere: it represented an effort to reorganize domestic spaces thoroughly. While this normalizing project was not fully implemented in the period examined here, more sustained efforts to carry it out came in the 1930s and 1940s.

39. Eduardo Archetti, *El mundo social y simbólico del cuy* (Quito: CEPLAES, 1992); M. J. Weismantel, *Food, Gender and Poverty in the Ecuadorian Andes* (Philadelphia: University of Pennsylvania Press, 1988).

40. National police chief of Alausí to the political administrator of Alausí, Alausí, May 15, 1922, AJPA 1922.

41. Ibid., June 21, 1922, AJPA 1922.

42. Petition from the Indians of Pizhillig and Quisla to the political administrator of Alausí, Alausí, September 2, 1919, AJPA 1919.

43. Wilfrido C. Puyol to the president of the cantonal junta of agricultural development of Alausí, Alausí, July 9, 1922, AJPA 1922.

44. Ezequiel Bermeo to the president of the cantonal junta of agricultural development of Alausí, Alausí, (n.d.) 1923, AJPA 1923.

45. Maldonado y Basabe, *Monografía*, 24.

46. Those large landowners who began to specialize in the production of dairy products in the 1910s, especially in Cotopaxi and Pichincha provinces, were precisely those who were praised as thoroughly modern (see chap. 5). Not only did they mechanize their farms and import livestock and pasture seeds but some of them also eliminated debt peonage on their own initiative before congress did so in 1918. We can assume that they voluntarily eliminated debt peonage due to their diminishing need for labor.

47. The spaces for negotiation and mutual constraint that existed in large estates have been explored by Andrés Guerrero in *La semántica de la dominación.*

48. Gavin Smith, *Livelihood and Resistance: Peasants and the Politics of Land in Peru* (Berkeley: University of California Press, 1989).

49. Based on evidence from Cotopaxi and Pichincha where dairy production expanded in areas with proximity to the railway. See Arcos and Marchán, "Apuntes"; and Trujillo, *La hacienda serrana.*

50. Alexandra Martínez Flores, "El conflicto hacienda-comunidad en la sierra norte: El caso de Paniquinra (Imbabura), 1841–1919," *Memoria* (Quito) 1, no. 1 (1990): 153–67.

51. See Patricia de la Torre Arauz, *Patrones y conciertos: Una hacienda serrana, 1905–1929* (Quito: Corporación Editora Nacional and Abya Yala, 1989); Guerrero, *La semántica de la dominación*; Martínez Flores, "El conflicto hacienda-comunidad"; Fernando Rosero Garcés, "Comunidad, hacienda y estado: Un conflicto de tierras en el período de las transformaciones liberales," *Ecuador Debate* (Quito) 12 (1986): 163–87. In haciendas owned by modernizing landowners in provinces closer to Quito, conflicts occurred somewhat earlier because they began to modernize on their own initiative before the late-1910s crisis began, and they were provisioning the urban

market of Quito rather than that of Guayaquil. Also, the modernization processes promoted by the Ley de Fomento Agrícola did not have the same effect in areas, such as the southern highlands, that were not crossed by the railway and were therefore farther from Quito and Guayaquil (Martha Moscoso, verbal communication, Quito, December 2, 1993).

52. It is tempting to attribute rural conflict to ruptures of a dehistoricized "moral economy" or, in Andean cases, of the principles of Andean "reciprocity" (see the criticism of the misuses of moral economy in Roseberry, *Anthropologies and Histories*, chap. 8). While reciprocity may have deep roots among Andean peoples, it can be used as a cultural resource to a variety of ends in historically specific fields of social relations. For examples of different uses of reciprocal exchanges see Benjamin Orlove, "Inequality among Peasants: The Forms and Uses of Reciprocal Exchange in Andean Peru," in *Peasant Livelihood*, edited by R. Halperin and J. Dow (New York: St. Martin's Press, 1977), 201–14; Michael Painter, "Re-creating Peasant Economy in Southern Peru," in *Golden Ages, Dark Ages: Imagining the Past in Anthropology and History*, edited by Jay O'Brien and William Roseberry (Berkeley: University of California Press, 1991), 81–106; Tristan Platt, *Estado boliviano y ayllu andino: Tierra y tributo en el norte de Potosí* (Lima: Instituto de Estudios Peruanos, 1982); and Smith, *Livelihood and Resistance*.

53. Clark, "Indians, the State and Law"; Martha Moscoso, "La tierra: Espacio de conflicto y relación entre el estado y la comunidad en el siglo XIX," in *Los Andes en la encrucijada*, edited by Heraclio Bonilla (Quito: Libri Mundi and FLACSO, 1991), 367–90; Silvia Palomeque, "Estado y comunidad en la región de Cuenca en el siglo XIX: Las autoridades indígenas y su relación con el estado," in *Los Andes en la encrucijada*, 391–418.

54. Guerrero, *La semántica de la dominación*, argues that the debts accumulated by *peones conciertos* were neither payable nor collectable. Instead, they guaranteed a stable labor force for the landowner and facilitated a better standard of living for the peasant.

55. National police chief of Alausí to the political administrator of Alausí, Alausí, July 21, 1922, AJPA 1922.

56. Indirect evidence that new varieties of lentils were being introduced into the region after the passage of the Ley de Fomento Agrícola also exists. In the early 1920s landowners from Alausí sent samples of lentils to the Ministry of Agriculture's experimental farm for testing to determine the nature of a new disease that had attacked the crop and how to prevent its spread. The appearance of crop diseases was common with the introduction of varieties that were not adapted to local patterns of climate, precipitation, and disease. The establishment of experimental farms in this era was aimed in part to assist in the adaptation of new varieties to local conditions. It is likely that the appearance of crop diseases in this conjuncture indicates the introduction of new crop varieties in the zone.

57. Maldonado y Basabe, *Monografía*, 31.

58. Political lieutenant of Gonzól to the political administrator of Alausí, Gonzól, May 15, 1924, AJPA 1924.

59. Political lieutenant of Sevilla to the political administrator of Alausí, Sevilla, November 5, 1921, AJPA 1921.

60. Florencia Mallon, "Economic Liberalism: Where We Are and Where We Need to Go," in *Guiding the Invisible Hand: Economic Liberalism and the State in Latin America*, edited by Joseph L. Love and Nils Jacobsen (New York: Praeger, 1988), 185. For elite debates see the other essays in Love and Jacobsen, *Guiding the Invisible Hand*; Paul Gootenberg, *Between Silver and Guano: Commercial Policy and the State in Postindependence Peru* (Princeton: Princeton University Press, 1989); idem, *Imagining Development*. For local perceptions of economic liberalism see Tristan Platt, "Divine Protection and Liberal Damnation: Exchanging Metaphors in Nineteenth-Century Potosí (Bolivia)," in *Contesting Markets: Analyses of Ideology, Discourse and Practice*, edited by Roy Dilley (Edinburgh: Edinburgh University Press, 1992), 131–58.

61. Petition from the townspeople of Alausí to the municipal council, Alausí, May 1906, ACMA 1906.

62. Municipal council president to the municipal police chief, Alausí, March 16, 1925, ACMA 1925.

63. Political lieutenant of Tixán to the political administrator of Alausí, Tixán, May 3, 1926, AJPA 1926.

64. Municipal police chief of Alausí to the governor of Chimborazo, Alausí, October 17, 1925, ACMA 1925.

65. Governor of Chimborazo to the political administrator of Alausí, Riobamba, October 28, 1925, AJPA 1925.

66. Ibid., May 6, 1930, AJPA 1930.

67. Municipal police chief to the political administrator of Alausí, Alausí, May 15, 1930, AJPA 1930.

68. E. P. Thompson, "The Moral Economy"; idem, "The Moral Economy Reviewed"; Charles Tilly, "Food Supply and Public Order in Modern Europe," in *The Formation of National States in Western Europe*, edited by Charles Tilly (Princeton: Princeton University Press, 1975), 380–455.

69. Ibarra, "Ambato," 273–74.

70. Petition from the merchants of Quito to the minister of the interior, Quito, November 6, 1907 (in *Registro Oficial*, November 19, 1907). See also the report from the governor of Guayas to the minister of foreign relations and justice, July 9, 1909, in *Registro Oficial*, August 2, 1909.

71. Comparative data from 1909 are available, but they should be read cautiously since they seem to include only merchants with a minimum of 1,000 sucres of capital. These data are summarized in the table below (excluding Achupallas, which was not included in the 1909 information):

Merchants in Alausí Canton, by Parish, 1909

Parish	Number of Merchants	Total Capital (sucres)	Range of Capital (sucres)	Average Capital (sucres)
Alausí	13	34,500	1,000–5,000	2,653.85
Huigra	6	26,500	1,000–10,000	4,416.67
Sibambe	8	9,000	1,000–1,500	1,125.00
Tixán	6	11,000	1,000–3,000	1,833.33
Chunchi	4	6,500	1,000–2,000	1,625.00
Guasuntos	5	6,500	1,000–2,000	1,300.00

Pumallacta	2	3,000	1,000–2,000	1,500.00
Totals	44	97,000		

Source: Compañía Guía Comercial y Agrícola, *Ecuador*, 448–49.

72. Ibarra, "Ambato," 267.

73. Ministro de Hacienda, *Informe . . . 1919*, 23–24; and *Informe . . . 1920*, 26.

74. To set these figures in context, the political administrator earned approximately 100 sucres per month, but he would usually also have had earnings from his property, commerce, or profession. In addition to his private practice, the municipal physician earned 80 sucres per month for treating the poor. Artisans, when they worked by day rather than by project, earned 1 sucre daily. Day laborers usually earned 20 centavos per day. Market vendors—that is, not the white, usually male, merchants who started new businesses in this period but the poor, illiterate market women selling small quantities of agricultural produce—earned net profits of 15 to 20 centavos per day.

75. Maldonado y Basabe, *Monografía*, 127.

76. Ibarra, "Ambato," 270–74.

77. Doreen Massey, "Places and Their Pasts," *History Workshop Journal* 39 (1995): 182–92.

78. Initially the municipality requested a 20,000-sucre indemnification for damages, while the company's first offer was 500 sucres. Eventually the company did come close to paying the full amount originally demanded by the municipality.

79. Municipal council session, February 21, 1907, ACMA LA-1907.

80. Ermel de la Cruz, *Alausí en marcha* (Quito: Editorial "La Unión," 1970), 26.

81. Barbara C. Schroder, "Haciendas, Indians, and Economic Change in Chimborazo, Ecuador" (Ph.D. diss., Rutgers University, 1984), 39.

82. De la Cruz, *Alausí en marcha*, 20–21.

83. Hernán Carrasco, "Democratización de los poderes locales y levantamiento indígena," in *Sismo etnico en el Ecuador: Varias perspectivas*, edited by CEDIME (Quito: CEDIME and Abya Yala), 29–69; Andrés Guerrero, "El levantamiento indígena de 1994: Discurso y representación política," *Memoria* (Quito) 5 (1995): 89–123; Galo Ramón, *El regreso de los runas: La potencialidad del proyecto indio en el Ecuador contemporáneo* (Quito: COMUNIDEC and Fundación Interamericana, 1993); Galo Ramón, coord., *Actores de una década ganada: Tribus, comunidades y campesinos en la modernidad* (Quito: COMUNIDEC and Abya Yala, 1992); León Zamosc, *Estadística de las áreas de predominio étnico de la sierra ecuatoriana: Población rural, indicadores cantonales y organizaciones de base* (Quito: Abya Yala, 1995).

84. Roseberry, "Hegemony and the Language of Contention"; see also Linda J. Seligman, "The Burden of Visions amidst Reform: Peasant Relations to Law in the Peruvian Andes," *American Ethnologist* 20, no.1 (1993): 25–51.

85. Thompson, *Whigs and Hunters*.

86. Corrigan and Sayer, "How the Law Rules," 21–53; Sayer, *The Violence of Abstraction*.

87. Gilbert M. Joseph and Daniel Nugent, "Popular Culture and State Formation in Revolutionary Mexico," in *Everyday Forms of State Formation: Revolution and the Negotiation of Rule in Modern Mexico*, edited by Gilbert M. Joseph and Daniel Nugent (Durham, NC: Duke University Press, 1994), 12–15. Compare Peter D. Evans, Dietrich Rueschemeyer, and Theda Skocpol, eds., *Bringing the State Back In* (Cambridge: Cambridge University Press, 1985).

88. Corrigan and Sayer, *The Great Arch*; Derek Sayer,"Everyday Forms of State Formation: Some Dissident Remarks on 'Hegemony,' " in Joseph and Nugent, *Everyday Forms of State Formation*, 367–77.

89. Michel-Rolph Trouillot, *Peasants and Capital: Dominica in the World Economy* (Baltimore: Johns Hopkins University Press, 1989), 184–85.

7

Beyond the Reach of Liberal Discourse

The Railway as a Source of Materials

Beyond the symbolic import and long-term economic and political effects of railway construction, the railway's appeal was as a physical object that could be appropriated for local use. The physical material of the rail line thus can be seen as an aggregate of highly valued resources for local economies, both during and after construction. Although in some cases it was possible to purchase certain items from the railway company, in many cases materials were stolen.

One of the most spectacular thefts of the fixed material of the railway occurred in 1903 when Bridge No. 66 disappeared overnight.[1] More often, however, theft involved the less dramatic pilfering of materials. For instance, wooden railway ties were of considerable use at the local level because they were often made of hardwood from the coast, not easily available in the highlands. (This would change after the railway was completed, when the massive movement of construction materials became possible.) In the town of Alausí, for instance, railway ties could be stolen during the construction period after 1902, when they were piled up at the train station waiting to be moved to the work site. In 1904 a local carpenter went on trial for the theft of wood that clearly belonged to the railway.[2] The value of the wood was only 12 sucres, but the case is interesting for what it reveals about how common was the stealing of ties. The carpenter and his workers testified that the wood, which they agreed had probably belonged to the railway company, had been supplied to them, piece by piece, by five different people, including the parish priest of one of the outlying villages. They insisted, too, that it was common knowledge that there were railway ties belonging to the company in the majority of houses in town. Rumor also had it that the source of these ties was an agent of the Ambulant Railway Police, who delivered it late at night to various tradesmen.

The railway also "supplied" other resources useful in local economies. The spikes that held the rails to the wooden ties were one such resource. In 1919 it was discovered that one hundred spikes had been removed from the rails just south of the town of Alausí.[3] Similarly, in 1923, spikes and pins were pulled up from three kilometers of track outside Ambato and sold to a local blacksmith.[4] In addition, a box of dynamite was stolen from one of the construction camps of the railway to Cuenca in October 1921.[5] These kinds of problems continued throughout the period under study, so that in 1930 the railway company lawyer complained that "it is alarming to see the frequency with which damages are caused to the railway line, with the intention of taking advantage of its materials. On repeated occasions there are robberies of the locks that secure the changes, [and of] the rails of the line, and the audacity of the delinquents even reaches the extreme of removing pieces of wood from the railway bridges."[6]

The railway also required a communications system that would allow the coordination of its trains and schedules.[7] By 1915, Ecuador had over 3,500 miles of telegraph lines,[8] and by 1926 the system had been extended to 6,000 miles.[9] One result was that the state could send orders more quickly and, in general, could govern more effectively through the rapid exchange of information. On the local level one sees a different result of the installation of telegraph and telephone systems: access to the new and often "renewable" resource of wire. Indeed, the state found it very difficult to maintain communications systems in working order because of the theft of wire, so that national and provincial authorities repeatedly ordered local officials to maintain a constant vigilance over the telegraph and telephone lines. By 1917 the theft of telegraph wire had become a serious problem for railway operation, provoking the company to officially complain to the minister of the interior and public works. Central authorities were aware that numerous individuals had pieces of the wire, and they made insistent appeals to and threats against local authorities to get them to collect the stolen material. In 1927 in the Alausí region, political lieutenants conducted a series of raids on indigenous communities in pursuit of telephone wire. However, "none could be found, except a couple of little pieces of no more than two or three meters in the huts of two Indians, but very old wire that they were using as clotheslines."[10] The authorities might have been more successful had they looked elsewhere for the wire: in one parish, an entire roll was found in the house of a former political lieutenant. In addition to telegraph and telephone wire, the wooden posts that supported the wires were often removed and used for firewood. Telephone line insulators were also stolen. In this context, it is understandable that telegraph offices usually had two permanent employees, an operator and a repairman.

These were not merely local problems. In 1917 the annual report of the general director of telegraphs to the minister of mail and telegraphs included a long section dealing with the theft of wire. The general director declared that these robberies were increasing to such an extent that they had become endemic, and he requested new legal provisions to allow him and his agents to punish these crimes more swiftly. In the previous year, they had managed to arrest and convict two people for stealing wire, but these had been the only convictions since the foundation of the telegraph. He also requested funds to reproduce portraits of those convicted, which would be posted in all of the telephone and telegraph offices in the national territory, "with the objectives of educating the neighborhood and striking fear in delinquents." As he pointed out, "All Ecuadorians have the strict duty of watching out for the proper conservation of the telegraph and telephone lines, since they represent a general benefit . . . thus I recommend that the appropriate authorities (including teachers in primary and high schools, priests in their parishes, and political lieutenants in the civil parishes), be encouraged to educate the public about their duties, by means of verbal explanations, chats, and admonishments, circulars, and so on."[11]

While evidence of the pilfering of materials is abundant in local archives, there are limits to what this information can reveal. It is certain that many kinds of materials were scarce in local economies, especially materials from other regions or available only through the international market. In addition to materials stolen from the railway company, other materials were purchased from the company. Article 10 of the 1897 contract between the Ecuadorian government and the Guayaquil and Quito Railway Company authorized the latter to import any materials it required for the construction or operation of the railway, free of customs duties. While it was also possible for municipalities and schools to apply for duty-free status for specific goods, greatly reducing their cost, the process involved was highly bureaucratic. However, imports destined for the railway company cleared customs rapidly, in as little as a month and a half, as compared with a year or more for municipal goods (and this dating from the time when the goods actually arrived in Ecuadorian ports).

Given the relative difficulties that Ecuadorians had in importing goods, government officials often obtained such goods from the railway company once those items were on national territory. Thus, in 1903 the railway company lent to the army the wooden frames and canvas to make tents, during one of its mobilizations. In the same period the company sold dynamite to the provincial government in Riobamba to be used in public works construction as well as for blasting local trails in the parish of Achupallas. In 1919 the municipality of Alausí bought a winch from the company building the railway from Sibambe to Cuenca. No doubt there were other similar purchases. Moreover, the company made old rails available for local bridge building throughout the period under consideration, and one can still see bridges around Alausí built on old rails for supports. In addition, along the Panamerican Highway throughout the central highlands there are upright rails serving as telephone poles. Thus, the railway provided many materials that might otherwise not have been available, and traces of these can still be seen inscribed on the Ecuadorian landscape.

What does the theft of materials tell us about local perceptions of the national project as embodied in the railway? Without additional information, we cannot regard these thefts as deliberate sabotage or, even more romantically, as resistance to capitalism or to the state. Nonetheless, it can be safely argued that these thefts reveal an alienation from the perspective of elites and the state about the importance of the railway. Despite continual assertions by central state officials—amounting almost to a mantra—that the railway was a redemptive work and of utmost importance to national progress and development, clearly not everyone believed that he or she had a stake in this grand project. And, as Chapter 6 pointed out, not everyone would profit from it in equal measure.

Besides the pilfering of materials by the local populace, there were numerous suggestions that lower-level political and police authorities either were directly involved in or otherwise profited from such robberies. Certainly, many local authorities were at least remiss in their duty to punish thefts of railway materials.[12] Their reluctance to do so was the cause of great frustration for the chief of the railway police, who did not himself have the authority to punish criminals; he could only investigate robberies and turn the guilty parties over to local authorities in the jurisdiction where the crimes had taken place. He found repeatedly that the thieves were set free without punishment. For local officials and police agents, railway construction probably just added more ways for them to profit from their positions, whether by stealing materials themselves or by participating in labor recruitment. The alienation of local officials from the liberal project may well have been associated, whether consciously or not, with the fact that the overall project of the liberal state involved an undermining of the independence of local officials and a strengthening of the central state (see Chapter 4).

Railway Company Profits and Practices

If there was pilfering from "below," in a sense there was also pilfering from "above," as the railway company made a good portion of its profits from rather dubious practices during the construction of the line. The railway operated at a profit only for a brief period in the 1920s, and again in the 1940s. If in some cases local populations proved to be insensitive to the broader significance of the railway, the company itself was similarly unaffected by the reveries of Ecuadorian elites and the state about the redemptive qualities of the project.

Some of the questionable practices engaged in by the railway company were the result of inadequacies of the initial construction contract. For instance, in article 21 of the original contract of 1897, the company was granted free use of any existing roads and bridges that it might need for the rail line; and, in fact, south of Guamote in Chimborazo province, the railroad occupied entirely the road built under García Moreno, rendering it useless for transit.[13] When the minister of public works objected to the destruction of the wagon road in 1903, Archer Harman responded that the company would exchange its right to use such roads and bridges if a financial clause in the contract was altered. Thus, it was agreed that for the remainder of the line (between Colta and Quito) the railway company would not use national roads, paths, or bridges and that the roads or paths crossed by the railway line would be left in perfect condition for transit.

After the rainy season caused damage to the line in early 1900, the company had agreed to increase the grade of the line significantly in exchange for the assurance that the principal line would run through Riobamba. Although the steep grade represented a significant shortcut in time and money for the company, it created problems for national commerce since only 45 tons of cargo per train could be moved up the line from the coast to the highlands (150 tons could be moved in the opposite direction). Nonetheless, the company did not fulfill its commitment to run the main line through Riobamba until 1924.[14]

Other company practices were more clearly outright violations of its contract. For instance, when the railway reached Quito in 1908, much of the line had been improvised, and the government refused to accept it as the first-class railway that had been contracted. Among other things, it lacked some of the supporting masonry, and it included secondhand material from railways in Panama and Costa Rica. As German traveler Hans Meyer observed as he rode along the line in 1903: "I have frequently examined the line and it is readily apparent that the railway company has fulfilled the deadlines stipulated in the contract by sacrificing the work's solidity. It is regarded in the following way, as one of the engineers who accompanied us explained, laughing: 'The most important thing is that the locomotive arrive in Quito by a certain date; then the government will take responsibility for the line, or we will run it with a financial guarantee from the government, and at that point all of the defects and poor construction can be repaired, at the state's cost.' "[15] (The government granted the company two years to improve the line in the "transaction contract" of 1908).

Other problems resulted from the company accountants' inclination toward "creative bookkeeping." In the original contract a distinction was made between construction expenses and operating expenses. The former were to be paid by the company, while the latter were to be paid from the revenues of railway traffic, with the government making up any deficit. It soon became clear that the company was hiding its profits. Subcontracting companies (of which Archer Harman and his associates were stockholders) were employed to provide various services to the railway. These companies made profits while the railway company itself remained forever on the verge of bankruptcy. Unwarranted charges were also attributed to "operating expenses": everything from Harman's yacht (fueled with the railway's coal), to a luxurious head office in New York, to extravagant salaries for the American directors and employees, to trips abroad.[16] When the Ecuadorian government attempted in 1925 to get the company to repair the railway, which had been damaged by landslides between Tixán and Bucay, the government's conditions for approving financing for the repairs included the elimination of the company's office in New York, the payment of all railway employees in Ecuadorian currency, and an equalization of the salaries of Ecuadorian and U.S. employees.[17]

In Ecuador, there was growing concern among the public, the press, and the government about company practices and the quality of railway service, gradually intensifying over time. During the 1910s the government periodically requested that the Office of Foreign Bondholders in London send out an independent accountant to audit the company's books.[18] The railway had been constructed primarily with British financing; and, under the terms of the renegotiation of Ecuador's foreign debt carried out by Archer Harman in order to finance the railway, the U.S.-based Guayaquil and Quito Railway Company was the primary debtor to the British, while the Ecuadorian government was simply the guarantor of the debt. Periodically, payments to the Foreign Bondholders were suspended, which put British diplomats in Ecuador in a difficult position since they had an explicit policy of showing to Ecuador a "united front" with the United States, at least in political matters. In 1919 the British Foreign Office and the Foreign Bondholders agreed not to foreclose on the railway after the State Department in Washington lobbied on the company's behalf, and the British consul in Quito submitted to the Foreign Office a long, detailed report about the status of the railway company in Ecuador.[19]

The British consul's report confirmed many of the Ecuadorian government's claims about railway company practices. The main points of the report were: first, that it was important to remember that it was the Guayaquil and Quito Railway Company and not the Ecuadorian government that was responsible for payment of the bonds and that the Office of Foreign Bondholders had previously recognized the responsibility of the railway company in this matter; second, that "the Americans running the railway company are thoroughly corrupt; they do in fact make profits on the railway company, but they manage to conceal them, with the result that they never make any contribution whatever toward paying the Bondholders"; third, that it was essential to examine the company's accounts directly, because the railway management had a close relationship with many Ecuadorian businesses, which would make it difficult to obtain witnesses against the company; and fourth, that to put pressure on the Ecuadorian government through diplomatic channels to make it pay interest on the bonds would be just what the company wanted as well as being unfair to the government, which had already indebted itself to provide funds to the company. The British Consul was concerned that a decision to pressure the Ecuadorian government in this matter would "react prejudicially upon His Majesty's Government's reputation for fair play."

These kinds of reports had little effect. In 1923 the British consul in Quito continued to see the railway as "a standing disgrace to the owners of it (the Americans) who have done nothing but exploit this country since President Alfaro was foolish enough to entrust Mr. Harman with the construction of the line. . . . The Guayaquil and Quito Railway is . . . the most miserable apology for a railway that exists, either in South or Central America, and that is saying a good deal. Enormous sums have been contributed, but could not have been applied to its construction."[20] Indeed, at no point was the railway company willing to admit fault. In 1924 the company president, Archer Shunk Harman (John Harman's son, and heir to his uncle Archer), suggested that what was needed to resume bond payments was that measures be taken to strengthen the Ecuadorian sucre, after which all problems would be solved.[21] He was convinced that if exports were increased sufficiently to create a favorable balance of trade, thus stabilizing the sucre, exchange rates would return to "normal," and the company would be able to "relieve the Government of more and more of the burden of the present foreign debt." The problem for Harman was that the railway's revenues were collected in Ecuadorian sucres, while bond payments had to be made in foreign currency. However, the exchange rate for Ecuadorian currency was never again to reach "normal" (which Harman considered to be the stable rate of exchange prior to the war, approximately two sucres per dollar), despite the extensive changes in fiscal policy recommended by economist Edwin Kemmerer in Ecuador after the 1925 July Revolution.[22]

There is also evidence that the service offered by the railway was not what Ecuadorians had hoped it would be. As the governor of Chimborazo province reported to the minister of the interior in 1914, striking just the right balance between the importance of the railway and its inadequacies, "The service of the railway leaves a great deal to be desired, due to low-quality rolling stock that is completely lacking in comfort for the traveler, as well as the frequent interruptions in traffic due to the line's imperfections and the constant crumbling of the retaining walls that support the tracks. This redemptive work, which despite its deficiencies has stimulated the country's progress in an astonishing manner, demands special legislation to remedy the innumerable complaints that are made daily by those who enjoy its benefits."[23]

As early as July 1907, when it became clear that the company would not finish railway construction to Quito in the time allotted by the original contract, the British consul in Quito reported confidentially to the Foreign Office that "if the Ecuadorian government should decide to take over the railway, they will find themselves with a real White Elephant."[24] In 1913 the new British consul in Quito stated that "the treatment at present shown by the Company to the Public would not be tolerated in any other country in the world."[25] The commonest complaints about the railway service included the fact that the trains seldom arrived on schedule, usually because the locomotives had broken down. In addition, the freight service was considered terrible by merchants and agriculturalists, and goods took up to two weeks to travel between Guayaquil and Quito in the early 1920s. It was suggested that a weekly through passenger service from the coast to the capital would be much more convenient since passengers were required to spend the night in Riobamba, which raised the price of the trip. However, this service would have required strengthening the track, which otherwise would not support greater speeds because of its faulty construction.[26]

In the early 1920s the railway company had increased tariffs by 25 percent, with the promise that this revenue would be dedicated to making bond payments, but instead had treated the money raised as profit. When in 1925 the company proposed to raise tariffs another 25 percent to repair the line, the Ecuadorian government refused to approve the plan. The government argued that tariffs were already too high, and it made it clear that it had lost faith in the company's promises about how the revenue generated would be used.[27] The impossibility of arriving at an agreement with the company to repair the line led the Ecuadorian government to purchase the railway's controlling interest. While the company had estimated that the damage would take two years and two million sucres to repair, the government restored the line in a few months, at a cost of three hundred thousand sucres.[28]

In view of the preceding discussion, one is tempted to conclude that there was an element of poetic justice in Archer Harman's death in Virginia in October 1911 as a result of being thrown from his favorite horse, named "Ecuador."[29] To be fair, however, while Harman appears to have become involved with the Ecuadorian railway as an adventurer, it went on to become his life's work, just as it did for his friend, Eloy Alfaro. The contradiction lies in the fact that the profit-making objectives of the U.S. company were in many ways incompatible with the much broader project of the Ecuadorian government and elites. For instance, the effort to use the railway to forge an internal market would have been facilitated by low tariffs, which were clearly not in the interests of the company. The wide-ranging national project of political, economic, social, and moral redemption that Ecuadorian elites saw embodied in the railway was a far cry from the opportunities for profit that the company perceived.

Ecuadorian public opinion was frequently aroused against the railway company during the construction period, as it met few of its deadlines, requested additional emergency funds, and, after negotiating favorable contract changes from the government, still did not fulfill its own responsibilities (such as running the main line through Riobamba). Perhaps the very fact that the railway company caused controversy meant that it served as a rallying point for Ecuadorians. At moments of particular tension, the railway was seen as a "Yankee octopus,"[30] and the willingness of the U.S. government to back up company claims with the occasional gunboat anchored off the coast fueled resentment.[31] The railway created such anti-American sentiment in Ecuador that British diplomats feared the political implications of being associated with it. Indeed, as the British consul in Quito reported in 1923, "It cannot truthfully be said that the American nation is in any way popular with Ecuadorians, who are beset with the constant dread that the United States on some pretext or other, preferably the railway, may intervene and treat this country as she has done with Nicaragua and other unfortunate Central American States that have come within the sphere of her Monroe Doctrine."[32] Thus, the distance between the company's interests and those of Ecuadorian elites and the state may have turned the railway into a national project in yet another way: by provoking nationalist sentiments that many Ecuadorians could share.

Notes

1. Governor of Chimborazo to the political administrator of Alausí, Riobamba, September 16, 1903, AJPA 1903.

2. Criminal case against M. Andrade, April 25, 1904, AJPA 1904.

3. Telegram from the minister of public works to the political administrator of Alausí, Quito, June 14, 1919, AJPA 1919.

4. Anton Rosenthal, "Death on the Line: Disease, Accidents and Worker Consciousness on the Railroads of Ecuador," paper presented at the Sixth Latin American Labor History Conference, Yale University, April 21–22, 1989.

5. Inspector of the Sibambe-Cuenca railway to the political administrator of Alausí, November 7, 1921, AJPA 1921.

6. Minister of the interior circular no. 83, transcribed in governor of Chimborazo to the political administrator of Alausí, Riobamba, December 2, 1930, AJPA 1930.

7. In addition to the telegraph, the first telephones in Ecuador were installed between Yaguachi and Chimbo in May 1887 to serve the railway. Crespo Ordóñez, *Historia del ferrocarril*, 34.

8. Pan American Union, *Ecuador: General Descriptive Data Prepared in April 1915* (Washington, DC: Pan American Union, 1915), 11.

9. Pan American Union, *Ecuador: General Descriptive Data* (Washington, DC: Pan American Union, 1924), 12.

10. Political lieutenant of Gonzól to the political administrator of Alausí, Gonzól, September 16, 1927, AJPA 1927.

11. Transcribed in Ministro de Correos y Telégrafos, *Informe que el ministro de correos y telégrafos presenta a la nación en 1917* (Quito: Imprenta y Encuadernación Nacionales, 1917), 84.

12. Governor of Chimborazo to the political administrator of Alausí, Riobamba, March 22, 1907, AJPA 1907; political lieutenant of Huigra to the political administrator of Alausí, Huigra, July 19, 1907, AJPA 1907.

13. Crespo Ordóñez, *Historia del ferrocarril*, 111.

14. Félix Flor M., *Páginas de historia contemporanea: La rectificación de la línea férrea de Riobamba* (Riobamba: Imprenta y Libreria "Nacional," 1924).

15. Meyer, *En los altos Andes del Ecuador*, 68.

16. Crespo Ordóñez, *Historia del ferrocarril*, 141, 183.

17. Moncayo Andrade, "El ferrocarril."

18. Mr. Jerome to the Foreign Office, Quito, June 21, 1913, No. 38293, 368/845, BCR/FO AHBC-Q.

19. Mr. Keyser to the Foreign Office, Quito, October 4, 1919, No. A525/314/54, 371/3709, BCR/FO AHBC-Q.

20. Annual Report of R. C. Mitchell to the Foreign Office, Quito, December 31, 1923, No. A895/895/54, 371/9542, BCR/FO AHBC-Q.

21. Mr. Goold (U.S. Embassy in London) to the Foreign Office, London, February 8, 1924, No. A903/903/54, 371/9542, BCR/FO AHBC-Q.

22. For a discussion of Kemmerer's reforms in Ecuador see Drake, *The Money Doctor*; and Rodríguez, *The Search for Public Policy*.

23. Annual report of the governor of Chimborazo province, in Ministro de lo Interior, Municipalidades, Policía, Obras Públicas, etc., *Informe . . . 1914*, 34–35.

24. Mr. Beauclerk to the Foreign Office, Lima, July 3, 1907, No. 27307, 368/119, BCR/FO AHBC-Q.

25. Mr. Jerome to the Foreign Office, Quito, August 16, 1913, No. 44472, 368/845, BCR/FO AHBC-Q.

26. R. C. Mitchell to the Foreign Office, Quito, April 16, 1924, No. A3488/903/54, 371/9542, BCR/FO AHBC-Q.

27. Moncayo Andrade, "El ferrocarril," 21.

28. Reyes, *Los últimos siete años*, 25–26.

29. Crespo Ordóñez, *Historia del ferrocarril*, 146.

30. Rosenthal, "Death on the Line."

31. Eva Loewenfeld, "The Guayaquil and Quito Railway, Ecuador," *Southwestern Social Science Quarterly* 27, no. 1 (1946): 68–93.

32. Annual Report of R. C. Mitchell to the Foreign Office, Quito, December 31, 1923, No. A895/895/54, 371/9542, BCR/FO AHBC-Q.

8

Social Space and the Railway, the Nation, and the Liberal State

The Uneven Effects of the Railway

If one of the aims and achievements of railway construction in Ecuador was national integration, it is nonetheless true that the railway connected only certain regions, in particular the Guayas basin with the north-central highlands. In fact, as the railway incorporated some provinces, it simultaneously isolated others. Thus, the incorporation and the isolation of regions and populations should both be seen as the result of modern processes: areas that were not incorporated did not simply remain outside of history, unchanged. This dual process of incorporation and isolation by the railway had differential effects not only among the provinces but also more locally, by proximity to the track.

The construction of the railway along the Chanchán River and through Chimborazo province, instead of along the Chimbo route proposed by Marcus Kelly through Bolívar, led to displacement of the *terratenientes* of Bolívar province. Moreover, Guaranda, the capital of Bolívar, had been a central point on the trip from the coast to the interior throughout the nineteenth century. An obligatory rest point, it was also where travelers hired fresh saddle and pack animals. In the 1860s and 1870s, with the initial construction of the railway from Yaguachi to Chimbo and the building of García Moreno's wagon road south of Quito along the highlands, Guaranda's position was threatened, but not irreversibly. In the period from 1888 to 1892, President Antonio Flores was skeptical about the possibilities of railway construction (understandably, because for twenty years Ecuadorians had been trying to put in a railway from Guayaquil to Quito). Flores thus emphasized road building instead. Under his administration, the importance of Guaranda was renewed through construction of a new and improved road along the traditional coast-highland route, which became known as the Vía Flores. The selection of the Chanchán route for the railway in 1900 sealed the decline of Guaranda, however, and throughout the liberal period Guaranda's residents complained that railway construction had meant the dearticulation and underdevelopment of their region. Lobbying for renewed incorporation was occasionally successful, as happened in 1906 when work was briefly undertaken on a railway that was meant to link Babahoyo, Guaranda, and Riobamba (one of the many lines never completed). But in the long run, Guaranda and Bolívar province were never to be quite so central again.

In the areas crossed by the railway, its construction led to the intensification of production in haciendas that had privileged locations and to the incorporation into production of new lands that had previously been considered marginal. A market in land was stimulated, and landed property began to acquire value as a factor of production rather than simply as a sign of nobility. In some cases, the new possibilities for profit meant that new groups invested in land, in addition to the traditional landed elite. These groups included merchants and industrialists, who either purchased land or rented *haciendas de asistencia pública* (the estates nationalized in 1908), especially after 1920.

In the central highland region, the fortunes of the Chimborazo elite rose because of the province's articulation with the coastal market through railway construction, expanding agriculture and livestock raising. The landowners of Tungurahua in turn became involved in fruit and vegetable production, large-scale commerce, and the industrialization of foods and leather. Research on the agrarian history of Cotopaxi province has shown that haciendas along the railroad were precisely those that were modernized for the production of dairy products.[1] The railway's proximity saved large landowners in the Guaytacama area, such as Enrique Gangotena Jijón, from making expensive investments in infrastructure, allowing them instead to invest in other variables that augmented their competitiveness, such as imported machinery, pasture seeds, and livestock breeds. That these landowners dominated the Sociedad Nacional de Agricultura also enabled them to lobby for policies that would advance their interests even further. Cotopaxi haciendas that were more distant from the railway, for instance, those in the zone of Cusubamba, found that their competitiveness did not remain static under these conditions but progressively diminished. Again, the train's route left them actively underdeveloped.

The uneven effects of the railway were felt not only in broad regional terms: in the laying of the rail line, even a single kilometer could make an important difference to a locality. A revealing conflict occurred in Alausí in 1923 between the owners of agricultural properties located between the Chanchán and Chimbo rivers and those whose property they had to cross, along the banks of the Chimbo, to reach the railway line—a route that they had been using since 1916. In December 1920 they requested permission to build a bridge over the Chimbo for the transport of their fruits and other produce, since their production had expanded significantly because of the new agricultural policies and access to new markets. In April 1923 the bridge was swept away by flooding of the river, and the landowners who used it began to rebuild. However, when only the wooden planks remained to be put in place, the bridge builders received notice from the owner of the lands that the route crossed, denying them transit. Even a cable used in the bridge construction was cast into the river by the landowner's employees. This route had also provided an outlet to Bucay (5 kilometers away), so that with the destruction of the bridge the landowners affected had been unable to transport their produce for over a month. The loss to them was "indescribable," and they petitioned the cantonal junta of agricultural development to provide them with "a permanent outlet for the expansion of our production."[2]

Clearly, the precise location of the railway made a crucial difference in the possibilities that agriculturalists had for taking advantage of the policies encouraging increased agricultural production and the opportunities presented by the railway in this regard. As they tried to benefit from these opportunities, their actions brought these neighbors into a new relation with each other. One kind of economic freedom that proximity to the railway allowed was the option to limit other producers' ability to use it. Thus, in 1928 there was a conflict between the Haciendas Moyocancha and Zula. In that year Julio Salem closed a road passing through his vast estate of Moyocancha, which previously had connected Zula with the village and railway station of Tixán. The administrator of the Zula hacienda recognized that this was an effort to limit his ability to market hacienda products, and he complained to the local political authorities. As we know, class can create solidarities. Nonetheless, for those who own the means of production, class also tends to bring its members into direct competition with one another.

To some extent one would be able to read the distribution of the most modern haciendas across the landscape of the Ecuadorian highlands in 1930 in the lay of the railway and its junctions with roads. However, this does not mean that the railway alone brought change since social relations on haciendas also influenced the possibility and form of agricultural expansion. And, of course, the policies that facilitated the expansion and/or modernization of haciendas resulted from successful lobbying by a sector of highland landowners at a particular conjuncture of national and international processes. Another way that local activity must be taken into account in reading the distribution of modernized haciendas involves the initial lobbying to have the railway pass through one region rather than another. In 1899, Colonel William Shunk, an American consultant on the possible routes of the Guayaquil-Quito Railway, rather poetically expressed how railway routes were chosen.[3] In a letter to Eloy Alfaro in September, he stated that "the best localization [of the line] is a point of capital importance; there are as many possible routes in a region as there are statues in a block of marble. But a master artist is needed, who will dedicate his time to find the Venus de Milo in that block. Similarly, in any given region, a master will necessarily encounter the best railway route, dedicating a great deal of time to the task. One can never be precipitous in such matters."[4] However, some scholars suggest that rather different processes were involved in the choice of routes. Maldonado Obregón states that Eduardo Morley's purchase of a cattle ranch near Huigra motivated him to build the line through Huigra while Archer Harman was abroad.[5] And Jorge Trujillo argues that the choice of the route through Chimborazo (rather than Bolívar) was determined by the lobbying of the large landowners who would benefit from the line.[6]

The importance of the precise route that the railway took was recognized by the residents of Riobamba. Although in the original railway construction contract of 1897 there was only to be a short branch line connecting Riobamba to the main line, the 1900 revision that allowed a steeper grade around Nariz del Diablo did so only on the condition that the main line would pass through Riobamba. By 1905, when the railway was inaugurated in Riobamba on a branch line from Luisa, it had become clear that the railway company intended to ignore this provision in its haste to reach Quito by 1907, as the contract specified it must. Riobambeños felt so strongly about having the railway pass directly through their town that the highland arm of the uprising that overthrew President Lizardo García in January 1906 was initiated in Riobamba.[7] Eloy Alfaro's plot to regain the presidency was supported by Riobambeños because they believed that only a strong leader could force the company to fulfill its commitment. Apparently, they had presented a petition earlier to García, and they perceived him to be indifferent to their complaint. Nevertheless, only eighteen years later, in June 1924, the main line of the railway was finally inaugurated in Riobamba. Since Riobambeños believed that the branch line from Luisa posed a continuing threat to their direct line, they marked the lifting of the tracks through Luisa in July 1924 with a great celebration.[8]

When the railway to link the southern highlands with the Guayaquil-Quito line was in its planning stages, Alausenos lobbied heavily but unsuccessfully to have the new track leave from Alausí rather than Huigra, which had been proposed by Eduardo Morley. In the end, it was built from neither Huigra nor Alausí, but from the Sibambe station at the foot of the Nariz del Diablo. Although the route from Huigra would have been more direct,[9] the route from Sibambe would pass through Chunchi, a more populated zone. Indeed, landowners in that parish donated the lands on which the line would be built. All evidence suggests that they were right to do so, because the difference of a few kilometers in the track's trajectory was critical. In contrast, in Guasuntos and Achupallas (parishes where neither railway passed), local elites got together in 1929–30 to promote the construction of a road fit for motor vehicles—the wave of the future.

The Reorientation of Transport

Despite its preeminence, the railway was not the only transportation route constructed during the liberal period. The Guayaquil-Quito Railway was meant to be the spinal column of an extensive system of railways, most of which was never built. It did, however, become the hub of a network of footpaths and horse and mule trails. Archival sources for this period are filled with reports of bridges being built and paths being opened.

The railway's central importance as the vertebrae of this system is demonstrated in two ways. First, the fact that the railway continued to be the best road available, even at the end of our period of study, is nicely underlined by the route of a 1928 foot race from Guayaquil to Quito, planned by the Federación Deportiva del Guayas (the Guayas Sports Federation) to celebrate the May 24 civic holiday. All of the way from Durán to Guamote the race was to be run along the train tracks; only between Guamote and Quito could it be run along a road.[10] A car rally was also held for the same celebration, but only between Riobamba and Quito. Second, although they were not eliminated, the routes of muleteers were reorganized as a result of railway construction. The main transportation route no longer passed through Babahoyo and Guaranda. Once the railway was completed to Guamote, for instance, all cargo to Cuenca from either the north-central highlands or the coast was discharged at Huigra to continue south on muleback.

Even over routes that were served by rail, we cannot assume that trains fully displaced muleteers. There is evidence that in some cases, muleteers actually drove their pack animals along the tracks. British geographer Reginald Enock, writing in 1913, commented that "the railway track is continually used as a horse and mule trail during the rainy season, with the result that the hooves of horses and mules loosen the wooden ties. The muleteers insist on using the line this way, despite all of the regulations that have been dictated to prevent it."[11] Local archives provide substantial evidence of these practices. In 1908, for instance, the villagers of Huigra sent a petition to the municipal council president in Alausí requesting that funds be approved for the construction and repair of local trails. They pointed out that the paths that most needed attention were those linking Huigra with Chunchi and Sibambe, which would stimulate the transport of food and merchandise. "Moreover, in this way we could avoid the continual mishaps that occur when the inhabitants of these neighboring villages, in the interest of trading, are compelled to occupy a long extension of the railway track, with the frequent result that the daily traffic of the trains occasions victims, especially when they travel with heavily laden pack animals."[12] Similarly, in 1914 the minister of public works sent a telegram to the governor of Chimborazo province pointing out that travel by foot and horseback along the rail line caused frequent accidents, as well as damaged the track. He suggested that the political lieutenants prohibit transit on foot or horseback along the line and that fines be imposed on any transgressor.[13]

During the construction of the railway from Sibambe to Cuenca the use of the rail line by muleteers became so common that railway administrators began to charge a one-sucre toll. We learn of this only because a railway company employee charged more than the agreed-upon rate and "the statements of mule-teers who have been prejudiced" were ordered collected.[14] By 1922 the villagers of Chunchi were using the Sibambe-Cuenca rail line as their regular trail for local travel, by foot, horseback, and mule.[15] The problems continued. In 1928 the general man-ager of the Guayaquil and Quito Railway Company insisted that instructions be sent to the authorities in Alausí "prohibiting the use of the railway tracks as a route for the transit of animals between places with proper trails. This traffic of animals is abun-dant; and, due to the rains, muddy ruts are now forming. Above all, where this abuse is most common is in the kilometer and a half to the south and north of Alausí, and the same around Tixán."[16]

Although innumerable footpaths and mule trails were built during the liberal period and many railway projects were in the works, before the 1920s there does not seem to have been much attention to building roads that could support vehicular traffic. Thus, in 1920 the trip of 233 kilometers from Quito to Tulcán still required five days. Similarly, it took three days of travel by horse or mule to reach Cuenca from Huigra. Indeed, it appears that the condition of roads throughout the first two decades of the twentieth century was much as had been described by the British consul in Guayaquil in 1905. In a report to the Foreign Office about automobile imports into Ecuador, the consul noted that the first importation as a business investment (as opposed to private use) was made in 1903–04, of three eight-passenger Daimler vehicles. They were found to be useless for traffic in the highlands, especially because of the steep grades of the road to Quito.[17] The Daimlers were subsequently shipped to Peru in search of a market. The second importation, in 1905, was of Brit-ish traction cars, which were sold to the Guayaquil and Quito Railway Company for conveyance of cargo from Riobamba to Quito and of construction materials for the line. Problems emerged, however, because their weight damaged the wagon road. In 1906 the only automobile that could successfully and repeatedly run the course between Quito and Riobamba be-longed to Archer Harman. Nonetheless, apparently the condi-tion of the road was so bad that after six or eight journeys even that car was practically destroyed. The poor condition of Ecuadorian roads in 1909 led the Paige-Detroit Motor Company to claim that the Paige automobile (available for import through a Guayaquil agent) was "the only automobile built for the altitudes and bad roads" of Ecuador.[18]

Despite poor connections between cities, sometimes automobiles were imported for use within cities. Prior to the railway, these vehicles were dismantled and transported over the Andes by mules and indigenous cargo bearers (on *lomo de indio*, as this method was called at the time). The transport of vehicles (and other kinds of machinery) became much easier with the construction of the railway, particularly after its completion to Quito in 1908. But even within days of the railway's 1902 inauguration in Alausí, allowing for rail transport on the difficult ascent through the tropical forest on the western cordillera, an automobile for the governor of Chimborazo province was sent from Alausí to Riobamba on *lomo de indio*. The following year another car, for a cabinet minister, was sent by this method from Alausí to Quito. As revealed by conflicts over their payment, indigenous cargo bearers resented this work for which they were often forcibly recruited. The completion of the railway would release local Indians from at least these unpleasant tasks.

Only in the 1920s did roads for motor vehicles begin to be constructed in many regions. In fact, in the early years of the decade a shift occurred in the assumptions underlying government reports. After years of promoting the construction of multiple rail lines, cabinet ministers began to object to the "railway politics" of the liberal period. As one complained, "In the heat of the ideals consecrated by the Liberal Revolution of '95, a violent, frenetic desire for material progress arose in the spirit of the diverse regions of the country, that departed from any serene vision of the reality of things, and, above all, from the reality of our fiscal and economic resources."[19] It was argued that Ecuador should construct transportation routes that were inexpensive and appropriate to the nation's economic situation, meaning "a system of modern and inexpensive roads, rectifying the onerous error of our railway fantasies."[20] By 1930 there was vehicular traffic between Quito and Babahoyo. Dry season roads permitting truck traffic began to cross the province of Los Ríos in the following decade, displacing muleteers. Still, in the 1940s, the number of vehicles was limited. Only in the 1950s, with the banana boom, was river transportation in the Guayas basin finally displaced by road transport and the railway undermined by the construction of new routes between the coast and the highlands. In addition, on March 20, 1929, President Isidro Ayora inaugurated the first regular commercial air link between Quito and Guayaquil, whose weekly service was undertaken by a subsidiary of Lufthansa.[21] At the end of our period of study, the Ecuadorian government also had begun to approve the lifting of the tracks on some of the many incomplete rail lines. Thus, by the late 1920s, the heady era of Ecuadorian railway construction was over.

The Movement of People through Space

Much of what has already been discussed involves not only the reorganization of spatial connections but also implied changes in how people can move through space. During the nineteenth century, movement around the national territory required substantial resources of time, money, energy, even courage. There can be no doubt that people did not undertake travel lightly. And for half of each year, travel between the highlands and the coast was nearly impossible. Indeed, the difficulties of movement between the coast and the highlands prior to railway construction are highlighted by the fact that when Eloy Alfaro marched triumphantly into Quito in 1895, it was the first time he had set foot in the nation's capital.

One aspect of the way that Ecuador was transformed by the railway is the emergence of vacation zones in the highlands. Seasonal migrations of Guayaquileños to Huigra and Alausí are considered in Chapter 6, but the implications are wider. A distinct climate, territorialized in a different space, became a resource for well-to-do Guayaquileños during the tropical rainy season. Their use of this space probably also involved a reorganization of their domestic life. The seasonal movement of a family to Alausí for the months of January to March entailed a separation between business time and leisure and family time, as household heads spent part of each week in Guayaquil and the remainder with their families in Alausí. Wintering elsewhere in this way was also fundamentally different from having a city home and a country home in the form of a working hacienda. In Alausí, there was no productive connection between most seasonal visitors and the land. The visitors were vacationers.

While only elites could move for months at a time to other regions, there is also evidence of an increase in day and overnight outings. For instance, in 1927 the senior class of the Riobamba high school arranged an overnight trip to Alausí to celebrate their graduation. Also, sightseeing in other parts of the republic emerged as a new activity directly associated with the railway. The fact that sightseeing was unusual prior to the railway is demonstrated by the experience of many Guayaquil-eños who made the trip to Quito in 1908 for the gala celebrations marking the rail line's inauguration. They could find no accommodations in the capital city, which had very few hotels at the time.[22]

The subjective experience of travel was profoundly transformed by the railway. In addition to reducing the time required to move from one place to another, the railway offered the possibility of traveling between the coast and the highlands without being exposed to the jungle on the ascent up the Andes. The railway distanced its passengers from nature, as travel required no direct contact with nature except as landscape.[23] Given the difficulty, fatigue, and danger involved in this trip previously, the possibility of passing relatively quickly through this zone without being directly exposed to nature is a significant change. While the railway can thus be seen as taming the wilderness, this was the case only in terms of people's experience of nature, rather than in any objective way. Indeed, in the section of the railway running through the tropics, the front of locomotives were periodically equipped with herbicide sprayers to distribute a solution of arsenic and niter over the line to discourage the plant growth that continually threatened to engulf and destroy the tracks.

There was also increased movement of subordinate groups over space as the railway stimulated a labor market, particularly by facilitating migrations from the highlands to the coast. Poor mestizos, following the rail line, moved in significant numbers during the 1910s and 1920s. A substantial migration of indigenous laborers from the highlands did not begin until later, probably in the 1930s or 1940s. However, seasonal labor migrations were stimulated earlier in areas brought into close contact with the coast by the railway, such as Alausí (as early as 1917). In 1922 the indigenous peasants of Pizhillig had declared that they were prepared to pack up their families and move elsewhere. Whether they were bluffing or not, the claim itself attests to the fact that mobility had become more feasible than ever before.

The Space of the Liberal State

The experience of space, and of the nation itself, was significantly transformed by the possibility of increased movement between regions. But the social experience of space was altered by the government's efforts to redraw the boundaries between public and private spaces during this period, in the process of redefining the appropriate sphere for state activity.

The appropriate arena for state action was redefined through processes of national incorporation. For instance, the sanitation campaign discussed earlier involved state officials entering homes to inspect their sanitary conditions. The campaign entailed an effort to reorganize domestic space as well. Not only were certain kinds of structures (double walls, thatched roofs) destroyed but the disposal of waste and the relative distribution of humans and animals in domestic areas were also regulated by public health inspectors. The justification for these measures was that people's private conduct affected the health of the larger society, particularly that of the populations of the interior cities.[24]

Because disease was spread by rats that traveled in the freight cars of trains, as well as by human travelers, a national institution—the Public Health Service—was created to deal with the problems associated with increased mobility. Another important form of movement was also facilitated by trains and similarly demanded the existence of national institutions to deal with it. As the railway was inaugurated in each subsequent town in Ecuador, the size of local police detachments was increased, especially in provincial capitals. This increase testifies to both the perceived danger of transients arriving in town and the new facility for moving stolen property, such as livestock (rumored, for instance, to be loaded onto trains in Huigra), presented by the railway. The integration of the police system was also enhanced by such measures as the improved circulation of information about criminals and stolen goods. Thus, the movement of people through space here involved an attempt to increase the state's own effectiveness over space, reducing the possibilities for anonymity.

The definitions of "public" and "private" were also modified during the liberal period. In general, there was a consistent effort to make religion a private matter and remove it from the public sphere. Prior to the Liberal Revolution, the clergy's use of indigenous labor had been not only condoned but also facilitated by political authorities. This was a privilege that the clergy, as a corporate group, had over another group defined by its racial and social characteristics. The liberal state moved quickly to condemn this practice in the early skirmishes with the Catholic Church that were fought prior to the full establishment of the secular state. The clergy were instructed to form labor contracts between private and equal individuals—a particular clergyman and a worker—rather than having state-sponsored access to workers based on the two parties' essentialized characteristics.

More broadly, there was an effort by the state to discourage public expressions of religious belief and ritual, in part by exerting more control over the use of public spaces such as streets and plazas. This effort was associated with the process of removing the Catholic Church from any interference with public affairs and relegating it to the realm of private belief. Perhaps the most important expression of this process in rural areas was the effort to eliminate those aspects of religious fiestas, such as village bullfights, that were seen as leading to excess.[25] In the documentary evidence from Alausí are many pleas for help that had been sent to authorities in the cantonal seat from political lieutenants in outlying parishes, who could not enforce the prohibitions on bullfights during the fiestas of San Pedro. Prior to such events they requested armed troops to control public behavior and afterward reported that they had remained hidden in their houses rather than confront the faithful on their own. When they were ordered to name and fine the infractors, they asked how could they possibly do so? A thousand or more Indians had "invaded" the village plaza.

Although requests for permission to hold bullfights as part of religious fiestas were consistently denied (despite the ineffectiveness of such denials), during the 1920s the increasing requests by mestizo townspeople to hold bullfights to celebrate civic festivities began to be granted. Permission was accompanied by the laborious efforts of the municipal council of Alausí during the first two decades of the liberal period to import musical instruments from abroad, hire a music teacher, and form a municipal band to perform at such events.[26] A redefinition of the kind of behavior that belonged in the public plaza was clearly under way.

The Ecuadorian liberal period also saw what David Nugent has suggestively called, in his analyses of Peru, the "annihilation of regional space by state power."[27] This phrase refers to the progressive incorporation of areas that had previously operated according to regional social, economic, and political dynamics into the logic of the central state, the national economy, and the imagined national community. Thus, in Ecuador during the liberal period, there was a centralization and homogenization of laws and institutions,[28] as well as efforts to make the state's presence more even in other ways. Indeed, one characteristic of the modern state is that, ideally, "state sovereignty is fully, flatly, and evenly operative over each square centimeter of a legally demarcated territory."[29] Efforts to achieve this were undertaken in many fields. Reform of primary education, for instance, was meant to extend state influence over a large proportion of the national population. Thus, early in the liberal period, it was declared illegal to use textbooks (or teachers) that had not been approved by the government (although local teachers protested that therefore the government should provide access to those texts, which it was slow to do). The establishment of a single national police code was another dimension of this project, and increasing surveillance was revealingly represented by several municipal police forces with the adoption of a single, staring eye on their letterheads.

The railway was another field in which the state's control over its territory became more extensive: the state's ability to quell insurrections, for instance, was greatly enhanced where troops could be moved by rail rather than on foot and horseback. In very direct ways, then, the railway facilitated a strengthening of the central state. That state power in Ecuador could be enhanced in the name of a liberal project—although liberalism as a body of theory argues precisely for a smaller state and less state intervention in the economic sphere—is a contradiction that appears in the historiography of other Latin American countries as well.[30] Indeed, although in Ecuador the government did not actually build the railway, it did push through its construction by an act of political will. Only by so doing could the conditions be created that would eventually allow for the free circulation of goods and labor, that is, for economic liberalism.

To understand the process of annihilating regional space and expanding the space of the liberal state in Ecuador requires attention to the relationship between the central state and subordinate groups. Together they undermined regional power structures, although only rarely should we see them as being in explicit alliance. Given the new facility to move around the national territory, for instance, local indigenous leaders in the late 1910s and 1920s began to engage in an important form of travel. They periodically journeyed from the Alausí area to Riobamba or Quito to present complaints or petitions to supra-local government authorities. Their having more direct access to superior political authorities often resulted in modifications of the abuses of local officials and landowners. Less frequently, indigenous leaders from Alausí also traveled to coordinate uprisings with indigenous leaders in other areas. This was another form of pressure that could be brought to bear on local social relations, and the results were often institutionalized through the passage of new laws to protect Indians, which then became the matrix for subsequent complaints and petitions to political authorities, when these measures in turn were disregarded at the local level.[31]

The sphere of state activity was further expanded into new spaces during the liberal period with the entry of state authorities into haciendas and indigenous communities, that is, into the rural hinterlands beyond the towns and villages where government officials were stationed. In the conflict between the Hacienda Moyocancha and the community of Pizhillig, discussed in Chapter 6, not only was Alausí's police chief invited into the heart of each of these places—at the instigation of the Indians—but he also directly intervened in a labor conflict, an unprecedented action. The conflict had been provoked by changes associated with new policies favoring agricultural expansion, but the same legislation that stimulated the changes also provided some of the tools for dealing with the conflicts that arose. In this case, the laws against obstructing local trails were integral to the overall project to encourage the increased production and movement of agricultural products, even though particular landowners' modernization efforts were prejudiced by customary transit through their properties. Once the law promoting agricultural development was passed, it became a resource for contention whose use could not be controlled by those who had designed it, with their own interests in mind. When local Indians engaged such laws to deal with the resulting problems, central state authority was called in where it had scarcely dared to tread previously.

As already noted, the railway also annihilated regional space by facilitating the movement of troops to quell rebellions by local caudillos. In 1924 the president of the railway company commented that the rail line had "made possible a closer linking together of the two distinct parts of the country—the coast and the interior—from a military point of view, providing for the quick transfer of troops, essential to national safety."[32] The British consul in Quito at the time agreed: "As a military asset the railway has been invaluable to the various governments in grappling with revolutionary movements, and they were so dependent on the railway for the transport of troops that they did not venture to urge the improvement of the line for commercial purposes, which appear to have been considered as of secondary importance."[33] We do not have to accept the consul's word that the military benefits of the railway were all that mattered to Ecuadorian governments to recognize that this was, nonetheless, an important use to which the railway was put.

This analysis can be taken further by looking at the effects of these processes at the local level. How did troops move prior to the construction of the railway? Given the difficulties of long-distance transport of supplies, the mobilization of soldiers had required multiple exactions at the local level—for pack animals and horses, for forage, and for agricultural and livestock products to feed the troops. Who provided these resources? While in the months during and immediately after the Liberal Revolution it was common practice to appropriate these goods from local conservatives who were combating the new government, in most cases it was indigenous peasants who suffered the brunt of these exactions. Those who provided pack animals either never saw them again or had to travel considerable distances to recover their property. Although, in principle, people were to be paid for the use of their animals or for the products they provided, such payments were the exception rather than the rule.

In this context, the railway allowed for a qualitative change in the relationship between the central state and indigenous peasants. Prior to railway construction, great resentment was generated by the recruitment of animals, forage, and food for the transport or maintenance of government officials or troops; afterward, in contrast, both troops and their provisions could be easily and rapidly moved by train.[34] The result was that the central state could more convincingly present itself as the protector of the Indians from local abuses, as it ceased to be perceived as a direct predator on their limited resources. In a rapid about-face before the railway had even been inaugurated in Quito, the provincial police commissioner in Riobamba sent a stern warning in 1907 to the police chief of Alausí pointing out that it was now absolutely illegal for local authorities to requisition animals from Indians, who instead deserved official protection since they were defenseless in the face of abuses.[35] However, the fact that this order was sent in response to local Indians' complaints to the provincial authorities throws doubt on how defenseless they really were. Nonetheless, it provides another example of how the annihilation of regional space, through the undermining of local powerholders by the central state, was carried out by way of complaints made by local Indians to central authorities. These processes were part of the construction of what Philip Abrams has called a new "idea of the state."[36]

The manner in which the central state seemed to speak through Indians during the liberal period has been summed up by Andrés Guerrero as a kind of state ventriloquism.[37] That evocative image should not, however, lead one to think that Indians themselves did not gain from the legal resources offered to them by the reformist project of the liberal state. While not all of their autonomous projects could be encompassed in and pursued through these channels, in many cases they were nonetheless able to use the spaces opened up by the central state to press for their own interests with surprising effectiveness, at least in dealing with some of their most immediate daily problems.[38]

The last three decades of the nineteenth century had seen a proliferation of local state officials with the accelerated creation of new cantons and parishes.[39] But this did not necessarily imply an intensified presence of the central state in those areas. Instead, this may simply have given local elites the possibility to more rigidly control the local population in their own interests. In contrast, during the liberal period, there was undoubtedly a process of increased central state control in local areas, at the expense of local officials and other powerholders. Henri Lefebvre has argued that we need to pay attention to both "command" and "demand" in the constitution and reconstitution of social space.[40] Command refers to how changing spatial organization can contribute to new forms of control from "above," by dominant groups and state authorities, while demand refers to how these changes may facilitate the assertion of claims from "below," or from subordinate groups. During the Ecuadorian liberal period, these processes occurred simultaneously, as two sides of the same coin.

Processes of national incorporation are contradictory and experienced in multiple ways. What David Harvey has referred to as the control of space[41] (that is, as the ability to use movement through space to one's advantage, as opposed to the control of specific *places*) benefited agricultural elites who wanted to move their products to market, and the state, which tried to achieve a monopoly over force within the national territory. But, in addition, subordinate groups could also use new spatial connections and improved communications and transport to their advantage. It may be that it was precisely the impossibility of any elite group to fully establish a project in its own interests that created the openings that allowed subordinate groups to pursue their own interests within the bounds of the liberal project. If that is the case, what has often been seen as an inadequacy of Ecuadorian liberals, or a deviation from the "normal" course of history, should be moved to the center of our analyses. The ongoing compromises between elite groups, and the subsequent possibilities opened to subordinate groups, may in fact be among those "peculiarities of the Ecuadorians" that have had the most profound effects on the historical construction of social relations in the nation.[47]

Notes

1. Arcos and Marchán, "Apuntes."
2. Petition to the president of the cantonal junta of agricultural development, Alausí, May 1, 1923, AJPA 1923.
3. Shunk had previously visited Ecuador when he was designing the intercontinental Panamerican Railway (an expression of Manifest Destiny), which was never built (see Crespo Ordóñez, *Historia del ferrocarril*, 42, 98). He was the father-in-law of Major John Harman and grandfather of Archer Shunk Harman, president of the railway company in the early 1920s.
4. Cited in Crespo Ordóñez, *Historia del ferrocarril*, 100.
5. Maldonado Obregón, *La historia del ferrocarril*, 78.
6. Trujillo, *La hacienda serrana*, 117.
7. This was not a popular insurrection, and descriptions of these events evoke the restricted nature of Riobamba elite society at the time. On the evening of December 31, 1905, one of the conspirators held a party attended by all of Riobamba's political and military authorities. At midnight, several guests stole away and took over the army barracks while the authorities and the rest of Riobamba high society were celebrating the New Year. See Un Riobambeño, *Para la historia: El ferrocarril de Riobamba y la revolución del 1 de enero de 1906* (Riobamba: Imprenta Municipal, 1906). For Eloy Alfaro's version of the uprising see Alfaro, "Historia del ferrocarril," 403–7.
8. Crespo Ordóñez, *Historia del ferrocarril*, 119, 162.
9. Eduardo Morley, *Comparación entre las líneas férreas Huigra-Cuenca y Sibambe-Cuenca* (Guayaquil: Imprenta Progreso, 1919).
10. President of the Federación Deportiva del Guayas to the political administrator of Alausí, Guayaquil, May 10, 1928, AJPA 1928.

11. Enock, *Ecuador: Geografía humana*, 317–18.

12. Petition from the residents of Huigra to the municipal council of Alausí, Huigra, March 1908, ACMA.

13. Transcribed in governor of Chimborazo to the political adminis- trator of Alausí, Riobamba, April 18, 1914, AJPA 1914.

14. Political lieutenant of Huigra to the political administrator of Alausí, Huigra, November 24, 1922, AJPA 1922.

15. Political lieutenant of Chunchi to the president of the cantonal junta of agricultural development of Alausí, Chunchi, May 8, 1922, AJPA 1922.

16. Minister of the interior to the political administrator of Alausí, Quito, February 3, 1928, AJPA 1928.

17. Mr. Cartright to the Foreign Office, Guayaquil, December 7, 1905, No. 3146, 368/39, BCR/FO AHBC-Q.

18. In their advertisement in Compañía Guía Comercial y Agrícola, *El Ecuador*, 300.

19. Ministro de Hacienda y Crédito Público, *Informe del ministro de hacienda y crédito público, 1922* (Quito: Talleres Tipográficos Nacionales, 1922), 12, 5.

20. Ministro de Hacienda y Crédito Público, *Informe anual del ministro de hacienda y crédito público, 1923* (Quito: Talleres Tipográficos del Ministerio de Hacienda, 1923), 66–67.

21. Deler, *Ecuador*, 204.

22. Crespo Ordóñez, *Historia del ferrocarril*, 127.

23. Compare Wolfgang Schivelbusch, *The Railway Journey: The Indus- trialization of Time and Space in the Nineteenth Century* (Berkeley: Univer- sity of California Press, 1986); Williams, *The Country and the City*.

24. Sanitation was also the justification for increasing surveillance and repression of "nonofficial" cemeteries (usually in indigenous communi- ties) as well as the slaughter of animals outside of regulated and taxed municipal slaughterhouses.

25. Even within the church hierarchy, concern was sometimes ex- pressed for the "excesses" of religious fiesta activity among Indians. See Congreso Catequístico, *Conclusiones aprobadas por el primer congreso catequístico de la arquidiocesis de Quito* (Quito: Tipografía y Encuadernación de la "Prensa Católica," 1916); Federico González Suárez, "Quinta instrucción pastoral sobre la evangelización de los indios," 1911, reprinted in *Federico González Suárez y la polémica sobre el estado laico*, edited by Enrique Ayala Mora (Quito: Banco Central and Corporación Editora Nacional, 1980), 385–410.

26. At the beginning, band members were forcibly recruited by the municipal police chief from among idle boys, troublemakers, and artisans' apprentices who were fined and threatened with imprisonment for miss- ing music practice. Compare Guy P. C. Thomson, "Bulwarks of Patriotic Liberalism: The National Guard, Philharmonic Corps, and Patriotic Jun- tas in Mexico, 1847–88," *Journal of Latin American Studies* 22 (1990): 31–68.

27. David Nugent, "Building the State, Making the Nation: The Bases and Limits of State Centralization in 'Modern' Peru," *American Anthro- pologist* 96, no. 2 (1994): 333–69; idem, "From Devil Pacts to Drug Deals: Commerce, Unnatural Accumulation and Moral Community in 'Modern' Peru," *American Ethnologist* 23, no. 2 (1996): 258–90.

28. Corrigan and Sayer, reflecting on Weber, suggest why this might be important: "Rational, calculating capitalism, for Weber, 'needs . . . law which can be counted upon, like a machine.' Stability and predictability of the legal environment are essential to it. This can be achieved only in the centralized and standardized jurisdiction of the modern state, with its monopoly of the legitimate use of force, and its bureaucratic apparatuses of enforcement. States are also environments within which other forms—too easily taken for granted—of standardization which facilitate calculation, for instance, of currency or weights and measures, can most readily be achieved" (*The Great Arch*, 183).

29. Anderson, *Imagined Communities*, 26.

30. See Love and Jacobsen, *Guiding the Invisible Hand*; Topik, *The Political Economy*; and idem, "State Interventionism."

31. Clark, "Indians, the State and Law."

32. Mr. Goold (U.S. Embassy in London) to the Foreign Office, London, February 8, 1924, No. A903/903/54, 371/9542, BCR/FO AHBC-Q.

33. R. C. Mitchell to the Foreign Office, Quito, April 16, 1924, No. A3488/903/54, 371/9542, BCR/FO AHBC-Q.

34. Similarly, in late 1902, the mail between Guayaquil and Quito began to pass through Alausí on the train, rather than requiring the government to recruit pack animals and drivers to fulfill one of its most basic services. Nonetheless, mail continued to travel south to Cuenca by horse and mule, with all of the attendant conflicts. Also, the intensification of work on railway construction after the arrival of several thousand Jamaicans could be undertaken only because provisions for them could be brought from Guayaquil by train.

35. Police commissioner of Chimborazo to the national police chief of Alausí, Riobamba, April 26, 1907, AJPA 1907.

36. Philip Abrams, "Notes on the Difficulty of Studying the State," *Journal of Historical Sociology* 1, no. 1 (1988): 58–89.

37. Guerrero, "Una imagen ventrílocua."

38. For instance, during the liberal period, Indians in Alausí succeeded in gradually dismantling the forced-labor recruitment system for municipal public works, through a judicious combination of work evasions and petitions to higher authorities (see Clark, "Indians, the State and Law").

39. See Deler, *Ecuador*, 187–89.

40. Henri Lefebvre, *The Production of Space* (Oxford: Basil Blackwell, 1991), 95.

41. David Harvey, *The Condition of Postmodernity* (Oxford: Basil Blackwell, 1989).

42. Compare the discussions of the "peculiarities of the English" by E. P. Thompson, *The Poverty of Theory and Other Essays* (New York: Monthly Review Press, 1978); and Corrigan and Sayer, *The Great Arch*.

Bibliography

Archival Collections

ACMA   Archivo del Concejo Municipal de Alausí (Archive of the Municipal Council of Alausí), 1895–1930

AJPA   Archivo de la Jefatura Política de Alausí (Archive of the Political Administrator of Alausí), 1895–1930

BCR/FO   British Consular Reports/Foreign Office series 25/99 to 25/112, 368/39 to 368/1898, and 371/3708 to 371/14224, covering the years 1895–1930, reviewed in the Archivo Histórico del Banco Central del Ecuador, Quito (AHBC-Q)

Government Reports and Documents

Ayudante de la Dirección de Sanidad Pública. "Informe que sobre la campaña sanitaria contra la peste bubónica, en las poblaciones de Huigra y Alausí, presenta el ayudante de la dirección de sanidad pública." In *Informe que Modesto A. Peñaherrera, ministro de lo interior, municipalidades, policía, obras públicas, etc., presenta a la nación en 1913*, 297–301. Quito: Imprenta y Encuadernación Nacionales, 1913.

Director de Sanidad Pública. "Informe de la dirección del servicio de sanidad pública al señor ministro de lo interior y sanidad, 1916–1917." In *Informe que el ministro de lo interior, policía, obras públicas, municipalidades, etc., presenta a la nación, 1917*, 463–76. Quito: Imprenta y Encuadernación Nacionales, 1917.

Ministerio de Obras Públicas. *Informe especial del ministerio de obras públicas sobre el ferrocarril trasandino al congreso de 1904*. Quito: Imprenta Nacional, 1904.

Ministerio de Previsión Social y Trabajo. *Informe que el ministro de previsión social y trabajo, Dr. Carlos Andrade Marín, presenta a la nación*. Quito: Talleres Gráficos de Educación, 1941.

Ministro de Correos y Telégrafos. *Informe que el ministro de correos y telégrafos presenta a la nación en 1917*. Quito: Imprenta y Encuadernación Nacionales, 1917.

Ministro de Gobierno. *Informe concerniente a las secciones de instrucción pública, justicia y beneficencia que presenta el ministro de gobierno a la convención nacional de 1896–1897.* Quito: Imprenta Nacional, 1897.

Ministro de Hacienda. *Informe que el ministro de hacienda, Dr. Alberto Gómez Jaramillo, presenta a la nación y a sus representantes al congreso de 1924.* Quito: Talleres Tipográficos del Ministerio de Hacienda, 1924.

————. *Informe que el ministro de hacienda presenta a la nación en 1918.* Quito: Imprenta y Encuadernación Nacionales, 1918.

————. *Informe que el ministro de hacienda presenta a la nación en 1919.* Quito: Imprenta y Encuadernación Nacionales, 1919.

————. *Informe que el ministro de hacienda presenta a la nación en 1920.* Quito: Imprenta y Encuadernación Nacionales, 1920.

Ministro de Hacienda y Crédito Público. *Informe anual del ministro de hacienda y crédito público, 1923.* Quito: Talleres Tipográficos del Ministerio de Hacienda, 1923.

————. *Informe del ministro de hacienda y crédito público, 1922.* Quito: Talleres Tipográficos Nacionales, 1922.

Ministro de Instrucción Pública. *Informe del ministro de instrucción pública al congreso ordinario de 1900.* Quito: Imprenta de la Universidad Central, 1900.

Ministro de Instrucción Pública, Bellas Artes, Correos, Telégrafos, etc. *Informe que el ministro de instrucción pública, bellas artes, correos, telégrafos, etc., presenta a la nación en 1916.* Quito: Imprenta y Encuadernación Nacionales, 1916.

Ministro de Instrucción Pública, Justicia, Beneficencia, etc. *Informe que el ministro de instrucción pública, justicia, beneficencia, etc., presenta a la nación, 1919.* Quito: Imprenta y Encuadernación Nacionales, 1919.

————. *Informe que el ministro de instrucción pública, justicia, beneficencia, etc., presenta a la nación, 1921.* Quito: Imprenta y Encuadernación Nacionales, 1921.

Ministro de lo Interior, Municipalidades, Policía, Obras Públicas, etc. *Informe que Modesto A. Peñaherrera, ministro de lo interior, municipalidades, policía, obras públicas, etc., presenta a la nación en 1914.* Quito: Imprenta y Encuadernación Nacionales, 1914.

Ministro de lo Interior, Policía, Beneficencia, Obras Públicas, etc. *Informe del ministerio de lo interior, policía, beneficencia, obras públicas, etc., a la nación en 1908.* Quito: Imprenta Nacional, 1908.

Ministro de lo Interior y Policía, Beneficencia, etc. *Anexos al informe del ministro de lo interior y policía, beneficencia, etc., al congreso ordinario de 1900.* Quito: Imprenta Nacional, 1900.

————. *Informe del ministro de lo interior y policía, beneficencia, etc., al congreso de 1899.* Quito: Imprenta Nacional, 1899.

————. *Informe del ministro de lo interior y policía, beneficencia, etc., al congreso ordinario de 1900.* Quito: Imprenta Nacional, 1900.

Ministro de lo Interior y Policía, Obras Públicas, etc. *Informe del ministro de lo interior, policía, obras públicas, etc., a la asamblea nacional de 1906.* Quito: Imprenta Nacional, 1906.

———. *Informe del ministro de lo interior y policía, obras públicas, etc., al congreso ordinario de 1902.* Quito: Imprenta Nacional, 1902.

———. *Informe del ministro de lo interior y policía, obras públicas, etc., al congreso ordinario de 1903.* Quito: Imprenta Nacional, 1903.

Ministro de Justicia y Cultos. *Informe del ministro de justicia y cultos al congreso ordinario de 1900.* Quito: Imprenta Nacional, 1900.

Secretario de Instrucción Pública, Correos y Telégrafos. *Memoria del secretario de instrucción pública, correos y telégrafos, etc., al congreso ordinario de 1905.* Quito: Tipografía de la Escuela de Artes y Oficios, 1905.

Periodicals

El Comercio (Quito), selected months, 1906–1930
Registro Oficial (Quito), selected months, 1897–1930
Revista de la Sociedad Nacional de Agricultura (Quito), 1918–1930
La Unión (Alausí), August 1914–May 1916

Secondary Sources

Abrams, Philip. *Historical Sociology*, ix–17. Ithaca, New York: Cornell University Press, 1982.

———. "Notes on the Difficulty of Studying the State." *Journal of Historical Sociology* 1, no. 1 (1988): 58–89.

Ackerman, Samuel. "The 'Trabajo Subsidiario': Compulsory Labor and Taxation in Nineteenth-Century Ecuador." Ph.D. diss., New York University, 1977.

Adas, Michael. *Machines as the Measure of Men: Science, Technology, and Ideologies of Western Dominance.* Ithaca, NY: Cornell University Press, 1989.

Alfaro, Eloy. "Historia del ferrocarril de Guayaquil a Quito." 1911. Reprinted in *Narraciones históricas*, 385–432. Quito: Corporación Editora Nacional, 1983.

———. *Mensaje especial sobre la obra del ferrocarril del sur dirigido a la convención nacional por el presidente interino de la república General Don Eloy Alfaro.* Quito: Imprenta Nacional, 1896.

Alfaro, Flavio. "Discurso." In *El ferrocarril del sur, 1908–1933: Breve relación de los principales festejos que se realizaron en Quito, el 24, 25 y 26 de junio de 1908, con motivo de la inauguración del tren en esta ciudad*, 43–45. Quito: Imprenta "Industria," 1933.

Anderson, Benedict. *Imagined Communities: Reflections on the Origin and Spread of Nationalism.* London: Verso, 1983.

Andrade, Roberto. "Discurso." In *El ferrocarril del sur, 1908–1933: Breve relación de los principales festejos que se realizaron en Quito, el 24, 25 y 26 de junio de 1908, con motivo de la inauguración del tren en esta ciudad*, 59–61. Quito: Imprenta "Industria," 1933.

Andrade Coello, Alejandro. *La ley del progreso*. Quito: Casa Editorial de J. I. Galvez, 1909.

Andrade Marín, Luciano. *Nuevos aspectos agrícolas: ¿Qué haremos de nuestros páramos?* Quito: Sociedad Nacional de Agricultura and Tipografía y Encuadernación de la "Prensa Católica," 1925.

Archetti, Eduardo. *El mundo social y simbólico del cuy*. Quito: CEPLAES, 1992.

Arcos, Carlos. "El espíritu de progreso: Los hacendados en el Ecuador del 900." *Cultura* 19 (1984): 107–34.

Arcos, Carlos, and Carlos Marchán. "Apuntes para una discusión sobre los cambios en la estructura agraria serrana." *Revista Ciencias Sociales* 2, no. 5 (1978): 13–51.

Arregui, Víctor Manuel. "Discurso." In *El ferrocarril del sur, 1908–1933: Breve relación de los principales festejos que se realizaron en Quito, el 24, 25 y 26 de junio de 1908, con motivo de la inauguración del tren en esta ciudad*, 52–54. Quito: Imprenta "Industria," 1933.

Ayala Mora, Enrique. "Estudio introductorio." In *Federico González Suárez y la polémica sobre el estado laico*, edited by Enrique Ayala Mora, 11–68. Quito: Banco Central and Corporación Editora Nacional, 1980.

———. *Historia de la revolución liberal ecuatoriana*. Quito: Corporación Editora Nacional and Taller de Estudios Históricos, 1995.

———. *Lucha política y origen de los partidos en el Ecuador*. Quito: Corporación Editora Nacional and Taller de Estudios Históricos, 1978.

Banco del Pichincha. *Banco del Pichincha: 80 años, abril 1906–1986*. Quito: Banco del Pichincha, 1986.

Baquerizo Moreno, Alfredo. *Mensaje del presidente de la república al congreso nacional de 1918*. Quito: Imprenta Nacional, 1918.

Barker, Diana Leonard. "The Regulation of Marriage: Repressive Benevolence." In *Power and the State*, edited by Gary Littlejohn, 239–66. New York: St. Martin's Press, 1978.

Barsky, Osvaldo, and Gustavo Cosse. *Tecnología y cambio social: Las haciendas lecheras del Ecuador*. Quito: FLACSO, 1981.

Beezley, William H. *Judas at the Jockey Club and Other Episodes of Porfirian Mexico*. Lincoln: University of Nebraska Press, 1987.

Blanksten, George. *Ecuador: Constitutions and Caudillos*. Berkeley: University of California Press, 1951.

Bradley, Anita. *Trans-Pacific Relations of Latin America*. New York: Institute of Pacific Relations, 1942.

Bromley, Rosemary D. F. "Urban-Rural Demographic Contrasts in Highland Ecuador: Town Recession in a Period of Catastrophe, 1778–1841." *Journal of Historical Geography* 5, no. 3 (1979): 281–95.

Bromley, Rosemary D. F., and Robert J. Bromley. "The Debate on Sunday Markets in Nineteenth-Century Ecuador." *Journal of Latin American Studies* 7, no. 1 (1975): 85–108.

Bulmer-Thomas, Victor. *The Economic History of Latin America since Independence.* Cambridge: Cambridge University Press, 1994.

Bureau of the American Republics. *Ecuador.* Washington, DC: Government Printing Office, 1892.

Burgos Guevara, Hugo. *Relaciones interétnicas en Riobamba: Dominio y dependencia en una región indígena ecuatoriana.* Mexico: Instituto Indigenista Interamericano, 1970.

Bustos Lozano, Guillermo. "La identidad 'clase obrera' a revisión: Una lectura sobre las representaciones del Congreso Obrero de Ambato de 1938." *Procesos* (Quito) 2 (1992): 73–104.

Calle, Manuel J. *Una palabra sobre el contrato ferrocarrilero.* Quito: Imprenta de "El Pichincha," 1897.

Cardoso, Fernando Henrique, and Enzo Faletto. *Dependency and Development in Latin America.* Berkeley: University of California Press, 1979.

Carrasco, Hernán. "Democratización de los poderes locales y levantamiento indígena." In *Sismo étnico en el Ecuador: Varias perspectivas,* edited by CEDIME, 29–69. Quito: CEDIME and Abya Yala, 1993.

Casagrande, Joseph B., and Arthur R. Piper. "La transformación estructural de una parroquia rural en las tierras altas del Ecuador." *América Indígena* 29 (1969): 1039–64.

Castro, Julio. "Páginas de una cartera de viaje: Un viaje con García Moreno en 1861." *Boletín de la Academia Nacional de Historia* 82 (1953): 174–219.

Chang Rodríguez, Eugenio. "Chinese Labor Migration into Latin America in the Nineteenth Century." *Revista de Historia de América* (Mexico) 46 (1958): 375–97.

Chatterjee, Partha. *The Nation and Its Fragments: Colonial and Postcolonial Histories.* Princeton: Princeton University Press, 1993.

Chiriboga Vega, Manuel. *Jornaleros y gran propietarios en 135 años de exportación cacaotera (1790–1925).* Quito: Concejo Provincial de Pichincha, 1980.

Clark, A. Kim. "Género, raza y nación: La protección a la infancia en el Ecuador (1915–1945)." In *Palabras del silencio: Las mujeres latinoamericanas y su historia,* edited by Martha Moscoso, 219–56. Quito: Abya Yala, DGIS-Holanda, and UNICEF, 1995.

———. "Indians, the State and Law: Public Works and the Struggle to Control Labor in Liberal Ecuador." *Journal of Historical Sociology* 7, no. 1 (1994): 49–72.

———. "Indigenous Ecuadorians and Imagined Political Communities during Two Economic Crises." Paper presented at the annual meetings of the Canadian Association of Latin American and Caribbean Studies, Toronto, November 1996.

Comaroff, John, and Jean Comaroff. *Ethnography and the Historical Imagination*. Boulder, CO: Westview Press, 1992.

Compañía Guía Comercial y Agrícola. *El Ecuador: Guía comercial, agrícola e industrial de la república*. Guayaquil: Talleres de Artes Gráficos de E. Rodenas, 1909.

Congreso Catequístico. *Conclusiones aprobadas por el primer congreso catequístico de la arquidiocesis de Quito*. Quito: Tipografía y Encuadernación de la "Prensa Católica," 1916.

Contreras, Carlos. *El sector exportador de una economía colonial: La costa del Ecuador (1760–1830)*. Quito: Abya Yala and FLACSO, 1990.

Corrigan, Philip, and Derek Sayer. *The Great Arch: English State Formation as Cultural Revolution*. New York: Basil Blackwell, 1985.

———. "How the Law Rules: Variations on Some Themes in Karl Marx." In *Law, State, and Society*, edited by Bob Fryer, Alan Hunt, Doreen McBarnet, and Bert Moorhouse, 21–53. London: Croom Helm, 1981.

Cott, Kennett. "Mexican Diplomacy and the Chinese Issue, 1876–1910." *Hispanic American Historical Review* 67, no. 1 (1987): 63–85.

Coverdale and Colpitts, Consulting Engineers. *Report on the Guayaquil and Quito Railway Co. of Ecuador*. Quito: Guayaquil and Quito Railway Co. Printing Department, 1930.

Crawford de Roberts, Lois. *El Ecuador en la época cacaotera: Respuestas locales al auge y colapso en el ciclo monoexportador*. Translated by Rafael Quintero and Erika Silva. Quito: Editorial Universitaria, 1980.

Crespo Ordóñez, Roberto. *Historia del ferrocarril del sur*. Quito: Imprenta Nacional, 1933.

Crespo Toral, Remigio. "Cien años de emancipación (1809–1909)." *La Unión Literaria* (Cuenca) 4th series, no. 2 (1909): 59–78.

de la Cruz, Ermel. *Alausí en marcha*. Quito: Editorial "La Unión," 1970.

de la Torre Arauz, Patricia. *Patrones y conciertos: Una hacienda serrana, 1905–1929*. Quito: Corporación Editora Nacional and Abya Yala, 1989.

Deler, Jean-Paul. *Ecuador: Del espacio al estado nacional*. Quito: Banco Central, 1987.

———. "Transformaciones regionales y organización del espacio nacional ecuatoriano entre 1830 y 1930." In *Historia y región en el Ecuador: 1830–1930*, edited by Juan Maiguashca, 295–353. Quito: CERLAC, FLACSO, and IFEA, 1994.

Demélas, Marie-Danielle, and Yves Saint-Geours. *Jerusalén y Babilonia: Religión y política en el Ecuador, 1780–1880*. Quito: Corporación Editora Nacional and Instituto Francés de Estudios Andinos, 1988.

Drake, Paul W. *The Money Doctor in the Andes: The Kemmerer Missions, 1923–1933*. Durham, NC: Duke University Press, 1989.

Ecuatorianos. *Doce millones de sucres: El ferrocarril de Guayaquil a Quito*. Quito: Imprenta "La Industria," 1932.

―――. *Ferrocarril trasandino: Hablen los números*. Guayaquil: Imprenta de "El Tiempo," 1902.

Enock, Reginald. *Ecuador: Geografía humana*. 1914. Reprint, Quito: Corporación Editora Nacional, 1980.

E. O. N. *Ferrocarril Alfaro-Harmann*. Lima: Imprenta del "Universo," 1897.

Espinosa, Roque. "Hacienda, concertaje y comunidad en el Ecuador." *Cultura* 19 (1984): 135–209.

Espinosa Tamayo, Alfredo. *Psicología y sociología del pueblo ecuatoriano*. 1918. Reprint, Quito: Banco Central and Corporación Editora Nacional, 1979.

Evans, Peter D., Dietrich Rueschemeyer, and Theda Skocpol, eds. *Bringing the State Back In*. Cambridge: Cambridge University Press, 1985.

Ferrocarril (documentos oficiales). Quito: Imprenta Nacional, 1898.

El ferrocarril de Guayaquil a Quito: Contratos y otros documentos importantes, 1897–1911. Quito: Talleres de "El Comercio," 1912.

El ferrocarril del sur y los derechos del Ecuador. Quito: Talleres de "El Comercio," 1916.

Flor M., Félix. *Páginas de historia contemporanea: La rectificación de la línea férrea de Riobamba*. Riobamba: Imprenta y Librería "Nacional," 1924.

Flores Jijón, Antonio. *Derecho público: Inmigración china*. Quito: Imprenta del Gobierno, 1889.

Fox, Richard G. Introduction to *Nationalist Ideologies and the Production of National Cultures*, edited by Richard G. Fox, 1–14. Washington, DC: American Ethnological Society, 1990.

Franco, Ernesto. *La verdadera defensa nacional*. Quito: Imprenta Nacional, 1923.

Glade, William. "Economy, 1870–1914." In *Latin America: Economy and Society, 1870–1930*, edited by Leslie Bethell, 1–56. New York: Cambridge University Press, 1989.

Gonzales, Michael J. "Chinese Plantation Workers and Social Conflict in Peru in the Late Nineteenth Century." *Journal of Latin American Studies* 21 (1989): 385–424.

González A., José Luis. "Breves notas sobre la industria textil en el Ecuador." *Boletín del Ministerio de Previsión Social, Trabajo, Agricultura e Industrias* 4 (1937): 37–45.

González Suárez, Federico. "Manifiestos de los obispos del Ecuador sobre la ley de matrimonio civil." 1902–3. Reprinted in *Federico González Suárez y la polémica sobre el estado laico*, edited by Enrique Ayala Mora, 243–90. Quito: Banco Central and Corporación Editora Nacional, 1980.

―――. "Primera instrucción pastoral sobre la participación del clero en política." 1907. Reprinted in *Federico González Suárez y la polémica sobre el estado laico,* edited by Enrique Ayala Mora, 313–82. Quito: Banco Central and Corporación Editora Nacional, 1980.

———. "Quinta instrucción pastoral sobre la evangelización de los indios." 1911. Reprinted in *Federico González Suárez y la polémica sobre el estado laico,* edited by Enrique Ayala Mora, 385–410. Quito: Banco Central and Corporación Editora Nacional, 1980.

Gootenberg, Paul. *Between Silver and Guano: Commercial Policy and the State in Postindependence Peru.* Princeton: Princeton University Press, 1989.

———. *Imagining Development: Economic Ideas in Peru's "Fictitious Prosperity" of Guano, 1840–1880.* Berkeley: University of California Press, 1993.

Gramsci, Antonio. *Selections from the Prison Notebooks.* Edited and translated by Quintin Hoare and Geoffrey Nowell Smith. New York: International, 1971.

Guerrero, Andrés. "Una imagen ventrílocua: El discurso liberal de la 'desgraciada raza indígena.' " In *Imágenes e imagineros: Representaciones de los indígenas ecuatorianos, siglos XIX y XX,* edited by Blanca Muratorio, 197–252. Quito: FLACSO, 1994.

———. "El levantamiento indígena de 1994: Discurso y representación política." *Memoria* (Quito) 5 (1995): 89–123.

———. *La semántica de la dominación: El concertaje de indios.* Quito: Libri Mundi, 1991.

Hale, Charles A. "Political and Social Ideas." In *Latin America: Economy and Society, 1870–1930,* edited by Leslie Bethell, 225–300. New York: Cambridge University Press, 1989.

Harman, John A. "The Guayaquil and Quito Railway in Ecuador, South America." *Engineering News* 52, no. 6 (1904): 115–19.

Harvey, David. *The Condition of Postmodernity.* Oxford: Basil Blackwell, 1989.

Hassaurek, Friedrich. *Four Years among the Ecuadorians.* 1867. Reprint, Carbondale: Southern Illinois University Press, 1967.

Hill, Christopher. *Reformation to Industrial Revolution.* New York: Pantheon, 1968.

Hu-DeHart, Evelyn. "Immigrants to a Developing Society: The Chinese in Northern Mexico, 1875–1932." *Journal of Arizona History* 21, no. 3 (1980): 49–86.

Ibarra, Hernán. "Ambato, las ciudades y pueblos en la sierra central ecuatoriana (1800–1930)." In *Ciudades de los Andes: Visión histórica y contemporánea,* edited by Eduardo Kingman Garcés, 223–79. Quito: CIUDAD, 1992.

———. *Indios y cholos: Orígenes de la clase trabajadora ecuatoriana.* Quito: El Conejo, 1992.

———. *"Nos encontramos amenazados por todita la indiada": El levantamiento de Daquilema (Chimborazo, 1871).* Quito: CEDIS, 1993.

Icaza, Jorge. *Huasipungo.* 1934. Reprint, Bogotá: Editorial Oveja Negra, 1985.

El Imparcial. "Editorial de 'El Imparcial,' 24 de junio de 1908." In *El ferrocarril del sur, 1908–1933: Breve relación de los principales festejos que se realizaron en Quito, el 24, 25 y 26 de junio de 1908, con motivo de la inauguración del tren en esta ciudad,* 14–16. Quito: Imprenta "Industria," 1933.

Un imparcial. *Breves observaciones que demuestran lo ruinoso que será para la nación el contrato del ferrocarril del sur.* Guayaquil: Imprenta de Gómez Hnos., 1897.

Imparciales. *Cuestión candente.* Quito: Imprenta de la Escuela de Artes y Oficios, 1898.

Jacques, Leo M. "Have Quick More Money Than Mandarins: The Chinese in Sonora." *Journal of Arizona History* 17, no. 2 (1976): 201–18.

Joseph, Gilbert M., and Daniel Nugent. "Popular Culture and State Formation in Revolutionary Mexico." In *Everyday Forms of State Formation: Revolution and the Negotiation of Rule in Modern Mexico,* edited by Gilbert M. Joseph and Daniel Nugent, 3–23. Durham, NC: Duke University Press, 1994.

Kasza, Gregory J. "Regional Conflict in Ecuador: Quito and Guayaquil." *Inter-American Economic Affairs* 35, no. 2 (1981): 3–41.

Landázuri N., Cristóbal. "Las sociedades indígenas de las cuencas de los ríos Mira y Chanchán, siglos XVI y XVII: Estudios de caso." *Revista de Historia de América* (Mexico) 106 (1988): 49–106.

Larrea Jijón, J. M. "Nuestra situación agrícola-económica." *Revista de la Sociedad Nacional de Agricultura* 1 (1919): 365–70.

Laski, H. J. *El liberalismo europeo.* Mexico: Fondo de Cultura Económica, 1992.

Lears, T. J. Jackson. "The Concept of Cultural Hegemony: Problems and Possibilities." *American Historical Review* 90 (1985): 567–93.

———. *No Place of Grace: Antimodernism and the Transformation of American Culture, 1880–1920.* New York: Pantheon, 1981.

Lefebvre, Henri. *The Production of Space.* Oxford: Basil Blackwell, 1991.

Lentz, Carola. "Los 'Pilamungas' en San Carlos: Un estudio de caso sobre la inserción de migrantes serranos como trabajadores eventuales en un ingenio azucarero de la costa ecuatoriana." *HISLA* 7 (1986): 45–63.

El libro de la ciudad de San Francisco de Quito hasta 1951–52. Quito: Ediciones CEGAN, 1951.

Lockhart, C. "Opening the Riches of the Andes." *The World's Work* 2, no. 6 (1901): 1271–77.

Loewenfeld, Eva. "The Guayaquil and Quito Railway, Ecuador." *Southwestern Social Science Quarterly* 27, no. 1 (1946): 68–93.

Love, Joseph L., and Nils Jacobsen, eds. *Guiding the Invisible Hand: Economic Liberalism and the State in Latin America.* New York: Praeger, 1988.

Lovell, W. George. "Surviving Conquest: The Maya of Guatemala in Historical Perspective." *Latin American Research Review* 23, no. 2 (1988): 25–57.

Lynch, John. "The Catholic Church." In *Latin America: Economy and Society, 1870–1930*, edited by Leslie Bethell, 301–69. New York: Cambridge University Press, 1989.

Maiguashca, Juan, and Liisa North. "Orígenes y significado del velasquismo: Lucha de clases y participación política en el Ecuador, 1920–1972." In *La cuestión regional y el poder*, edited by Rafael Quintero, 89–159. Quito: Corporación Editora Nacional, 1991.

Maldonado Obregón, Alfredo. *Memorias del ferrocarril del sur y los hombres que lo realizaron, 1866–1958*. Quito: Talleres Gráficos de la Empresa de Ferrocarriles del Estado, 1977.

Maldonado y Basabe, Rodolfo. *Monografía de la provincia de Chimborazo*. Riobamba: Imprenta "Nacional," 1930.

Mallon, Florencia E. *The Defense of Community in Peru's Central Highlands*. Princeton: Princeton University Press, 1983.

———. "Economic Liberalism: Where We Are and Where We Need to Go." In *Guiding the Invisible Hand: Economic Liberalism and the State in Latin America*, edited by Joseph L. Love and Nils Jacobsen, 177–86. New York: Praeger, 1988.

———. *Peasant and Nation*. Berkeley: University of California Press, 1994.

Manrique, Nelson. *Yawar mayu: Sociedades terratenientes serranas, 1879–1910*. Lima: IFEA and DESCO, 1988.

Martínez, Luis A. *La agricultura del interior: Causas de su atraso y modos de impulsarla*. Quito: Imprenta La Novedad, 1897.

Martínez Flores, Alexandra. "El conflicto hacienda-comunidad en la sierra norte: El caso de Paniquinra (Imbabura), 1841–1919." *Memoria* (Quito) 1, no. 1 (1990): 153–67.

Marx, Leo. *The Machine in the Garden: Technology and the Pastoral Ideal in America*. New York: Oxford University Press, 1964.

Massey, Doreen. "Places and Their Pasts." *History Workshop Journal* 39 (1995): 182–92.

Mehta, Uday S. "Liberal Strategies of Exclusion." *Politics and Society* 18 (1990): 427–54.

Mena Villamar, Claudio. *Ecuador a comienzos de siglo*. Quito: Abya Yala and Letranueva, 1995.

Meyer, Hans. *En los altos Andes del Ecuador: Viajes y estudios*. 1907. Reprint, translated by Jonas Guerrero. Quito: Universidad Central, 1940.

Mintz, Sidney W. *Sweetness and Power: The Place of Sugar in Modern History*. New York: Penguin Books, 1985.

Moncayo Andrade, Abelardo. "Discurso." In *El ferrocarril del sur, 1908–1933: Breve relación de los principales festejos que se realizaron en Quito, el 24, 25 y 26 de junio de 1908, con motivo de la inaug-*

uración del tren en esta ciudad, 8–10. Quito: Imprenta "Industria," 1933.

———. "El problema del ferrocarril del sur y la compra del control." 1925. Reprinted in *Pensamiento económico de Abelardo Moncayo Andrade*, 1–41. Guayaquil: Archivo Histórico del Guayas and Universidad de Guayaquil, 1981.

Morley, Eduardo. *Comparación entre las líneas férreas Huigra-Cuenca y Sibambe-Cuenca*. Guayaquil: Imprenta Progreso, 1919.

Moscoso, Martha. "La tierra: Espacio de conflicto y relación entre el estado y la comunidad en el siglo XIX." In *Los Andes en la encrucijada*, edited by Heraclio Bonilla, 367–90. Quito: Libri Mundi and FLACSO, 1991.

Muñoz, Leonardo J. *Testimonio de lucha: Memorias sobre la historia del socialismo en el Ecuador*. Quito: Corporación Editora Nacional, 1988.

Muratorio, Blanca. *The Life and Times of Grandfather Alonso: Culture and History in the Upper Amazon*. New Brunswick, NJ: Rutgers University Press, 1991.

Noboa, Alejandro. *Recopilación de mensajes dirigidos por los presidentes y vicepresidentes de la república, jefes supremos y gobiernos provisorios a las convenciones y congresos nacionales desde el año de 1819 hasta nuestros días*. Vol. 5. Guayaquil: Imprenta "El Tiempo," 1908.

Nugent, David. "Building the State, Making the Nation: The Bases and Limits of State Centralization in 'Modern' Peru." *American Anthropologist* 96, no. 2 (1994): 333–69.

———. "From Devil Pacts to Drug Deals: Commerce, Unnatural Accumulation and Moral Community in 'Modern' Peru." *American Ethnologist* 23, no. 2 (1996): 258–90.

Ojeda, Ramón. *La agricultura y el estado: Carta agrícola al Sr. Dn. Emilio Estrada*. Quito: Imprenta de Julio Sáenz R., 1912.

———. "Efectos del ferrocarril en la agricultura y la ganadería." 1927. Reprinted in *Pensamiento agrario ecuatoriano*, edited by Carlos Marchán, 647–56. Quito: Banco Central, 1986.

Orellana, J. Gonzalo. *Guía comercial geográfica*. Guayaquil: Imprenta de la Escuela de Artes y Oficios de la Sociedad Filantrópica del Guayas, 1922.

Orlove, Benjamin. "Inequality among Peasants: The Forms and Uses of Reciprocal Exchange in Andean Peru." In *Peasant Livelihood*, edited by R. Halperin and J. Dow, 201–14. New York: St. Martin's Press, 1977.

Painter, Michael. "Re-creating Peasant Economy in Southern Peru." In *Golden Ages, Dark Ages: Imagining the Past in Anthropology and History*, edited by Jay O'Brien and William Roseberry, 81–106. Berkeley: University of California Press, 1991.

Palomeque, Silvia. *Cuenca en el siglo XIX: La articulación de una región*. Quito: FLACSO, 1990.

————. "Estado y comunidad en la región de Cuenca en el siglo XIX: Las autoridades indígenas y su relación con el estado." In *Los Andes en la encrucijada*, edited by Heraclio Bonilla, 391–418. Quito: Libri Mundi and FLACSO, 1991.

Pan American Union. *Ecuador: General Descriptive Data*. Washington, DC: Pan American Union, 1924.

————. *Ecuador: General Descriptive Data Prepared in April 1915*. Washington, DC: Pan American Union, 1915.

Pérez Marchant, B. *Diccionario biográfico del Ecuador*. Quito: Escuela de Artes y Oficios, 1928.

Phelan, John Leddy. *The Kingdom of Quito in the Seventeenth Century: Bureaucratic Politics in the Spanish Empire*. Madison: University of Wisconsin Press, 1967.

Pineo, Ronn F. "The Economic and Social Transformation of Guayaquil, Ecuador, 1870–1925." Ph.D. diss., University of California at Irvine, 1987.

————. "Guayaquil y su región en el segundo boom cacaotero (1870–1925)." In *Historia y región en el Ecuador: 1830–1930*, edited by Juan Maiguashca, 251–94. Quito: CERLAC, FLACSO, and IFEA, 1994.

————. "Misery and Death in the Pearl of the Pacific: Health Care in Guayaquil, Ecuador, 1870–1925." *Hispanic American Historical Review* 70, no. 4 (1990): 609–37.

Platt, Tristan. "Divine Protection and Liberal Damnation: Exchanging Metaphors in Nineteenth-Century Potosí (Bolivia)." In *Contesting Markets: Analyses of Ideology, Discourse and Practice*, edited by Roy Dilley, 131–58. Edinburgh: Edinburgh University Press, 1992.

————. *Estado boliviano y ayllu andino: Tierra y tributo en el norte de Potosí*. Lima: Instituto de Estudios Peruanos, 1982.

Polanyi, Karl. *The Great Transformation: The Political and Economic Origins of Our Time*. Boston: Beacon, 1944.

Quevedo, Belisario. "La sierra y la costa." 1916. Reprinted in *Ensayos sociológicos, políticos y morales*, 187–94. Quito: Banco Central and Corporación Editora Nacional, 1981.

Quintero, Rafael. "El estado terrateniente del Ecuador (1809–1895)." In *Estados y naciones en los Andes*, vol. 2, edited by Jean-Paul Deler and Yves Saint-Geours, 397–418. Lima: Instituto de Estudios Peruanos and Instituto Francés de Estudios Andinos, 1986.

Ramón, Galo. *El regreso de los runas: La potencialidad del proyecto indio en el Ecuador contemporáneo*. Quito: COMUNIDEC and Fundación Interamericana, 1993.

Ramón, Galo, coord. *Actores de una década ganada: Tribus, comunidades y campesinos en la modernidad*. Quito: COMUNIDEC and Abya Yala, 1992.

Reyes, Oscar Efrén. *Los últimos siete años*. Quito: Talleres Gráficos Nacionales, 1933.

Un Riobambeño. *Para la historia: El ferrocarril de Riobamba y la revolución del 1 de enero de 1906*. Riobamba: Imprenta Municipal, 1906.

————. *Riobamba y el ferrocarril*. Quito: Tipografía de la Escuela de Artes y Oficios, 1905.

Rodríguez, Linda Alexander. *The Search for Public Policy: Regional Politics and Government Finances in Ecuador, 1830–1940*. Berkeley: University of California Press, 1985.

Rodríguez Pastor, Humberto. *Hijos del celeste imperio en el Perú (1850–1900)*. Lima: Instituto de Apoyo Agrario, 1989.

————. "El inmigrante chino en el mercado laboral peruano, 1850–1930." *HISLA* 13–14 (1989): 93–147.

Roseberry, William. *Anthropologies and Histories: Essays in Culture, History, and Political Economy*. New Brunswick, NJ: Rutgers University Press, 1989.

————. "Hegemony and the Language of Contention." In *Everyday Forms of State Formation: Revolution and the Negotiation of Rule in Modern Mexico*, edited by Gilbert M. Joseph and Daniel Nugent, 355–66. Durham, NC: Duke University Press, 1994.

Roseberry, William, Lowell Gudmundson, and Mario Samper Kutschbach, eds. *Coffee, Society, and Power in Latin America*. Baltimore: Johns Hopkins University Press, 1995.

Rosenthal, Anton. "Death on the Line: Disease, Accidents and Worker Consciousness on the Railroads of Ecuador." Paper presented at the Sixth Latin American Labor History Conference, Yale University, April 21–22, 1989.

Rosero Garcés, Fernando. "Comunidad, hacienda y estado: Un conflicto de tierras en el período de las transformaciones liberales." *Ecuador Debate* (Quito) 12 (1986): 163–87.

Saint-Geours, Yves. "Economía y sociedad: La sierra centro-norte, 1830–1875." In *Nueva historia del Ecuador*. Vol. 7, *Epoca republicana I*, edited by Enrique Ayala Mora, 37–68. Quito: Corporación Editora Nacional and Grijalbo, 1990.

————. "La sierra centro y norte (1830–1925)." In *Historia y región en el Ecuador: 1830–1930*, edited by Juan Maiguashca, 143–88. Quito: CERLAC, FLACSO, and IFEA, 1994.

Samaniego Ponce, José. *Crisis económica del Ecuador: Análisis comparativo de dos períodos históricos (1929–1933)-(1980–1984)*. Quito: Banco Central, 1988.

Sarasti, Manuel. "El consejo de estado y el depósito de los dos millones." In *Ferrocarril del sur: Juicios imparciales*, 49–95. Guayaquil: Imprenta de "El Tiempo," 1892.

Sayer, Derek. "The Critique of Politics and Political Economy: Capitalism, Communism, and the State in Marx's Writings of the mid-1840s." *Sociological Review* 33, no. 2 (1985): 221–53.

————. "Everyday Forms of State Formation: Some Dissident Remarks on 'Hegemony.' " In *Everyday Forms of State Formation:*

Revolution and the Negotiation of Rule in Modern Mexico, edited by Gilbert M. Joseph and Daniel Nugent, 367–77. Durham, NC: Duke University Press, 1994.

———. *The Violence of Abstraction*. Oxford: Basil Blackwell, 1987.

Schivelbusch, Wolfgang. *The Railway Journey: The Industrialization of Time and Space in the Nineteenth Century*. Berkeley: University of California Press, 1986.

Schroder, Barbara C. "Haciendas, Indians, and Economic Change in Chimborazo, Ecuador." Ph.D. diss., Rutgers University, 1984.

Scott, James C. Foreword. In *Everyday Forms of State Formation: Revolution and the Negotiation of Rule in Modern Mexico*, edited by Gilbert M. Joseph and Daniel Nugent, vii–xii. Durham, NC: Duke University Press, 1994.

Sears, Alan. "'To Teach Them How to Live': The Politics of Public Health from Tuberculosis to AIDS." *Journal of Historical Sociology* 5, no. 1 (1992): 61–83.

Segal, Daniel A. "Nationalism, Comparatively Speaking." *Journal of Historical Sociology* 1, no. 3 (1988): 301–21.

Seligman, Linda J. "The Burden of Visions amidst Reform: Peasant Relations to Law in the Peruvian Andes." *American Ethnologist* 20, no.1 (1993): 25–51.

Smith, Carol A. "Origins of the National Question in Guatemala: A Hypothesis." In *Guatemalan Indians and the State, 1540 to 1988*, edited by Carol A. Smith, 72–95. Austin: University of Texas Press, 1990.

Smith, Gavin. *Livelihood and Resistance: Peasants and the Politics of Land in Peru*. Berkeley: University of California Press, 1989.

———. "The Production of Culture in Local Rebellion." In *Golden Ages, Dark Ages: Imagining the Past in Anthropology and History*, edited by Jay O'Brien and William Roseberry, 180–209. Berkeley: University of California Press, 1991.

Sociedad Nacional de Agricultura. *Primer Congreso de Agricultores: Programa*. Quito: Tipografía y Encuadernación de la "Prensa Católica," 1922.

Stewart, F. B. *Manejos de Mr. Harman*. Quito: Imprenta de "La Prensa," 1910.

Taylor, Anne-Christine. "El Oriente ecuatoriano en el siglo XIX: 'El otro litoral.' " In *Historia y región en el Ecuador: 1830–1930*, edited by Juan Maiguashca, 17–68. Quito: CERLAC, FLACSO, and IFEA, 1994.

Thompson, E. P. "Eighteenth-century English Society: Class Struggle without Class?" *Social History* 3, no. 2 (1978): 133–65.

———. "The Moral Economy of the English Crowd in the Eighteenth Century." In *Customs in Common: Studies in Traditional Popular Culture*, 185–258. New York: New Press, 1991.

———. "The Moral Economy Reviewed." In *Customs in Common: Studies in Traditional Popular Culture*, 259–351. New York: New Press, 1991.

———. *The Poverty of Theory and Other Essays*. New York: Monthly Review Press, 1978.

———. *Whigs and Hunters: The Origin of the Black Act*. New York: Pantheon, 1975.

Thomson, Guy P. C. "Bulwarks of Patriotic Liberalism: The National Guard, Philharmonic Corps, and Patriotic Juntas in Mexico, 1847–88." *Journal of Latin American Studies* 22 (1990): 31–68.

Tilly, Charles. "Food Supply and Public Order in Modern Europe." In *The Formation of National States in Western Europe*, edited by Charles Tilly, 380–455. Princeton: Princeton University Press, 1975.

Topik, Steven. *The Political Economy of the Brazilian State*. Austin: University of Texas Press, 1987.

———. "State Interventionism in a Liberal Regime: Brazil, 1889–1930." *Hispanic American Historical Review* 60 (1980): 593–616.

Torres, Víctor Rafael. *Provincia central "Los Andes" cuya capital es Alausí*. Alausí: n.p., 1937.

Trouillot, Michel-Rolph. *Peasants and Capital: Dominica in the World Economy*. Baltimore: Johns Hopkins University Press, 1988.

Trujillo, Jorge. *La hacienda serrana, 1900–1930*. Quito: Abya Yala and Instituto de Estudios Ecuatorianos, 1986.

Tyrer, Robson Brines. *Historia demográfica y económica de la audiencia de Quito*. Quito: Banco Central, 1988.

Weismantel, M. J. *Food, Gender and Poverty in the Ecuadorian Andes*. Philadelphia: University of Pennsylvania Press, 1988.

Whymper, Edward. *Travels amongst the Great Andes of the Equator*. 1892. Reprint, Salt Lake City, UT: Peregrine Smith Books, 1987.

Wiles, Dawn. "Land Transportation within Ecuador, 1822–1954." Ph.D. diss., Louisiana State University and Agricultural and Mechanical College, 1971.

Williams, Raymond. *The Country and the City*. New York: Oxford University Press, 1973.

———. *Keywords*. New York: Oxford University Press, 1976.

———. *Marxism and Literature*. New York: Oxford University Press, 1977.

Wolf, Eric R. "Closed Corporate Peasant Communities in Mesoamerica and Central Java." *Southwestern Journal of Anthropology* 13 (1957): 1–18.

———. *Europe and the People without History*. Berkeley: University of California Press, 1982.

———. "Types of Latin American Peasantries." *American Anthropologist* 57 (1955): 452–71.

————. "The Vicissitudes of the Closed Corporate Peasant Community." *American Ethnologist* 13 (1986): 325–29.

Wolf, Eric R., and Sidney Mintz. "Haciendas and Plantations in Middle America and the Antilles." *Social and Economic Studies* 6 (1957): 386–412.

Wolf, Teodoro. *Geografía y geología del Ecuador*. 1892. Reprint, Quito: Editorial Casa de la Cultura Ecuatoriana, 1975.

Yerovi, A. L. "Refutación de un informe." In *Ferrocarril del sur: Juicios imparciales*, 3–48. Guayaquil: Imprenta de "El Tiempo," 1892.

Zamosc, León. *Estadística de las áreas de predominio étnico de la sierra ecuatoriana: Población rural, indicadores cantonales y organizaciones de base*. Quito: Abya Yala, 1995.

Index

Latin American Silhouettes
Studies in History and Culture

William H. Beezley and
Judith Ewell
Editors

Volumes Published

William H. Beezley and Judith Ewell, eds., *The Human Tradition in Latin America: The Twentieth Century* (1987).
Cloth ISBN 0-8420-2283-X
Paper ISBN 0-8420-2284-8

Judith Ewell and William H. Beezley, eds., *The Human Tradition in Latin America: The Nineteenth Century* (1989).
Cloth ISBN 0-8420-2331-3
Paper ISBN 0-8420-2332-1

David G. LaFrance, *The Mexican Revolution in Puebla, 1908–1913: The Maderista Movement and the Failure of Liberal Reform* (1989).
ISBN 0-8420-2293-7

Mark A. Burkholder, *Politics of a Colonial Career: José Baquíjano and the Audiencia of Lima*, 2d ed. (1990).
Cloth ISBN 0-8420-2353-4
Paper ISBN 0-8420-2352-6

Carlos B. Gil, ed., *Hope and Frustration: Interviews with Leaders of Mexico's Political Opposition* (1992).
Cloth ISBN 0-8420-2395-X
Paper ISBN 0-8420-2396-8

Heidi Zogbaum, *B. Traven: A Vision of Mexico* (1992). ISBN 0-8420-2392-5

Jaime E. Rodríguez O., ed., *Patterns of Contention in Mexican History* (1992). ISBN 0-8420-2399-2

Louis A. Pérez, Jr., ed., *Slaves, Sugar, and Colonial Society: Travel Accounts of Cuba, 1801–1899* (1992).
Cloth ISBN 0-8420-2354-2
Paper ISBN 0-8420-2415-8

Peter Blanchard, *Slavery and Abolition in Early Republican Peru* (1992).
Cloth ISBN 0-8420-2400-X
Paper ISBN 0-8420-2429-8

Paul J. Vanderwood, *Disorder and Progress: Bandits, Police, and Mexican Development*. Revised and Enlarged Edition (1992).
Cloth ISBN 0-8420-2438-7
Paper ISBN 0-8420-2439-5

Sandra McGee Deutsch and Ronald H. Dolkart, eds., *The Argentine Right: Its History and Intellectual Origins, 1910 to the Present* (1993).
Cloth ISBN 0-8420-2418-2
Paper ISBN 0-8420-2419-0

Steve Ellner, *Organized Labor in Venezuela, 1958–1991: Behavior and Concerns in a Democratic Setting* (1993). ISBN 0-8420-2443-3

Paul J. Dosal, *Doing Business with the Dictators: A Political History of United Fruit in Guatemala, 1899–1944* (1993). Cloth ISBN 0-8420-2475-1 Paper ISBN 0-8420-2590-1

Marquis James, *Merchant Adventurer: The Story of W. R. Grace* (1993).
ISBN 0-8420-2444-1

John Charles Chasteen and Joseph S. Tulchin, eds., *Problems in Modern Latin American History: A Reader* (1994). Cloth ISBN 0-8420-2327-5
Paper ISBN 0-8420-2328-3

Marguerite Guzmán Bouvard, *Revolutionizing Motherhood: The Mothers of the Plaza de Mayo* (1994).
Cloth ISBN 0-8420-2486-7
Paper ISBN 0-8420-2487-5

William H. Beezley, Cheryl English Martin, and William E. French, eds., *Rituals of Rule, Rituals of Resistance: Public Celebrations and Popular Culture in Mexico* (1994). Cloth ISBN 0-8420-2416-6 Paper ISBN 0-8420-2417-4

Stephen R. Niblo, *War, Diplomacy, and Development: The United States and Mexico, 1938–1954* (1995). ISBN 0-8420-2550-2

G. Harvey Summ, ed., *Brazilian Mosaic: Portraits of a Diverse People and Culture* (1995). Cloth ISBN 0-8420-2491-3   Paper ISBN 0-8420-2492-1

N. Patrick Peritore and Ana Karina Galve-Peritore, eds., *Biotechnology in Latin America: Politics, Impacts, and Risks* (1995). Cloth ISBN 0-8420-2556-1   Paper ISBN 0-8420-2557-X

Silvia Marina Arrom and Servando Ortoll, eds., *Riots in the Cities: Popular Politics and the Urban Poor in Latin America, 1765–1910* (1996). Cloth ISBN 0-8420-2580-4 Paper ISBN 0-8420-2581-2

Roderic Ai Camp, ed., *Polling for Democracy: Public Opinion and Political Liberalization in Mexico* (1996). ISBN 0-8420-2583-9

Brian Loveman and Thomas M. Davies, Jr., eds., *The Politics of Antipolitics: The Military in Latin America*, 3d ed., revised and updated (1996). Cloth ISBN 0-8420-2609-6 Paper ISBN 0-8420-2611-8

Joseph S. Tulchin, Andrés Serbín, and Rafael Hernández, eds., *Cuba and the Caribbean: Regional Issues and Trends in the Post-Cold War Era* (1997). ISBN 0-8420-2652-5

Thomas W. Walker, ed., *Nicaragua without Illusions: Regime Transition and Structural Adjustment in the 1990s* (1997). Cloth ISBN 0-8420-2578-2   Paper ISBN 0-8420-2579-0

Dianne Walta Hart, *Undocumented in L.A.: An Immigrant's Story* (1997). Cloth ISBN 0-8420-2648-7 Paper ISBN 0-8420-2649-5

Jaime E. Rodríguez O. and Kathryn Vincent, eds., *Myths, Misdeeds, and Misunderstandings: The Roots of Conflict in U.S.-Mexican Relations* (1997). ISBN 0-8420-2662-2

Jaime E. Rodríguez O. and Kathryn Vincent, eds., *Common Border, Uncommon Paths: Race, Culture, and National Identity in U.S.-Mexican Relations* (1997). ISBN 0-8420-2673-8

William H. Beezley and Judith Ewell, eds., *The Human Tradition in Modern Latin America* (1997). Cloth ISBN 0-8420-2612-6 Paper ISBN 0-8420-2613-4

Donald F. Stevens, ed., *Based on a True Story: Latin American History at the Movies* (1997). ISBN 0-8420-2582-0

Jaime E. Rodríguez O., ed., *The Origins of Mexican National Politics, 1808–1847* (1997). Paper ISBN 0-8420-2723-8

Che Guevara, *Guerrilla Warfare*, with revised and updated introduction and case studies by Brian Loveman and Thomas M. Davies, Jr., 3d ed. (1997). Cloth ISBN 0-8420-2677-0 Paper ISBN 0-8420-2678-9

Adrian A. Bantjes, *As If Jesus Walked on Earth: Cardenismo, Sonora, and the Mexican Revolution* (1998). ISBN 0-8420-2653-3

Henry A. Dietz and Gil Shidlo, eds., *Urban Elections in Democratic Latin America* (1998). Cloth ISBN 0-8420-2627-4   Paper ISBN 0-8420-2628-2

A. Kim Clark, *The Redemptive Work: Railway and Nation in Ecuador, 1895–1930* (1998). ISBN 0-8420-2674-6

Joseph S. Tulchin, ed., with Allison M. Garland, *Argentina: The Challenges of Modernization* (1998). ISBN 0-8420-2721-1

Louis A. Pérez, Jr., ed., *Impressions of Cuba in the Nineteenth Century: The Travel Diary of Joseph J. Dimock* (1998). Cloth ISBN 0-8420-2657-6 Paper ISBN 0-8420-2658-4

Guy P. C. Thomson, *Patriotism, Politics, and Popular Liberalism in Nineteenth-Century Mexico: Juan Francisco Lucas and the Puebla Sierra* (1998). ISBN 0-8420-2683-5

June E. Hahner, ed., *Women through Women's Eyes: Latin American Women in Nineteenth-Century Travel Accounts* (1998). Cloth ISBN 0-8420-2633-9   Paper ISBN 0-8420-2634-7